Thanks are due to:

Paul Fuller-for reading the manuscript and suggesting amendments;
Terence Meaden-for the bones of Chapter One;
John Macnish-for permission to quote from
Cropcircle Apocalypse

THIS IS No. 79 .....of 300

C 2003 P.D.Rendall & Past-Track Publications
PO Box 1429,Bristol BS169XQ

All rights reserved. No part of this publication may be reproduced in any form or by any means - graphics, electronic or mechanical, including photocopying, recording, taping or information storage and retrieval systems - without the prior permission in writing of the publisher.

A catalogue record for this book is available from the British Library

ISBN 09531331-1-7

Printed by Catford Print Centre, Catford, London, UK.
Tele:02086950101.........Fax:02086950566

CEREAL KILLERS
BOOK ONE – THE INNOCENT YEARS

Page 1...*Prologue*

   3...Chapter 1...**Undeniable Evidence:** *White Horse-Blackbird-High Noon-Dark Deeds*

   10.Chapter 2...**Our Paths Will Cross:** *The View from a hill-Funny Haircut, Funny Name*

   20.Chapter 3... **The Story So Far:** *Aliens and Weather*

   25. Chapter 4...**Where Do We Go From Here?:** *New Circles-Magic Circles-Psychic Circles*

   31. Chapter 5...**Colour Developments:** *Dark Deeds-White Flag-Red Faces-White Lights*

   44.Chapter 6...**High On A Hill :** *Blackbird-High Hill-Noises Off-Evolution*

   54.Chapter 7...**Lows and Highs :** *The Cropwatcher-Colin Talks-Maiden Bradley-More eyewitnesses-More Support*

   62. Chapter 8...**Remember, Remember the Month of November:** *Meetings-More Meetings and Chat*

   78. Chapter 9..**The Best Laid Plans:1991.** *Our Plans-Their Plans-Promises of help- The First Circles of 1991*

   104. Chapter 10..**Reality is an Illusion:** *Fake? No-Duplicity? Yes!*

   116. Chapter 11..**Just for the Record:** *Blue Hill gets under way-Terence & the Press-Farmer Brown-NTV-Out in the Cold*

   129. Chapter 12..**Warm Wet Circles:** *Rain-More Rain-Circlevision move in-Circles appear under suspicious circumstances*

   143. Chapter 13..**The Short Straw:** *Alton Barnes again-The Sun appears-Jim Schnabel appears-the Son of God appears-Doubts appear*

   156. Chapter 14..**Wonderful Circles:** *More Hoaxes-The Vortex makes an appearance-Baldrick-Dundry*

   164. Chapter 15..**Trickery:** *Barbury and the Straws-The Great American Confession-Upton Scudamore-A Chorost of disapproval-Hoaxes*

   177. Chapter 16..**Harvest Home:** *Hoaxes and more Hoaxes-Harvest-Jim's Theory-Blue Hill finishes after 60 days on the hill*

   190. Chapter 17..**Trouble in the Stubble:** *The Tomlinsons-the Skeptics again-Clench Common-Doug and Dave*

Footnotes
Bibliography

CEREAL KILLERS
The true story of one group's research into the mystery of the
Crop Circles
BOOK ONE – The Innocent Years
PROLOGUE

By the time I got involved with Crop Circles they had become a phenomenon which had developed into an obsession; an obsession which led to a battle between two opposing camps, each following a different trail of belief towards the common goal: Who or What made Crop Circles. At first, both sides had worked together then, as one side scored a solo success, so the other had been forced to re-think and try different methods to keep up. This invariably led to friction and a parting of the ways between Colin Andrews and Pat Delgado, who believed in an 'other worldly' explanation, and physicist/meteorologist Dr Terence Meaden to whom the answer lay in the wind.

After the split, the success of Andrews and Delgado's book *'Circular Evidence'* put increasing pressure on Meaden, who lost a lot of ground in the wake of its publication and the resulting publicity. Meaden's theory was that electrostatically charged whirlwinds made the circles - but he felt that he had evidence that the circles had been created in this way since ancient times and been seen by our ancestors as 'messages from the gods'. The whirlwind idea was frequently expostulated, but the other part of the theory was far from ready for publication.

Meaden lacked both publicity and financial backing. Whereas Andrews and Delgado appeared regularly on BBC Birmingham's *'Daytime Live'*, appealing for more information and being called 'Scientists', Meaden, (a *real* scientist) was struggling to get beyond the local Wiltshire papers. It didn't seem to matter that he had the cautious backing of other scientists here and abroad and of some leading members of the British UFO Research Organisation (*BUFORA*). These latter people saw, in his theory, an answer to many UFO sightings. The media preferred to listen to Andrews and Delgado.

It was the wild claims of the 'Aliens and Unknown Energies' brigade, which drove my friends and I into the Meaden camp in 1990. From being merely helpers in 1990, we, along with Paul Fuller of *BUFORA*, became the mainstay of *'Operation Blue Hill '* the *CERES* (Circles Effect Research - the group started by Meaden) cropwatch in 1991 and arguably the longest running cropwatch to date.

As most devotees of the circles phenomenon know, 1991 was the year of more circles, more complex formations and humiliation for the researchers when two elderly jokers, Doug Bower and Dave Chorley, revealed that they were behind the entire game. They'd apparently started it all, way back in the 1970's and carried on until it all got too much; too many people were copying them and too many people were making money out of the whole business. They pooh-poohed Andrews and Delgado for not noticing that they (Doug & Dave) were taking part in their group meetings then going out to make circles, almost to order, on the basis of what they'd heard folk speculate at the meeting. They also criticised Terence Meaden for claiming to have a scientific explanation for circles that they'd made with planks of wood.

But Meaden had already suffered his ritual humiliation. Juniper, the company making the *Equinox* documentary, had 'set him up' with a set of fake circles. The professor had fallen into the trap and declared them genuine. So had Busty Taylor, one-time friend of

Andrews and Delgado and now a leading light in the Centre for Crop Circles Studies (CCCS). But when the documentary came out, it was Meaden's humiliation that was shown in full, not Taylor's.

After this, the subject faltered as more revelations came out. John Macnish who had been behind the *'Daytime Live'* camera and production and had masterminded the 1990 *'Operation Blackbird'* and 1991 *'Operation Chameleon'* camerawork, was convinced that Doug and Dave were telling the truth. He followed them around during the summer of 1992 and filmed them making circles under a variety of conditions. His subsequent video and book brought him a lambasting from the 'believers'.

Then there was Jim Schnabel, an American who'd 'infiltrated' all camps during 1991 and produced a book *'Round in Circles'*, which laid bare the personalities behind the investigators and the fakers. In it, he revealed that he and two friends had been behind the majority of complex formations made during 1992 and how easy it was to deceive the watchers. Scorn was, in turn, poured upon him by many whose fun he had ruined.

But still the subject lingers on. Some investigators found a ready market in the USA and lecture and write articles about crop circles and the 'strange phenomena' they insist are associated with them. Here in the UK there's still a steady stream of publications, and the tourist spots still sell postcards and books of the circles.

My story is one of mystery, intrigue, deceit and misguided intention - which in fact surround the entire history of the circles phenomenon. The events are recreated from the daily diaries I kept for nearly six years, tape recordings and interviews. But remember- this isn't a history of the circles affair: it's *my* story and it is the true story of the events of 1991 and of previous and subsequent summers; of the way in which the scientists were caught out. There will, of course, be some people who will disagree with what's said, but there's nothing untrue or deliberately malicious in these pages. I was present at many events over the years and saw many things that have been badly misinterpreted. I've seen people believe things which didn't happen; conceal things which did and make wild claims about crop circles which wouldn't stand up to close scrutiny. And these were things that happened to BOTH sides.

So, be you followers of crop circles; mystics or psychologists – read on: there's something in these pages for you all. But, remember: ***Nil Nisi Triticum Depressum!*** – **It's only flattened corn!**

P.D.Rendall
South Gloucestershire,
2003

Chapter One
"UNDENIABLE EVIDENCE"
White Horse-Blackbird-High Noon-Dark Deeds
Wednesday 25th July, 1990

The red disc of the sun dipped below the western horizon and the heat of the summer day now gave way to the cool of evening. As dusk fell, so a quiet air of anticipation descended upon the cluster of tents and vehicles that comprised the camp, perched on the very edge of the escarpment. On the side of the hill, the ancient chalk figure of the white horse gazed timelessly down on the twinkling lights, which outlined the streetplan of the small Wiltshire town of Westbury.

From tents and from makeshift dens, eager eyes scanned the rapidly darkening fields below through high-powered binoculars. Interested locals venturing near the camp could hear groups of watchers talking in low voices: now in Japanese, now in German which, with the English and American accents heard, indicated the multi-national flavour of this research project, code-named '*Operation Blackbird*'.

Away to the right, a group of youngsters camped in a tent passed around the cider and argued softly about who was to take the first watch. The still summer air was sweet with the smell of grass, mixed with the occasional breath of cigarette smoke as one of the watchers lit another fat roll-up. The still air emphasised the sounds of the night: the occasional burst of noise from the not-to-distant cement works sounded, to some, like the distant bustle of a city. By the side of a blue mini-bus, a member of a Japanese film-crew unfolded a camp-stool and settled himself down comfortably.

And so the night wore on. The beautiful pallet of colours which dusk had splashed across the western sky now gave way to sharp, starlit, darkness: there was no moon. From time to time a bat would swoop around the tall telescopic mast which protruded from the roof of the control van. From the top of the mast, the remote-controlled infra-red camera kept a watchful vigil over the cereal-fields of farmer Jonathan King far below.

In the control van, the young watchers sat in front of the flickering monitors. Despite the darkness, the infra-red picture of the fields showed up well on the black-and-white VDU's, although because of the distance, it wasn't possible to pick out fine detail. Inside the van it was hot and stuffy. The van door had been left open, but this did little to alleviate the sultry atmosphere. However, the recent events at the small village of Alton Barnes, some twelve miles east of the camp, were enough to ensure that enough adrenaline flowed to stave off the effects of tiredness. It was at Alton Barnes that the largest and most spectacular crop circles formation yet seen had been discovered. It was to discover what made it and all the other formations that '*Blackbird*' had been set up.

Midnight came and went. With each passing hour and nothing but an unchanging screen to look at, a degree of boredom began to creep in. An Intercity express showed briefly on the screens as a momentary streak of white light as it hurried through the landscape, heading west. One of the watchers yawned, opened a can of Coke and checked that the video recorders were running. For two nights now the monitors had been watched intently and the picture had been the same. In spite of the adrenaline, eyelids began to droop.

Suddenly, the screens came alive with images, small points of light which appeared to float above the crops. The watcher jerked awake and stared at the screen in amazement as the triangular darts of light began to slowly revolve. What the hell was going on? Was the phenomenon they'd all come here to see actually happening in front of his eyes? He elbowed his colleague and together they sat and watched open-mouthed, as the mysterious lights began to etch shapes into the cornfield....

'*Operation Blackbird*' had begun the weekend previously. A convoy of vehicles made up of a variety of cars and vans laden with expensive cameras and surveillance equipment, had wound its way up the track to the top of White Horse hill. Topping the hill were the imposing remains of the hill-fort, named Bratton Castle after the nearest village. More than 3,000 years old, the ramparts were still formidable obstacles, in spite of the passage of years. Situated on the very edge of the northern scarp of Salisbury Plain, the camp and its environs normally provided a spot for picnickers and walkers. Summer weekends would see the flat area behind the ramparts alive with people flying kites or playing football or cricket. The steep slopes of the hill also provided an excellent spot for the dare-devil antics of hang-glider flyers, who would hurl themselves off the top and swoop out over the countryside on 'thermals' of warm air.

On the very edge of the castle the '*Blackbird*' team set up camp. One by one the cameras were connected to recorders and monitors and a network of black cables snaked back across the grass to the control van. A mobile generator provided the necessary power supply. Amid the steady to and fro of eager helpers, the camera teams started testing their equipment. The project was multi-national; Japan's Nippon TV, led by producer Ogawa, was the biggest single financial backer of the project. British interests were represented by BBC Birmingham, whose Pebble Mill studio team, filming for the '*Daytime Live*' programme's '*Cropwatch*' slot, were led by producers John MacNish and David Morgenstern. ' *We're here to film a crop-circle happening,*' said Morgenstern in an interview with the BBC One o' clock news. '*...We want to show that it's not a hoax...*'.

The BBC were also using the services of Skystalk Surveillance, a specialist company led by Scotsman Mike Carrie, and whose telescopic camera mast was to dominate the skyline. Not to be out-done, the American TV crew from ABC television installed a satellite dish to beam pictures across the Atlantic to the USA. Thermal-image cameras were set up on the hilltop and aimed down into the crop fields.

Also present was the Army. They owned the land - part of the crop-belt leased to farmers to help distance the public from Britain's biggest war-games training ground - and as such had to be told about a high-tech surveillance operation of this kind operating on the edge of MOD property. Others who were advised of the presence of the 'Blackbird' team were the farmers who worked the land on which circles were confidently expected to appear, and the owners of Bratton Castle, English Heritage. The project was supposed to be secret, and was expected to last three weeks.

Through the hustle and bustle of the camp, the two Leaders strode to and fro; checking a camera here and a look-out position there, and stopping from time to time to speak to reporters and give interviews for TV. As instigators of *Operation Blackbird*, Colin Andrews and Pat Delgado had worked with the BBC on the arrangements for the project for months. Colin, a Test Valley Council employee responsible for electrical advice and civil-defence communications, had found his connections with police and army personnel useful when setting up the project. An enthusiastic and dedicated circles researcher who believed the strange shapes in the fields were caused by an '...*unknown intelligence, possibly involving an aerial component*....' [1], Andrews was responsible for the bulk of the pre-planning of the operation. His knowledge of electronics, apart from being useful where such high-tech equipment was being used, had also allowed him to protect his home from intruders with a sophisticated system whereby people approaching his front door set off alarm bells and had their photo taken by a hidden camera.

His colleague, Pat Delgado, a retired engineer at one time employed by the Australian Commonwealth Public service on secondment to NASA's Woomera base, was the more experienced circles researcher, having been investigating the phenomenon since 1981. Pat also believed in the 'unknown intelligence' theory, but was more inclined to include 'unknown energies' in his theory. However, of the two, Colin Andrews was the more dominant personality, and after the pair teamed up (having been introduced to each other by physicist and meteorologist Dr Terence Meaden - who was pursuing a weather-based reason for the circles), moved swiftly to stamp his authority on the search for a 'solution' to the phenomenon.

The publication in 1989, of their joint book '*Circular Evidence*', left no-one in any doubt at all that the solution sought by Andrews and Delgado was of a paranormal flavour, centring on otherworldly intelligence. The book went on to be a best-seller and at the time of '*Blackbird*', Andrews and Delgado were riding on the crest of a wave of supreme optimism.

And so it began, a vigil planned to last three weeks during which Andrews and Delgado were sure they would at last find the answer to the circles which had been baffling people for nearly a decade. However, on the second night, whilst the screens were alive with darting images, neither Andrews nor Delgado were present. Home, comfortably tucked up in their respective beds, they were blissfully unaware of the rising excitement at the camp, where the video recorder was capturing every movement of the flitting lights caught by the infra-red camera. As the observers watched, they could see the circles growing in size before their very eyes; whatever was out there was manifestly warmer than the surrounding air!

Little was spoken, such was the astonishment of the watchers at seeing the spectacle unfolding on the screens in front of them. They stared, they recorded and they waited. And, as the darkness of night withdrew, they could at last make out distinct markings in the field below. It was 04.30, British Summer Time.

As the stars grew dimmer and daylight brighter, it didn't require binoculars to see that an amazing complex pattern of circles and lines lay before them: such a complex formation had never been seen before. It was at this point that someone decided that they had better get in touch with Andrews and Delgado.

It was around five o' clock that morning when the telephone rang in the Andover home of Colin Andrews. A brief conversation, and Andrews rushed to dress, barely able to suppress his excitement. Before leaving home, Andrews phoned Bratton farmer Peter Gale. The farmer was none too happy at being disturbed so early, but agreed to Andrews' request to '...*come on over and verify that the circles are on your land*...'.

Colin Andrews was on top of the world as he drove the 40 miles to Blackbird; elated as he crossed the wide field inside Bratton Castle, and jovial as he joined the team at the edge of the escarpment. Gazing down at the complex of circles half-a-mile to the north, he studied the video recording of the night's events and grinned with delighted satisfaction; they had it taped!

Not everyone was happy. Farmer Gale arrived at the camp, peered down into the crop fields and demanded to know why he'd been dragged all the way up to the hill at this hour. The circles, it appeared were not on his land at all, but were on land owned by neighbouring farmer Jonathan York. Peter Gale was not amused at being summoned away from his work for nothing, and suggested that it might have been a good idea if the *Blackbird* organisers had found out whose land was whose before starting the project. Then he stalked off amidst profuse apologies from those present.

But this was just a minor hiccup and after someone phoned the correct landowner, the spirits of those present rose higher as they began to realise just what they appeared to have on film: Undeniable Evidence of crop circles forming!

Andrews was still beaming broadly when Pat Delgado arrived on site at 07.45.

The night watchmen had carried out their instructions to the letter: In the event of an occurrence, no-one was to go into the field where circles appeared until The Leaders arrived. Then, and only then, would a previously arranged plan of action be carried out. So as the sun climbed higher into the azure blue sky over Bratton, there they all were, together at the top of the hill; researchers, investigators and TV crews, peering down through camera sights, binoculars and a mounted telescope at the incredible sight below them.

No one was at the bottom, checking out the circles.

News of the formations travelled fast, and soon Andrews and Delgado were confirming the situation to the growing crowd of spectators. Confidently facing the gathering throng, Colin Andrews told them that a guard was being placed at the field to prevent unauthorised entry and that things looked good for the research project.

After dispatching several youthful members of his team complete with portable two-way radios, to stand guard over farmer York's land, Andrews then joined Delgado and between them the two men started to phone reporter after reporter from a long list of names. Each reporter so contacted was informed of the events and told that he or she had a couple of hours to get to Bratton , as the circles would not be inspected until after ten that morning. In the meantime, the television reporters were busy, and BBC Breakfast TV was first with on-site live interviews. Videos of those early-morning interviews express the excitement and hyped-up importance of the situation well...

Colin Andrews: '...*Well, we do have a major event here...very much excitement as you can imagine. We do have two major ground markings...*(they) *have appeared in front of all the surveillance equipment, performing absolutely to form for us. We had a situation at approximately 3.30 am this morning. On the monitor, a number of orange* lights taking the form of a triangle...it is a complex situation and we are analysing it at this very moment, but there is undoubtedly something here for science...' [2].

Nicholas Witchell (BBC newsreader): '...I'm sure you have the nation agog. Are you quite sure you couldn't have been the victim of some elaborate hoax last night?...'

Colin Andrews: '...No. Not indeed. We have high-quality equipment here, and we have indeed secured on high-quality equipment a major event...we do have something of great, great significance...yes, we have everything on film and we do have, as I say, a formed object over the field...we are doing nothing more now until we have helicopters over the top, to film in detail what we have, before anyone enters the field...'.

In a later interview, Andrews had this to say: '...as far as the hoax situation is concerned, undoubtedly now we've secured here on...high quality material, that it indeed...is **no hoax**..'" (My emphasis. PDR).

By the 8.30 news bulletin, Nicholas Witchell (himself the author of a book about the Loch Ness monster) was looking convinced, and millions of viewers and radio listeners as well were beginning to believe that Colin Andrews and his team had the mystery solved.

As the morning wore on, numbers on the hill grew rapidly as people rushed to Bratton to see for themselves. Radio cars from BBC Wiltshire Sound and Bristol's GWR FM stations arrived at the top of the hill. A plump lady, who bore a resemblance to comedienne Dawn French, and who was acting as a sort of 'chief marshal', was ordering people around and preventing those deemed *'persona non grata*' from stepping over the roped boundaries of the camp into *'Blackbird* territory'.

The number of waiting newsmen and women rose to 50 and passed that as the sun climbed higher. At first as excited as the *Blackbird* team, before long voices were heard from the gathered reporters complaining about the 'unreasonable waiting', and of the way they were being 'herded around' by *Blackbird* marshals.

Privately, in some quarters all those within the hallowed boundaries didn't share the supreme confidence exhibited by Colin Andrews that morning. Producer John Macnish was re-running the video tapes, and was baffled by the fact that, when the tapes were run backwards to the 'point of creation' the circles gradually faded away instead of disappearing suddenly. All previous eyewitness accounts told of circles forming in the space of a few seconds; If this was the case, the formations on tape would be expected to vanish suddenly when the tape was rewound- they didn't. Not only that, but from above the circles were quite ragged and rough – quite unlike the circles found in other places, such as Alton Barnes. Something wasn't quite right.

Another 'helper', Julie Blay, was puzzled by something she could see through a telescope: '...*The circles looked so serene and beautiful, but-*,' she later said, '-*There was something strange about them. In the centre of each circle was a touch of colour - a blue spot or something. I told Pat and Colin how odd this seemed to me, but they didn't heed its significance..*' [3]

In fact, in response to Julie's query, she was told that the blue patches were '...Just part of the phenomenon, we'll find out later what *it means...*'. How very prophetic those words turned out to be!

And so it transpired that at 10.30 that morning, the two Experts at last descended to the field in which the phenomenon had manifested itself. Accompanied by Andrew Potter, one of their team of watchers, Andrews and Delgado strode purposefully into the wheatfield. They were followed and filmed by camera crews from Nippon and BBC TV. As the procession grew nearer to the circles, so Pat Delgado began to spread his arms wide. He could, he said, feel the invisible energies emanating from the circles. As Pat began to dowse these energies with his bare hands, he became more absorbed by what he was doing, and failed to notice his fellow researcher's expression as Andrews walked into the second of the nearest pair of circles.

Closely followed by Andrew Potter, Andrews had entered the circle and headed for the blue patch at the centre, the same blue patch that Julie Blay had seen from the hill. It was this very patch of colour which Andrews now stood staring at, a look of horror and dismay on his face. Eventually he found his voice. '...*Pat..,*' he cried, '...*We've been had!*'

Delgado stopped dowsing and hurried to where his partner was standing. In the centre of the circle lay a piece of circular blue and green coloured card marked with astrological designs; it was part of a board game. On top of the board was placed a crude wooden cross, fashioned from twigs. Closer inspection revealed the board had probably originally been square or oblong in shape, and that the corners had been snipped off, thus effectively removing the manufacturer's name.

They could almost hear the sounds of someone, somewhere laughing!

Then the moment was shattered by the sound of aero - engines. Everyone looked skywards as three light aircraft flew low over the field and, still in formation, headed east. {4}

Pat Delgado stood and stared at the board with disappointment etched into his face. He looked around at the roughly flattened crop. His mouth opened and closed soundlessly. '...*Oh, dear...*' he managed at last. The TV men were, by now, looking into the other circle and sure enough there was another of the boards, complete with wooden cross. In all, six boards and crosses were discovered in the formation. It was now obvious that a hoax of monumental proportions had been perpetrated. Andrews and Delgado stood dejectedly in the cornfield and wondered just what the hell they were going to tell the crowd of reporters waiting on the hill.

Firstly, however, they had to say something for the cameras in front of them. All the while those cameras had been kept running, monitoring their disappointment. With a stunned looking Pat by his side, and Andrew Potter standing behind him, Colin Andrews spoke to the BBC. His expression could best be described as 'pained'.

'...*Somebody's had a laugh. they've had a joke. They've actually done none of us any good...these sort of things only set the research back. We have a serious job to be doing here...it's taken us off the - completely off of the project and frankly it's...funny for about sixty seconds, and then I find it very, very sad...'*

There was considerable delay before the two men returned to the waiting reporters. Well over an hour had passed since the media had been left on the bare hillside to fry in the heat of the summer sun. This was High Noon at the Bratton Castle Corral, and Delgado and Andrews came close to being metaphorically shot to pieces. What they had to say pleased no one.

After all the hype and the waiting, the news that it was a hoax after all didn't please the press. Some were hopping mad. They'd had more than enough of being pushed around and made to wait for what turned out to be nothing. Andrews and Delgado were left in no doubt as to what a large proportion of the reporters they'd summoned to Wiltshire hours before now thought of them.

In spite of the fact that the *'Blackbird'* team had made a monumental gaffe in not looking closely at the circles before summoning the press, by the time Andrews appeared on the BBC's One o'clock News he'd recovered sufficiently to brazen it out. With *'Daytime Live'* producer David Morgenstern standing by him, he told the nation: '*...At the end of the day, we have here, a hoax which certainly we can use...to our advantage...we can ensure* [sic] *all of you that this is a real phenomenon...this clearly is a hoax, and we were able to identify that immediately...'*

However confident he tried to sound, it was clear that a body blow had been dealt to *'Operation Blackbird'*. Andrews and Delgado had been 'undressed in public' as it were, and had suffered humiliation in front of the world's media. *Operation Blackbird* had become 'Operation Red Face'.

So just who had pulled off this well-publicised trick - one of the few great hoaxes to be monitored and filmed in the presence of unsuspecting film crews? A hoax that had been delivered just two weeks after Alton Barnes, the most famous crop-circles complex of all time, had raised excitement about crop-circles to fever pitch across the world? What motives could have directed such an elaborate hoax?

With my *CERES* colleague, Roger Davis, I stood on the hill above the White Horse as the sun set that day over the *'Blackbird'* circus and wondered just where all this was leading.

Chapter Two
OUR PATHS WILL CROSS
The view from a hill-funny haircut, funny name

24th July 1988

The fine light drizzle began to drift down again from the lead grey clouds which hung low over the Wiltshire countryside. I switched on the windscreen wipers and steered my Capri out of Avebury and onto the B4003. With my (then) girlfriend, Jacqui Griffiths, I'd set out that afternoon on a photographic trip to the ancient stones, only to be continuously thwarted by the showery weather. At length we decided to set course for home. The sentinel stones of the Avenue, grey and shiny with rain and fuzzy-outlined in the drizzle, were the subject of attention only by sheep, which huddled in their shelter as Avebury slipped behind in the rear - view mirror, and the car approached the junction with the busy A4.

'I fancy a pub meal,' said Jacqui, gazing out of the car window at the rain. As it would be gone eight o' clock when we reached Bristol, where we lived, I was only too happy to agree with this. The decision made, I waited for a couple of lorries to thunder past in clouds of spray before turning right onto the A4. Sod's Law being what it is, the drizzle now stopped and, whilst the sun didn't quite manage to penetrate the gloom, the clouds were now paler and at least it got a little brighter. Shortly, the mound of Silbury Hill loomed large ahead of us.

It was now almost seven o' clock and, whilst opening time was imminent, it would be at least a further half-hour before most pubs started to serve food. So, when Jacqui suggested climbing Silbury Hill to pass away half-an-hour, I agreed in lieu of anything better to do.

The mysterious Silbury Hill is the largest prehistoric man-made mound in Europe. Covering some five and quarter acres, and standing 150ft high, its purpose is still unknown, even after many archaeological digs over the years. I knew that there was a lay-by just the Marlborough side of the hill, and had it in mind to park there. As we approached the lay-by, Jacqui gave a surprised gasp. 'Look!' she cried, pointing ahead. In a field on the left-hand side of the road was the most amazing sight. A series of circular depressions of varying sizes were present in the green crop! I let out an exclamation of surprise and hastily pulled over into the lay-by. Switching off the engine I looked at my companion.

'Are we going to investigate?' I enquired. '*We certainly are!*' came back the emphatic reply.

Neither Jacqui nor myself were complete strangers to the Crop Circles mystery, having read various articles about the circles by UFOlogist Paul Fuller in the magazine *'The Unknown',* and also articles in the esoteric news-sheet *'Viewpoint Aquarius'*, published by UFO fan and goldfish expert, Rex Dutta. This, however, was the first time either of us had seen circles 'for real'.

As I had my camera gear with me, the first steps we took were to cross the busy road with the idea in mind now to climb Silbury Hill to get some photographs of the crop circles from the top. It took only a few minutes to arrive at the fence that had been erected to prevent people from climbing the ancient mound. A notice warned that *'...erosion of the hill, and damage to flora and fauna...'* would be the result of allowing sightseers to climb Silbury. Like most people, we completely ignored the sign and climbed over the fence.

After a breathless and somewhat slippery scramble to the top we stopped to get our breath back and to look down on the fields. The sight was even more spectacular than from the road. Below, in the green wheat, a large circle had been flattened. Some distance out from this central circle was four smaller 'satellite' circles, seemingly equidistant from the larger circle and from each other. The formation resembled the figure 5 on a dice.

I took my trusty Canon from the camera bag and fired off a few frames on the scene below. Luckily I had a 400 ASA Ektachrome slide film in the camera, which I hoped would allow me to get reasonable pictures in the dull conditions caused by the clouds coming over again. For a while, I moved to and fro across the top of Silbury, taking photos from different angles.

Then we slid back down the damp side of the hill to see what we could from close range. Before long we were standing at the gate to the field in which the circles lay. Fixed to the gate was a piece of cardboard, crudely stuffed into a plastic bag. On the card was written *'Please do not enter field'*. There was no farm anywhere in sight to ask permission to enter, so, after a quick discussion we decided that if we kept to the tractor lanes we'd not damage any crop and our consciences would be clear! Besides, from the top of Silbury, we'd already seen people walking in the circles, although these people were now conspicuous by their absence.

By this time several other cars had pulled up in the lay-by, their occupants standing in a cluster and gazing in amazement at the circles. We climbed over the gate and, keeping to the very edge of the field, made our way to the tractor lane which would lead us to the central circle. We walked with ease along the path between the waist high wheat, and were soon in the large circle. It was incredible! The wheat had been swirled round in a neat clockwise pattern and pressed flat to the ground. Where the circle edge met the rest of the crop, the wheat suddenly stood again. The edges were almost perfect. It was just as if a large, spinning disc had descended into the crop, pressed it flat, and then vanished. However, right overhead were three-phase electric power cables, so that ruled out any 'nuts and bolts' aerial object theory straight away, be it helicopter or UFO: the cables ran across the entire pattern.

I took photos of the main circle and moved off to photograph the satellites. That done, I looked round for Jacqui and was surprised that she was no-where to be seen. Hastening back to the main circle, I found her on her knees in the corn, fiddling with something.

Puzzled by her behaviour, I asked what she was doing. Continuing to fiddle, she said, 'I remembered I had a small bar magnet in my bag, but I haven't anything to suspend it from. I'm trying to tie it with a hair. Then...', she continued, '...I can see if there's any magnetic field here.'

Daft as this sounded, she had to be awarded full marks for ingenuity, as a moment or so later she stood up with the magnet suspended from a hair! Standing still in the middle of the circle, she waited until the swinging the magnet sorted itself out. All we discovered from this experiment, was which way north was. There was no deviation of the makeshift 'compass' in any of the circles.

Visits to each satellite in turn elicited the information that the crop swirl in the northernmost satellite was clockwise, whilst the other three were anti-clockwise. By the time we left the field, again by means of the tractor lanes, Jacqui and I were still very much in awe of what we'd seen. I noticed that a small group of people had by now assembled at the gate, and hoped the farmer was not among them.

The group at the gate consisted of a ginger-haired girl, several men and an elderly couple. As soon as we reached the gate, these folk started asking questions: *'What was it like in the circles? What do you think caused them? Did you feel anything?'* - were typical of the questions asked. It became an impromptu 'press conference', with Jacqui and I trying to answer as best we could, bearing in mind that neither of us had ever before been in a corn circle!

It was while Jacqui was talking to the ginger-haired girl, that I became aware of a small man at the back of the little knot of people. He was about 45-ish, of average height and build, and his hair was cut short, with a little fringe. On the whole there was absolutely nothing that would normally have made this man stand out in a crowd, but for one thing: On his shoulder was a video camera and the winking red light told me that it was running - we were being filmed!

Moving out of sight of the camera, I saw that the man followed me with the lens. The elderly lady was now speaking, telling Jacqui that a 'UFO' had been seen over this very field a night or so previously. She looked at me. Did we think this could have been responsible for the circles ? Still aware of the little man who was attempting to keep me in the lens of his video camera, I pointed out the power lines. No, I didn't think anything as material as a UFO could have caused the circles. Nothing could 'land' there because of those power cables. No, it looked to me like some kind of aerial 'vortex' may have caused the circles. The old lady looked disappointed.

As the people began to talk amongst themselves, speculating on what causal factor had been at work in the wheat, so Jacqui and I took the opportunity to ease our way out of the 'conference'. Climbing over the gate, we called out 'goodbye' to the others and headed for the car, still being filmed by the man with the video camera! (Later, looking back on the incident, I wondered why I hadn't challenged the cameraman straight away; let's face it, it was a bit of a cheek).

We'd only just had time to reach the Capri and unlock the doors, when the cameraman approached. He didn't introduce himself but straight away asked what we thought of the circles. Something about the man, maybe it was just his attitude, made me wary of him. The stranger asked lots of searching questions, but wouldn't answer any himself, becoming vague when asked what he thought of it all.

'Do you contribute to any magazines?' asked Jacqui. He shrugged his shoulders. 'I might - then again, I might not,' he smiled. It was an enigmatic smirk, rather than a friendly grin. By now he'd been joined by a middle-aged woman with short, curly blond hair. She didn't have much to say, and stood around with a bored, vacant expression on her face.

'Have you ever heard of a magazine called *'The Unknown'*, and do you know why it stopped publication?' Jacqui said, referring to the A5 magazine of that title which had stopped appearing on bookshelves some months previously; no - one seemed to know why. An interesting little mag., it had covered all sorts of subjects from ghosts and UFO's to corn circles. Perhaps, if he was a contributor to such magazines, this man knew the reason.

No such luck. The cameraman looked blankly at her. 'Never heard of it,' he said.

'I've got copies of a magazine called *'Viewpoint Aquarius,'* went on Jacqui, 'It's got all sorts of theories in it, about the formation of circles. Trouble is,' she went on, 'I don't know where to send off for further copies of it, as I've lost the address.'

'Get it through *'Flying Saucer Review',*' said the man.

'That's all very well,' said Jacqui, 'But that's not easily available where I live. You can't walk into W.H.Smith and find that sort of mag. on the shelf!'

'That's easily solved!' grinned our new companion. 'Give me your address and I'll send you the FSR address.'

By now, I was becoming increasingly uneasy with this guy. There was nothing I could put my finger on, save for the way he asked a lot and told little. His whole manner was too casual for my liking. I tried to indicate to Jacqui that I didn't think she should give the stranger her address, but she didn't understand my sly dig in her ribs.

Fishing in her shoulder bag, Jacqui found an envelope to write her address on. This done, she gave it to the man, who smiled and put it in his pocket. He wrote something on a piece of paper and handed it to Jacqui.

'Ah, Mr. Taylor!' The newcomer was a tallish man, whom I recognised as being part of the 'audience' back at the gate. He was dressed in cord trousers and tweed jacket, and on his head was a battered Stetson. When he spoke, it was with an obviously well - honed accent, probably the result of a good public school, and he had something of the bearing of a military man about him.

A small boy, presumably his son, accompanied him. The newcomer and our mystery cameraman quite obviously knew each other well, and I listened intently as the conversation centred around the apparent flying activities of the man called 'Mr. Taylor'. It seemed that at some time in the recent past, the well-spoken newcomer and Taylor had been up in a plane flown by Taylor for the purpose of photographing the circles. The newcomer was trying to arrange another flight.

'When do you want to go?' asked Taylor.

'Not for a day or so,' replied the other. 'I've just come from Petersfield and have to get back. I'll be in contact.'

'OK,' said Taylor. 'I'll wait to hear from you.'

The newcomer turned on his heel and left, walking a short distance to an estate car packed full of camping gear. Taylor turned to Jacqui (it was noticeable that it was to her that he directed all his attention...) and resumed his questioning.

'I saw you bending down in a small circle,' he said, 'What were you doing?'

Jacqui looked at him strangely. 'Nothing,' she said. Taylor persisted; 'What did you do, what did you find?' When all he got was a shake of the head in reply he said; 'What did you see?'

'We didn't see anything,' retorted Jacqui, sharply.

What was this man up to? What business was it of his what we'd seen or found?

But he didn't give up.

'What do you think caused the circles ?' demanded Taylor - you had to hand it to him, this bloke was persistent!

'It looks as if some sort of vortex has flattened the crop and then ascended away,' I said finally, hoping that this would satisfy Taylor's strange curiosity. Taylor just looked bemused.

'Anyway,' I turned to Jacqui, 'It's time we went and got some food.'

'Why not use the *'Waggon & Horses'* down the road?' suggested Taylor. 'That's not a bad pub.'

'Damn the man!' I thought. 'It's almost as if he's aware of our intentions...'.

Aloud I said, 'We might, or we might go somewhere nearer home'.

Taylor shrugged. 'I'm going to climb Silbury and take some more film before the light goes,' he said. This I thought, was a fairly futile occupation as it was now dusk. My face must have conveyed my unspoken thoughts because, with another of his enigmatic grins, Taylor set off in the direction of the ancient hill with his female companion in tow.

Jacqui and I said nothing to each other until we were in the car and speeding off along the A4. 'What did you make of *HIM*?' I said.

'I don't know.' replied Jacqui. 'He seemed to want to know all about what we were up to in that field. I didn't like his attitude much.'

'Nor me,' I agreed. 'He was far too nosey - and he was filming us.'

Jacqui looked startled. 'When?'

'When we were talking to those people at the gate - didn't you notice?'

'No, I bloody didn't!' she exclaimed angrily, 'He's got a cheek! Still,' she added, 'We know his name and address. 'F.C.Taylor',' she read from the piece of paper which the man called Taylor had given her, '.. He lives in Andover. He's even put down his phone number....'

I pulled up in the car park opposite the *'Waggon & Horses'* in Beckhampton, and switched off the engine. I locked up the car we crossed the road to the pretty thatched pub. Entering the bar, we were pleased to see that it was not too crowded and we had no trouble in finding a seat, so after ordering food, we retired to a pew-type seat near the door with our drinks and held a post-mortem on the events of the last hour.

'What did you make of those circles?' I said, after a long pull on my pint of 6X.

'Weird!' Jacqui replied. ' I've seen plenty in magazines, but when you see them in real life - they're so perfect.'

'I agree. I've wondered what they looked like close up, and now I know. Rog will be interested to know what we've seen. In fact,' I went on, 'He'll want to come up here with us to see for himself!'

'Rog' was Roger Davis, a long - time friend of mine and companion in earth - mysteries investigations. Rog and I had been at school together, and over the years, we'd followed 'ley-lines'; visited many an ancient site; practiced dowsing, and drunk many a pint of real ale in the process.

Soon, the food arrived and it was time to stop talking and start eating; the plaice and chips was good. In between mouthfuls, I asked Jacqui what she thought Taylor's part in all this was.

'No idea,' was the reply.

'He must have some influence, y'know,' I went on , 'To be able to get his hands on a plane whenever he wants to. He's also too bloody inquisitive for my liking. Shifty looking bloke too! What are you looking at me like that for?'

Jacqui was giving me furtive glances and inclining her head to one side. I slowly looked round and there, right behind me, was F.C.Taylor and his female companion. The Mona Lisa smile was still on Taylor's face. They must have heard every word...

'How long has he been there?' I hissed.

'Don't know,' came the answer, ' I've only just noticed him.'

Deliberately avoiding the subject of crop circles, Jacqui and I carried on with our meal in comparative silence. Shortly, Jacqui got up to go to the loo. She hadn't been gone more than a minute, when Taylor, who'd been to the bar, suddenly walked swiftly to the door and went out into the road. Less than a minute later he was back, the grin this time somewhat sheepish. He sat down next to me.

'I thought your young lady had gone outside,' he said, 'I've just spoken to the wrong person!'

It crossed my mind to ask him why he should have wanted to follow Jacqui out of the pub anyway, but at that moment, she returned and took her seat. Taylor turned to his female companion and said: ' I've just spoken to the wrong girl!' The blonde woman still looked bored stiff and said nothing. Taylor turned back to me. 'What do you think of those circles?' he said.

God's teeth! Didn't the man ever give up?

'I really don't know,' I replied, carefully and non-committally.

'You must have some idea,' he insisted.

'Do you film many circles?' said Jacqui, butting in.

'Quite a few,' replied Taylor. 'All over the place. You've got to be careful though. I know a place in Hampshire, near Winchester in fact, where the Farmer will shoot first and ask questions later.'

'How do you manage to find the time and money to do this?' enquired Jacqui.

Taylor paused for a moment. 'I'm a driving-instructor,' he said shortly, as if that explained it all. Presumably driving-instructors must be wealthy people if they flew aircraft as well...

'Where did you learn to fly?' I asked.

'That was some time ago, now,' said Taylor, evasively.

'Did you learn to fly with the air force?'

Taylor laughed. 'No.'

'And you find these circles, do you?' I said.

'I'm almost always first at the site of a new circle,' he replied. 'And I've worked with a chap who put forward the idea of the weather being responsible. He's appeared on television with his theory.'[1]

'Have you ever published anything on the subject of circles?' asked Jacqui, trying the same question she'd had no reply to back at the lay-by.

'My friends and I are trying to publish our findings,' Taylor said darkly, 'but we're encountering a lot of problems. People don't want to know.'

'What sort of problems?'

'Just problems. My friend Pat Delgado is trying to write about it, but there's these problems...'

'Come on,' I urged, 'tell us!'

F.C.Taylor gave me a strange look. Then he turned to Jacqui and changed the subject.

'Do you recognise the shapes?'

'What shapes?' retorted Jacqui, taken by surprise.

'The shape that those circles formed back at Silbury. You must know it.'

'Must I?'

'Yes. Look at it again - you'll recognise it.'

'Oh,' said Jacqui, glancing at me with a puzzled look on her face.

'What do the farmers think about all this,' I asked, determined to get back into the conversation. 'Surely they must get annoyed at the damage to the crop?'

'Oh, they do,' agreed Taylor. 'As I said just now, there's a chance that you'd get shot if you went into some circles near Winchester. You know,' he went on, 'Many strange things happen to people investigating circles, like camera lenses melting and bending... and - other things'

He'd said something similar back at the layby, and that had been enough to make me take my camera gear into the pub with me. However, this sounded a bit far-fetched. Still, I had to admit that I'd had trouble taking photos in the South circle at Avebury the year before. Although I'd later attributed this to a flat battery in the camera, nevertheless it had been an odd event. [2] Recalling this incident, and listening to Taylor's strange claims, I did wonder what the connection might be, and just hoped that the pictures of that day's corn circles would come out ok.

Turning my thoughts back to Taylor again, I tried to take the opportunity to find out who the bloke we'd nicknamed the 'military man' was.

'Does your friend get involved with these strange happenings?' I asked.

Taylor looked puzzled. He frowned, 'Which friend?'

'The one who spoke to you back at the car park; the man who wanted to fly in a plane with you on a photographic trip.'

F.C.Taylor relaxed. 'Oh, him. Yes, he comes with us on occasions. He's got friends in high places. *Powerful friends.*'

However Taylor meant it to sound, this last statement came out like a threat. It was time to take the offensive.

'Why did you video us?' I demanded. 'Isn't it polite to ask before doing something like that to total strangers?'

Again the grin. 'No, not really,' relied Taylor. 'I like to keep a record of people who are interested in the circles.'

'Why?'

Taylor shrugged. 'It's an interest of mine. I'm as interested in the people who research the circles as I am in the circles themselves. Then when we meet again, I recognise them and remember what they were saying and doing when we last met.'

'But we've never met you before, and the chances of us ever meeting again are pretty remote,' I protested. Taylor chuckled, then became serious. He leaned forward and said in a matter - of - fact voice: 'Our paths will cross. Make no mistake about it - *our paths WILL cross*!'

Why did this man talk in riddles? Just then that instantly - recognisable voice boomed from behind: 'Ah, Mr. Taylor! A word with you! '
It was the 'military man' from the lay-by, who was supposed to be on his way to Peterborough, or somewhere like that. Neither of us liked the idea of being 'interrogated' by TWO of these strange people, so we took advantage of the newcomer's arrival, made our excuses and left the pub rapidly.

Before the summer was out that year, the field opposite Silbury Hill had produced another set of five circles, interlinked with the original set. On a visit to these new circles with Roger Davis, Jacqui and I noticed that there appeared to be another formation of circles away across the fields to the left of the Devizes road. We set off to investigate and, sure enough, there was another set of five circles in the 'dice' formation. These however, were fairly rough, and we deemed them to be hoaxes, probably copied from the Silbury formations.

But then a doubt formed: as these new circles were not easily visible from the road, did it mean that the 'new' circles were not that new, and were in fact 'practice' circles and that hoaxers had been able to make the Silbury ones more convincing?

There, our interest in the circles might have stumbled to a halt if it had not been for an item about the circles on the BBC West local affairs programme *'Points West'* during the week following the second visit to the circles.

The item concerned a Wiltshire local authority worker named Roy Lucas, who'd been trimming hedges with a tractor flail near Windmill Hill, not far from Avebury, when he'd seen what he described as 'spinning columns of mist' a few fields away. When he later went to the area, Circles were discovered in the crop. Lucas was not claiming that the 'columns of mist' he saw had caused the actual circles found, but believed it was possible that they were responsible for other circles, as did a meteorologist, Dr Terence Meaden, who was also briefly interviewed on the programme. He postulated that it was a form of spinning wind, a 'vortex' that caused all crop circles.

I had never heard of the meteorologist, nor his interest in the circles, and it was coincidental that on a visit to my parents later that same week, that my Mother gave me a small cutting she'd taken from the *'Daily Mail'* at some time in the recent past. The cutting was a letter to the paper from - Dr Terence Meaden! Dr Meaden was appealing for anyone who came across crop circles to send him the information. I thought it might be a good idea to contact the scientist...

But first, having now been 'bitten' by the circles bug it was to another part of Wiltshire that we went next to look for more crop circles. In an old copy of *'The Unknown'*, Jacqui had read that circles were often found in the corn fields below Bratton Castle, the Iron Age fort on the slopes above the Westbury White Horse. I knew the area well, having worked in Frome for a while some years previously, so, one fine day in late August Jacqui and I headed for Westbury.

The trip was not in vain, for there, in the wheatfield below Bratton Castle, were several circles! As we looked down from the ramparts, in a field to the right was a shape not unlike a snowman; a smaller circle on the same axis as a larger one, and just touching the edge of the latter. Beyond this, was a single small circle, with a ragged edge. The ragged-edged circle was not at all distinct, even through binoculars, but it could easily be ascertained that the large circle was swirled clock-wise, the smaller one anti-clockwise.

In another field to the left, was a large isolated single circle, which was swirled anti-clockwise, while near the edge of the field by the road, were two small circles, not touching each other. The left hand one was swirled clock-wise; the right-hand one anti-clock-wise. There also appeared to be a further small circle, way over the other side of the road, adjacent to the railway line, but it wasn't very clear. These were duly photographed.

All the slides I took of crop circles that summer came out well. There were no further dealings with F.C.Taylor, and, as Christmas approached, the subject was kept alive by the photo's and the occasional evening of speculation over a pint or two of real ale in front of a roaring log fire in the comfort of our local pub, the 'Bull'. It was there that we hit on the idea of sending F.C.Taylor a Christmas card with a 'dice' formation drawn on it. A week later F.C. sent a reply: inside the card, written in a tiny scrawl, were the words: *'Our paths WILL cross - you wait and see'.* [3]

Chapter Three
THE STORY SO FAR...
Aliens and Weather

It was a cold, wet Saturday in January 1989. Jacqui and I were in the Clifton area of Bristol where we'd been browsing around the antiques markets. Jacqui suddenly fancied a bar of chocolate and went into a newsagent to buy one. I followed her in and found her with a bar of chocolate in one hand, and a copy of some esoteric magazine in the other hand. I peered over her shoulder.

The mag. was entitled *'Link-Up'* and claimed to be a *'...Network of Expanding Consciousness...'*. Wow, man! Far out! What the hell was she doing with that? Jacqui had, I knew, gone through a 'Hippie' phase a few years back, but was now totally against all this 'expanding consciousness' stuff. So what was she doing with the mag?

She handed it to me without a word. *'Round and round in Circles'* it said; *'Circles in the fields, and circles in the sky'*. I flipped through the pages and what I saw on page 4 was enough to make me buy the mag straight away: the name that leapt out at me from the pages of writing was that of F.C.Taylor!

On the way home in the car, Jacqui read bits of the article out to me. It seemed that Fred Taylor (that was our driving instructor and his nickname was 'Busty'!) worked closely with an electrical engineer called Colin Andrews, who in turn apparently co-ordinated a small team of scientists and engineers who researched the circles every year. Colin Andrews apparently felt that that the circles were 'evolving' too fast for them to be a product of Nature, and felt that there was a 'more extra-ordinary explanation' - but wouldn't say what.

This sounded to us like a touch of the mystics. Next, the article mentioned Dr Terence Meaden, who forwarded some interesting views about his theory. Firstly, Meaden said that more circles than ever before had been found in the vicinity of Salisbury Plain, and that he considered that this increase was only because more people were out looking for them. Then there was an explanation of how he believed the circles to be formed: by a type of temporary, stationary whirlwind, which pressed down on the crops. The wind, it seemed, was diverted around obstacles such as hills, met up on the other side, and in turbulent areas caused 'eddies'. These in turn caused the 'whirlwind'. To both Jacqui and myself, this sounded perfectly feasible. I could picture a similar effect in a smoothly running stream, where a rock or something was placed in the way of the flow. Little 'whirlpools' would form downstream of the obstacle. So was this what made Crop Circles?

Just to put a dampener on this, the magazine had consulted weather experts at the Met. Office in Bracknell, who appeared to think that Meaden's Vortex was too rare to explain the many circles and their consistent formations. Then a couple called Martin and Petronel Payne, who worked on a farm in Hampshire, said that they were convinced that the circles were the result of an extra-terrestrial visitation.

Well, everyone was entitled to their opinion, so I supposed that it was quite in order for them to claim that the circles were the results of 'Flying Saucers'. The circles did look very much as if some sort of round, spinning object had descended into the crop - that much couldn't be denied. Though why any 'alien' would land in Wiltshire alone was beyond me . However, that question was soon answered, because the article not only claimed that the circles mainly formed in a rough 'triangle' formed by linking Wantage,

Winchester and Warminster, but went on to say that this was also an area of considerable Military activity. The inference was plainly that the 'Aliens' or what have you, were spying on the military exercises.

Somebody, I thought, has been reading too many of the books from the Mystical Bookshop. 'Triangles', 'Aliens' and now the Military! It was symptomatic of the 'Bermuda Triangle' tripe and the 'Warminster Thing' flap of the late 1960's. Next the article said that Colin Andrews had hinted that the loss of a Harrier jet over Salisbury Plain in October 1987, where the pilot 'mysteriously' ejected and was killed, was due in some way to the Circles! It appeared to me that this Andrews bloke was jumping to some pretty strange conclusions, because not only was the unfortunate pilot's body found in a *nearby* field and *not* the one in which circles appeared *two years* later, but the problem had been due to failure of the Harrier's canopy ejection firing system, as a contact at RNAS Yeovilton had later explained.[1]

Later in the evening, when Jacqui was looking at the article in more depth, she suddenly exclaimed: 'Hey - this Andrews bloke knows Pat Delgado!'

'So?' I didn't see the connection.

'Don't you remember? Delgado is the man Taylor spoke of at the pub last year. And I know where I've seen his name before - he's the one who wrote about the 'Delgado Effect' in *'The Unknown'*. ' Now I remembered. In the article, the author had claimed to have invented a form of perpetual motion. We'd done a bit of research and found that it had really been discovered in the 1930's, and was apparently due to air currents or something similar which kept a rotor moving without any visible means of propulsion. Delgado had 're-discovered' this and given his name to it.

And F.C.Taylor claimed that he'd never heard of the *'Unknown'*!

The article also mentioned Professor Archie Roy. Professor Roy was professor of Astronomy at Glasgow University, and he, to all intents and purposes found the circles 'a most intriguing mystery'. Paul Devereux, the then Editor of *'The Ley Hunter'*, and the man who'd recently run the 'Dragon Project' a long-standing research project at the Rollright Stones in Oxfordshire, was of the opinion however, that it was not extra-terrestrials who caused the crop circles. He didn't venture what his personal opinion was.

'There's more,' went on Jacqui. 'Delgado and this Colin Andrews are writing a book about the circles, and it should be in the shops by February 1989. That's pretty soon, I wonder if I could order it?' she mused. 'That's interesting,' she continued, 'there's a preview of the book here and - Oh, my God! - there's mention of 'strange lights in the sky', 'energy beams', 'ley lines', the 'Earth Goddess healing herself', and -listen to this! Colin Andrews claims that his parent's dog was violently sick when they took it into a circle!'

Oh, dear. The usual stuff. Was this lot aging hippies left over from the Warminster business? Perhaps we'd soon find out; Jacqui vowed to order the book as soon as she could get into Bristol again.

The next we heard of crop-circles was on another visit to my parents. This time it was my father who had some information for me.

'BBC *'Points West'* had a bit about crop circles on *'Person to Person'* last week,' he said. 'As you know, it's repeated on BBC Radio Bristol, so I taped it for you.'

This was good news! I'd been on late shift, and hadn't seen the *'Person to Person'* topical phone - in slot on the local current affairs programme. I eagerly took the offered cassette, and promising to copy it and return the original, hurried back home to listen.

'Person to Person' was a phone in/interview slot run at that time by one - time musician and latterly Radio Bristol DJ, John Turner. The usual format was for Turner to pose a question and invite people to comment for broadcasting the following week. The question for this programme was: "Corn Circles". Turner opened the phone-in by describing the circles and some of the claims associated with them.

The first callers were an elderly couple, who told of an experience that they'd had the previous year, near Winchester. They'd seen a circle in a field between Winchester and Petersfield, and were of the opinion that 'no-way could a whirlwind have travelled across that field'. They went on to say they were sceptics, but then related a UFO sighting, which they categorically believed in - without investigation. They also said that they believed the circles to be the landing sites of UFO's, and that they believed there were people 'out there'!

Before introducing the next caller Turner mentioned something about Dr Terence Meaden. It seemed that Meaden too had a book out on the subject - but most of Turner's comments were lost in a wave of static interference. The next person to call had mistaken the subject and wanted to talk about Witches, and was followed by a caller who had a slightly wacky theory that the circles were caused by 'pranksters' who sprayed the young crop with a 'strong spray' (he couldn't say what) and this caused the mature crop to fall down. It was an idea to be repeated from time to time as the investigation progressed, but at this stage it was all news to me.

The next caller was from Bath, and introduced himself as Richard Green [2]. Richard had visited the site of some circles, near Avebury, one evening, with a lady friend. They'd experienced 'energy levels' and 'had an experience' whereby the girl turned to 'white light' and Green himself ' *...had communication - just as if these space people were talking to me...'*. This prompted John Turner to ask: *'...you aren't putting me on, are you?...'* *'No,'* was the answer. Green went on to say he thought the space-people were *'...caring for us...it's about looking after us...I felt their space-ship was above us...'* and he saw *'...flashes of green light... going into Silbury Hill!*

'...You won't mind me asking you...you weren't on anything-were you?' asked Turner.

'No. Not at all,' came the answer.

Green claimed that he was 'in tune' with the aliens, and, as such, believed he was 'chosen' to be a communicant. I wasn't convinced.

Turner then related an incident which had happened to him back in the Sixties, where he'd been driving past Silbury Hill with folk singer Ralph McTell one night, and was overtaken by a flash car. Shortly afterwards, Turner's car broke down. When he was towed to a garage, there was the same sports car, which had previously overtaken him. Both cars had, oddly, suffered burnt-out wiring.[3] Turner confessed that he found the whole thing 'most extra-ordinary'. The mystery deepened.

Then an ex-army man came on the phone to relate a story of how he'd been on exercise on Salisbury Plain some years before, and had seen a bright light which hovered over him and his colleagues for ten minutes or so, during which time the ammunition in the soldiers' machine-guns 'fused' together. The theme of the programme was getting well away from crop circles!

At last the programme came to the man whose side of the story I wanted to hear: Dr Terence Meaden. Dr Meaden had, he said, been investigating crop circles since the day he'd seen a couple of them in a field near the Westbury White Horse, in 1980. He went on to describe the areas from which he had no account of circles being found, and appealed for eye-witness accounts of circles being formed. The more I listened to this scientist, the more I liked his theory: It had substance. He would not be drawn on whether or not he believed the tale previously recounted by Richard Green. Meaden had written a book as well, which was to be published shortly. Dr Meaden gave his address, and I resolved to send off for a copy of his book, to add to the Andrews/Delgado book, which Jacqui had ordered.

When I played the *'Person to Person'* tape to Jacqui a day or so later, her first reaction was: 'I know that bloke!'

'Which bloke?' I asked.

'Richard Green, who had the 'alien contact' at Silbury. When I lived in Plymouth,' she said, 'There was a bloke named Richard Green who was the 'friend of a friend'. He was a bit of a fantasiser; y'know the sort - he had a vivid imagination. He was also an Acid-head.'

'You mean he took LSD?'

'From time to time, yes. He wasn't addicted, so far as I recall, but he did drop Acid on occasions; most people in that group did. Except me,' she hastened to add.

I leaned back on the sofa. 'Do you reckon he was on a trip when he had his experience, then?' I said.

'Could be,' she muttered. 'Acid-heads always reckon the trip is better when shared with someone, and he did have a girl with him...'

The next day, Jacqui phoned directory inquiries and attempted to find out if this Richard Green was on the phone, but she had no success. As luck would have it, my parents had also videoed the *'Person to Person'* item when it was broadcast on 'Points

West'. I didn't have a video at that time, and Jacqui's was a Betamax, whereas my folks' machine was VHS. It didn't help that Rog was in possession of a Betamax as well. But a viewing at my folks' place proved that the 'Richard Green' in question was undoubtedly the same one that Jacqui was referring to. So much for HIS evidence!

Over the rest of February and during March, I spent a lot of time working in the area of Westbury, Wilts, and this helped to keep the subject of the circles fresh in mind. Noting that in previous years, the early circles seemed to arrive in May, Jacqui, Rog and I made a point of visiting various sites between us to see if there were any 'visitations'. During the merry month we managed to visit Bratton and Silbury several times but - nothing doing. May turned into flaming June (which wasn't) and still we continued our patrols.

It was to Dr Meaden that we turned next.

I wrote to the meteorologist asking if I could buy a copy of his book, mentioning that I'd heard all about it on the BBC. Within a week or so I received a letter from Dr Meaden, thanking me for my enquiry and advising me that the book was available, and that I should send a cheque to him. I did so, and got a copy of the book back almost by return of post. A note accompanied the book: '...*Book enclosed. Hope you enjoy it. Phone if you come across any circles. Terence Meaden...*'

Just a glance through the pages of Meaden's book *'The Circles Effect and its Mysteries'* showed that this was indeed all I'd hoped it would be: a scientific book which looked into the mystery from a sensible and scientific viewpoint. Full of diagrams, information, photographs and, importantly, eye-witness accounts of circles forming. This book became essential bed-time reading for the next week! So now we had both sides of the story so far.

Chapter Four
WHERE DO WE GO FROM HERE?
New circles-Magic circles-Psychic circles

June 1st 1989

Where we went next was Cheesefoot Head, on the hunt for circles. .Neither Jacqui nor I had the faintest idea where Cheesefoot Head was other than that it was in Hampshire and near Winchester. The roadmap we had showed nothing of that name so it was going to be a bit hit and miss. We spent a morning wandering around Hampshire to no avail and paused at lunchtime for a snack at a pub. There we decided to ask some locals where Cheesefoot Head was. To our surprise, nobody seemed to have a clue until one chap said he'd heard of a place that he thought was pronounced '*Chezzafoot*' but didn't know where it was. On second thoughts, he said, it might be south of Winchester. And so it proved to be. We left Winchester on the A272 towards Petersfield, acting on a hunch as this town had been mentioned in some article we recalled seeing. We were in luck. A mile or so out of town we found the unmistakable location of the Devil's Punchbowl at Cheesefoot Head. We parked in the car park and hurried to the edge of the bowl to be met by disappointment – there were no circles there.

On the 11 June we went, with Rog, to Bratton. Here we found that the roads up to the white horse were closed by the police and local council. Measures to prevent New Age travellers camping on top of the horse were in place. We could see no circles anywhere.

On June 19 Jacqui and I went back to Bratton – still no circles. At this point, we were thinking that travellers were possibly responsible for some of the circles and the lack of travellers and lack of circles at Bratton was significant. If the roads and parking spots were blocked, we reasoned, any hoaxers couldn't make circles without being spotted, and that year - none formed anywhere near the horse.

June wasn't a particularly good month weather – wise. Undeterred by the seemingly daily rain we were watching for the first circles to appear and following the weather signs thought to herald the right conditions for the type of wind vortex as suggested in Dr Meaden's book. Sunday 25th June was a lovely day. That evening the signs were right. A cold front approached and passed over Wiltshire. Monday dawned with heavy showers and strong winds, which continued into Tuesday, dying out in the afternoon. Early that evening, Jacqui came in with the news that circles had formed in Wiltshire!

Great! Where?

'Near Calne. Jim Crow [1] phoned me at work and told me that a mate of his had seen them.'

It seemed that the circles were in a field to the left of the A4, between Calne and Beckhampton. Later, the two of us set out for Wiltshire. Parking in a layby opposite the White Horse at Calne, we stood at the roadside and surveyed the circles. There appeared to be about seven circles, two fields away from the road. We looked around to see if there was a farm in sight, so we could ask permission to enter the field. As with the previous summer's circles site, there was not a farmhouse to be seen. We'd have to chance it. Carrying the camera gear and a notepad, we set off around the field boundary. It took about twenty minutes to make our way to the circles. We noted that the main formation was similar to that at Silbury the previous year: a large central circle with four satellites. Only this time there was an additional circle next to one of the satellites. Of these circles, the three 'northern' satellites were swirled anti-clockwise, and the main circle and the other two satellites, clockwise. Some yards away were two small circles, which had been made so close to each other that they touched, with only a few strands of standing corn between them.

We measured the circles as best we could, not having a long tape, and took photos. By now, more people had seen the circles and were threading their tortuous way towards us. But it was a man with his dog, striding straight across the crop leaving an unmistakable trail which caused us to leave the field as quickly as we could in case the farmer should arrive. Back on the road again, we looked at the plan Jacqui had drawn. Something about the formation bothered us, and we went up onto the hill above the White Horse to get a better look. Sure enough, when viewed from the hill, the formation resembled - a Celtic cross! What were we to make of it? The weather conditions as set down by Dr Meaden, had been right for circles to appear - and they had. But a cross?

We returned the next night with Rog. Again we took the long way around the field boundary to gain access to the circles. More photos were taken and we were just about to leave when some other 'visitors' arrived to view the circles and told us that fifteen more circles had appeared in a field between Silbury Hill and Avebury.....

Twenty minutes later we were at the bottom of Silbury Hill, and a further ten minutes saw us standing on top of the hill gazing to the north at the group of circles below. There were several sets of the 'dice five' formation, similar to those which had attracted our attention the year before. Whether it was the look of the circles or where they were - I don't know, but for some reason we decided that they were probably fakes without going down to see them at close quarters, and retired to the nearest pub. [2]

By the end of July, the Andrews/Delgado book 'Circular Evidence' was climbing the bestseller list and we at last managed to obtain a copy. It didn't take long to discover that while 'Circular Evidence' contained many spectacular photographs of Crop Circles, the underlying message in the text hinted that the whole phenomenon was probably to be attributed to 'Aliens'. The many references to 'lights in the sky' and so on served to press the point home. What a disappointment! We'd really thought there would be a sensible, detached viewpoint instead of a lot of un-substantiated, circumstantial evidence wrapped up in the old 'Aliens' theme. To our minds, although having only seen at first hand a relatively small number of circles, the answer seemed to lie with the 'Natural' rather than the 'Supernatural'. Even if it was to be found that a freak of the weather was causing these circles, surely this in itself was cause for excitement?

Meanwhile, Andrews and Delgado were riding high on a wave of publicity. The press and TV were helping them no end. It seemed that every TV report concerning circles was accompanied by New Age music and shots of dramatic cloud effects to add to the 'air of mystery' the report was to about to set. Whatever the TV/radio channel, more often than not it was Andrews and Delgado who got the mention, whilst Dr Meaden was only occasionally interviewed, and then usually just on local radio. It was on one such broadcast, which we picked up, on July 3rd, that the Professor, stated that there were '....140 circles in Wiltshire and 5 in Hampshire...' !

Jacqui and I were on holiday for the first week or so in July so it was left to Rog to investigate the Silbury area on July 6th. There was nothing new to be seen. Even the rain looked the same. Four days later he went there again and although the weather had bucked up, there were no new circles. Where the hell were they all then? Of course, it was our limited knowledge of the subject, which was leading us to concentrate on the areas we knew. The circles were appearing in places we'd never been to before. Jacqui and I returned from our holiday and went straight to Bratton to see if any circles had formed. They hadn't. We drove over to Silbury and were rewarded with the sight of a new set of 'dice', which had joined the first formations to the area. From the hill, the new arrivals looked pretty good, but away in a field to the right were a couple of smaller, rougher circles. These, we decided straight away, were hoaxes because of their roughness. We didn't investigate them closer.

James Belsey, of the *'Bristol Evening Post'* reviewed both Meaden's *'Circles Effect and its Mysteries'*, and *'Circular Evidence'*, on July 14th that year. He also claimed to review a new publication by Paul Fuller and Jenny Randles of BUFORA, called *'Mystery of the Circles'*. [3] In reality, whilst claiming scepticism for the mystics viewpoint, Belsey openly admitted that he *'...couldn't wade through...'* Fuller and Randles' booklet (less than a third the size of *"Circular Evidence"*) and found Meaden's book *'...dauntingly and off-puttingly technical...'*. But however sceptical he claimed to be, Belsey filled half a page with a review of *'Circular Evidence'* finally adding his own theory that circles may be formed by 'scar tissue' on the earth's surface, caused by old buildings and the like.

This sort of review was typical of the press reaction to the circles. Perhaps it was a means of providing light relief from stock market wobbles and Mrs. Thatcher's poll tax problems but the press seemed to always dismiss the meteorological theory and concentrate more on the mystical side of the subject. As the subject got into its stride in the 1990's, you could bet your life that there would be more air time given to the UFO/mystical viewpoint than Terence Meaden got. In the end, events would prove that it was probably just as well.

Tuesday July 18th 1989

The weather meantime had at last become more like summer. We decided to pay another visit to Cheesefoot. With Rog squeezed in the back of my Capri 2.8, Jacqui and I set off for Hampshire in the afternoon. We had a good, fast run down and arrived at the punchbowl, which was bathed in lovely early evening sun. Parking in the nearby carpark we made our way to the edge of the bowl. There was not a mark in the crop. What now?

Now concerned a theory I had developed concerning dowsing effects reputed to be found in and around the circles we'd read about. The theory went something like this: many circles were being discovered in places which were near military bases or training grounds[4]. I knew that long pipelines ran underground to these sites and were marked by white 'stiles' in hedgerows. I figured that if there was something in the dowsing game, then it was most probably picking up something from these underground pipes. I'd noticed a couple of these 'white stiles' either side of the A272 as we approached the punchbowl, so the three of us walked back along the side of the busy road until we came to them. We crossed the road and elected to follow the pipeline across a couple of fields in case we came across any circles. We hadn't gone far before we came across a couple of men walking towards us. They told us that there was a large crop circle in the next field...

Excitedly, we hurried across the field and through a gap in the hedge. Sure enough, in a field of ripening wheat, was a magnificent circle. Not just any old ordinary circle, though, this one had a long, curved tapering tail coming from it. Inside the crop was pressed perfectly flat. The men we'd spoken to earlier came back into the circle to do some measuring and, as the sun set over Hampshire, a helicopter came up out of the dusk and hovered overhead for a while. Presumably it was a civvie chopper as the markings were not military registration marks. We imagined the occupants to be taking photos. It was a perfect summer's evening for it. We did likewise.

Leaving the 'circle-tail' we made our way back towards the car, only to come across the remains of two more circles which had been harvested. Only the bent remains of stems were left and Jacqui straight away christened them 'Dead' circles. The name stuck. These were also photographed before we finally left the cornfields and made our way back to the car. Leaving Cheesefoot Head we made our way down the hill and into Winchester, thence to the A34 and A303 and homeward.

Over the next four weeks nothing much happened. We heard of no new circles to see and so dedicated much time to making sense of Dr Meaden's book. Once one realised that it was, in effect, an academic book written for academics, then things became clearer. It was definitely not aimed at the 'popular' market. Nevertheless, the theory was feasible. Electrically-charged whirlwinds could be responsible for crop circles. The theory was about to be put to the test.

It was the first Saturday in August. I was working a late shift and left for work at about 13.30. Later that afternoon I had a phone call. It was Jacqui. 'I've just seen a whirlwind!' she announced. It transpired that she'd decided to go out somewhere and was driving out of Pucklechurch when, passing the Remand Centre, she'd noticed the trees on the right-hand side of the road swaying violently. Surprised, as it was a fine summer's day, she'd pulled over to look. The cause was a 'whirlwind' which came out of the trees and onto the road, where it faded away. After I'd come home from work that evening it was too late to do anything about investigating, but the next day we cycled the half-mile from my house to the field; The crop of grass had been cut and harvested but there were some clumps of hay lying around. Looking further we were stunned to find circular traces in the remaining grass!

The grass stems had been twisted into a semblance of a circle. Had the grass been longer, there seemed to be little doubt that a fairly good circle might have been left. There was a snag – the 'circle' was a few hundred yards away from where Jacqui had seen the 'whirlwind' pass over the field boundary. Nevertheless, it was a circle of sorts and it had appeared roughly in line with Meaden's theory. Across the field was a small hill of sorts which concealed an underground reservoir – could this 'hill' have been the place which caused the vortex to form? Undaunted by the roughness of the formation, we took photos and that evening I urged Jacqui to write down exactly what she'd seen and we'd send the report off to Dr Meaden for his comments. Some time after sending the report off, we received a note from Terence Meaden asking if we could send him copies of the photos that we'd taken. This was done. On September 19th I had another letter from Dr Meaden

– he considered the report of the Pucklechurch circle important enough to want to publish our report in his magazine, the '*Journal of Meteorology*' and also include it in his latest book on the subject! Needless to say we gave permission!

These were the times when earth mysteries researcher Andrew Collins was riding high on the crest of a wave of success with his books about '*The Black Alchemist*'. [5] Jacqui, Rog and myself were all keen followers of these tales and had the books. We even had plans to attend Collins' 'Psychic Questing' conference in London the following month. Ever ready to keep an open mind about things, the three of us gathered at my place one September evening and debated whether '...extra-magical influences could cause additional electrical disturbances in the atmosphere leading to the creation of crop circles...'. The motion was not carried!

We talked at length about the Andrews/Delgado cropwatch of 1989 – '*Operation White Crow*' which had featured in an edition of the New Age magazine '*Kindred Spirit*'. It was noticeable even at that stage how crop circles did not arrive when fields were being watched, but quickly formed either somewhere else during a watch or near the watch site when the watchers were not there. This was given deep meaningful attention by the mystic believers who saw in this proof that 'they' were watching the watchers. We decided it showed that hoaxers were watching the watchers! Evidence for this was present in the (overlooked by most) fact that when the roads to and around Bratton camp in Wiltshire were closed to keep out travellers, no circles had formed. Or it proved that 'the Aliens' were afraid of the police!

Another letter from Terence Meaden told of a crop circle in the village of Kelston, near Bath. On the evening of 26th September, Jacqui and I set off to look for this formation and found it, harvested and 'dead' in a field near the 'Old Crown' inn. The weather was poor and the formation, a ringed single circle, was difficult to pick out and although it was only seven in the evening, clouds made it too dark to photograph. We did note that the circle had formed beneath power lines, in the manner of the previous year's Silbury set. What significance lay here we couldn't think, unless the power lines were a sighting mark in the dark for possible hoaxers.The following afternoon I returned on my motorcycle and successfully photographed the formation.

Autumn and October passed colourfully by, with only the 2nd anniversary of the 1987 Great Hurricane and the San Francisco earthquake being noteworthy events. Unless you count my taking out a subscription for the '*Journal of Meteorology*' ! We spent more time with Jim Crow and in particular attended a magical ceremony one weekend. Jim was part of a group of 'magicians' who were seemingly incensed by Andy Collins '*Black Alchy*' (as we nicknamed it) work. Not to be outdone by Collins' group and their well-publicised finding of seven swords [6], Crow and his friends had started searching for similar weapons. Crow himself had, through a series of dreams, been 'led' to a junk shop where he found a blade inscribed with 'Gaelic and runic' marks. He said he'd show it to us at the Psychic Questing conference. He also warned us to pretend not to know him at the event. Collins, he said, had: '...*Got a memory for people...don't ever underestimate him*...'. Very mysterious but we hadn't a clue what he was on about!

Crow's group was upset that Andy Collins was visiting the west in connection with some search for the 'Holy Grail' and were desperate to outdo him by producing some major magical stuff in the west. To this end, they'd decided that they would do no less than predict/influence the forthcoming birth of the Duchess of York's next child. We were invited to attend.

On the day in question, Jacqui and I met up with Jim Crow and his group in Glastonbury. We moved on to Street and, on a hill near some 'sacred stones' [which looked all the world like a stile to me...] the ceremony was performed. Much waving of ceremonial swords was accompanied by the ritual chanting of the group, colourful robes blowing in the wind. When it was done, they confidently predicted that Fergie would have a son, who would be the reincarnation of Mary, Queen of Scots (!). As we know, she didn't and it wasn't! The only interesting thing which happened was when one of the group, a gypsy-looking woman in her fifties, predicted that Jacqui and I wouldn't stay together. She was right on this point!

Little more happened that Autumn. Rog was off the scene for a while as his mother had been taken ill. Jacqui and I spent a lot of time delving into the '*Black Alchemist*' and the subject of Psychic Questing and finding holes in both. We went to the Questing Conference in London on October 14th and were disappointed. The bill promised many 'names' from the world of Earth Mysteries, including John Michell. He didn't show, nor did Graham Phillips or Martin Keatman [7] and various unknown people filled the spaces. The feline-like Andy Collins was everywhere, organising and arranging. During the intervals I was pleased to see Mary Caine, of Glastonbury Zodiac fame, so had a chat to her, which made up for some of the disappointments. I also got talking to a very old lady who was into Crop Circles. She'd studied the recent circle found near Leicester and was very interested in the subject. When I mentioned the *Journal of Meteorology* however, she lost interest in the conversation!

Jim Crow's mystic blade (which he showed us only when Andy Collins wasn't around) turned out to be nothing more than an old Scottish bayonet!

Christmas came and with it the now usual exchange of cards with Busty Taylor.

Chapter Five
COLOUR DEVELOPMENTS
Dark deeds-White flag- Red faces-White lights

January 1990 started with almost three weeks of severe storms and gales across the West Country. Trees were blown down and there was much flooding. Crop Circles were largely forgotten and we spent much time going round antiques markets and museums. However, the local BBC news programme *Points West* ran a piece about circles, including lots of dramatic cloud effects and New Age music. The UFO brigade got lots of publicity whilst Dr Meaden was hardly mentioned. I wrote to the BBC in an effort to 'put the record straight' that there was another explanation to be considered other than the paranormal. All I got back was a polite letter of acknowledgement.

Another incident served to distract us from the crop circles. One day I was showing some pictures of crop circles to the owner of the shop where I had my photos processed. He was fascinated. I explained that I thought they were caused by a meteorological phenomena but that many saw them as being caused by UFO's. Danny [1] looked at me and said '...I don't believe in UFO's, but...'. He stopped and looked embarrassed before telling me the tale.

It seemed that a few weeks before, during one of the stormy nights, he and a friend had been driving from Mangotsfield, on the outskirts of Bristol, towards Pucklechurch where they were going for a pint. As they passed through the village of Shortwood, Danny had seen what he described as a '..ball of fire, about the size of a double-decker bus...' fly fast and low across the sky in a north west-south east direction, before vanishing below the horizon. He and his friend had been so shocked by this that when they reached Pucklechurch (which is on a hill) they fully expected to find that a light aircraft had crashed there. To their lasting amazement, there was no trace of the 'ball of fire'.

Knowing Danny, I asked if he'd already had a few.

'Yes, I had – but Don (his friend, a local businessman) was driving and he hadn't had a drop at that stage'.

This was an amazing tale. I got Danny to write down the details and a day or so later, told Rog. We plotted the course of Danny's flying ball of fire on the map and saw that if it had missed Pucklechurch, then in theory it would have hit the hills in the region of Lansdown, near Bath. If it missed that area, then the ground dropped away and the object could have passed on its way right over Bradford-on Avon and into deepest Wiltshire without meeting any further obstructions.

The next weekend Rog and I set off to look for traces. We were stunned to find that where a row of trees crowned Freezing Hill, next to Lansdown, there was now a gap! We climbed the hill and found two or three trees had been knocked or blown down! The trees had already been cut up by the farmer, so there was little hope of seeing any sign that the trees had been hit by anything. It was plain to see that if they had been knocked over by some low-flying object then that object would have henceforth had many miles of low ground over which to recover its height. What had Danny and Don seen? Could it have been a meteorite? Who better to ask than a physicist and meteorologist? I wrote a letter to Dr Terence Meaden, asking his opinion. I never received a reply.

We never got to the bottom of that one, but the gap in the trees on Freezing Hill remains as a reminder of the incident.

What with this, the magical ceremonies and psychic questing, Crop Circles were very much on the back-burner: Well, it was the 'Close Season'. However, during February, events took a startling new turn. BBC TV's *Daytime Live* programme, which had taken over the *Pebble Mill at One* slot, ran an un-seasonal piece on Crop Circles. On it were Colin Andrews and Pat Delgado pleading for help from members of the public during the coming summer and asking for all sightings of circles to be sent to them at the BBC Pebble Mill studio! Horrifyingly, they were being described as *'Scientists...'*

This was a coup for them and no mistake! Where, we wondered, was Dr Meaden in all this; Surely *he* was a scientist? Andrews and Delgado we knew were well into the UFO idea and were now 'consultants' to *Flying Saucer Review.*

No sooner had this shock landed than the *'Bristol Journal'* was giving lots of space to the work of a group of local UFO enthusiasts calling themselves 'Bristol Quest'. Headed by spokesman Richard Tarr, *Quest* claimed that UFO's were regularly flying over south Bristol, passing over Dundry Hill and disappearing towards Somerset. The 'saucers' had bright lights on them and red and green flashing lights as well. In fact they were very, very similar to what one could see most nights as aircraft, inbound to Bristol Airport, took up their position in the landing circuit.....

Laughable, and we couldn't see why the paper was giving this sort of rubbish space. What wasn't laughable was Tarr's claim that UFO's and crop circles were connected. Hopefully, something would soon be heard of Terence Meaden; But it wasn't Meaden who next got in the news but a dead cat. The charred remains of the cat were found on Clevedon beach and the newspapers made much of a possible Black Magic connection. Further articles in the Bristol Evening Post claimed that there was an increase in Black Magic rites in the West Country. 'Top People' were claimed to be involved. All this kept the magic theme going.

The spring arrived and nothing was heard about circles; UFO groups got more space in papers and magazines. About now, Jacqui, Rog and I started going to meetings of a small group of Bristol Flying Saucer enthusiasts. They were a mixed group of various ages and met at members houses. I'm not sure how we got involved with them although it may have been via a Jim Crow/Crop Circles connection. I recall giving them a talk about circles one night.

It was May before we were really aware of the circles scene again. One morning I received a surprise phone call from the chap who'd written the first crop circles articles I'd seen: Paul Fuller.

The voice on the phone was quiet, polite and extremely knowledgeable on the subject of crop circles. Paul was a director of the British UFO Research Organisation (BUFORA). Apparently he and another director, Jenny Randles, were working with Dr Meaden on the correllation between certain UFO sightings and car-stop cases, and the electrically-charged vortex which Dr Meaden named the Plasma-vortex and which he claimed made crop circles. Jenny and Paul were currently writing a book on the subject – could they have permission to use my photos and text from the Pucklechurch circle case to use in their book?

I was flattered. Of course they could. Paul explained that I would be eligible for a free copy when the book was published. We had much in common and got on well. Talk soon got round to other researchers and the subject of F.C.Taylor came up. I explained all about the incident at Avebury in 1988. Paul told me that 'Busty', who had supplied most of the photos for Andrews/Delgado's book, had apparently fallen out with them for some reason and whilst he still thought that there were strange forces at work, he'd waved the white flag and was now working with Terence Meaden. Paul promised to follow up the conversation with a letter of confirmation and rang off with the hope that we'd meet sometime during the summer.

Two things now happened. The first was that we decided that Terence Meaden was obviously at a disadvantage where the press was involved. It has been said that drama sells newspapers; regrettably, the TV channels were as bad. They were only interested in promoting the possibility that there was some sort of 'supernatural' element where the crop circles were involved. This was a distortion of the truth, but the truth didn't seem to matter to the TV people. So, when Terence Meaden put a note in the *Journal of Meteorology* asking for volunteers to assist with the 1990 'crop watch' – we wrote off volunteering our services. This time, I received a reply! Dr Meaden would be pleased to accept our offer of assistance and the crop watch would be held during June and July of that year. He would advise us further.

The next thing that happened was the advert in *J.Met.* advertising a unique event: there was to be an international conference on Crop Circles in Oxford on 23rd June. Apparently, Dr Meaden was also a director of an organisation known as *TORRO* (Tornado and Storm Research Organisation). *TORRO* it seems, held an annual conference on weather-related subjects. This year, the subject was the circles. Tickets were £20 each for non-J.Met subscribers, £15 for subscribers. We wanted to go! But there was a problem: I was the one who'd taken out the subscription. We could pay the difference or, as we were all to help with the cropwatch that summer, try to get three tickets for the lower rate.

I tried for the lower rate. It worked! I sent off the cheque for £45 and soon after received the tickets and programme of events. Here was yet another surprise...one of the speakers was none other than Busty Taylor! Paul Fuller had said Busty was now working with Meaden but this was unexpected! Busty was scheduled to give a 15 minute presentation of his video and photographic record of the circles. Other speakers were all from a scientific and academic background, including two professors from Japan. All in all it was an impressive line-up of people giving various levels of backing to Meaden's theory. We looked forward to the conference with eager anticipation.

During the early part of June we kept in touch with Paul Fuller who explained all about how, in 1988, he'd been the subject of furious solicitors' letters after he claimed, in private correspondence to someone, that certain claims made by Andrews/Delgado about their work status were somewhat exaggerated. Although it seemed that Fuller was correct, Andrews and Delgado had managed to threaten him with a libel suit if he didn't send them written apologies. Fuller could not contest this from a financial point of view and was advised by his solicitor to send apologies. This he begrudgingly did. The circular twosome then promptly published the apologies! Fuller had to suffer the embarrassment of having his name dragged through the dirt. All the more galling was the fact that he had proof that what he'd said in the letter about Andrews and Delgado was fairly insignificant, but true!!

And these two were appearing weekly on *Daytime Live* collecting information from the general public....

Saturday June 23rd 1990

The day of the First International Conference on Crop Circles dawned and, Jacqui driving, the three of us set off for Oxford via the M4 and A420. We found the venue, Oxford Polytechnic, and parked. Soon, we were in the building, mingling with the delegates and visitors and sampling the free coffee and biscuits. Jacqui managed to embarrass herself by spilling coffee over the shoes of one of *TORRO*'s directors, Dr Elsom! I'd never seen her go so red before! We saw Paul Fuller briefly, but there wasn't time to chat as the show was about to begin…

Dr Terence Meaden began an introductory talk, in which he welcomed everyone and explained that the conference had been a sell-out. He told us that the day before had seen a tour of circles sites in Wiltshire and Hampshire, led by himself and including a group of scientists and press/TV people. They'd visited circles in a variety of places Rog, Jacqui and I had never heard of, but those we had, included Cheesefoot Head and Bishop's Cannings-the latter the site of a spectacular four-ringed quintuplet set of circles (we didn't know about this one). They'd also been to a place not far from Cheesefoot where a spectacular new shape had recently appeared-a 'dumb-bell' (two circles joined by a corridor). There was also a set of small, individual circles at a place called 'Furze Hill' [we'd never heard of that either] and these were described as a 'vortex shower'.

The next person on stage was Busty Taylor. Busty gave a splendid film/slide show of circles, including the small ones of the 'vortex shower' which he called 'grapeshot'. It was all very straightforward with none of the mystery and intrigue he had spun when we'd first met him.

Next came the second (Meaden was the first) of a veritable procession (should that be a 'study'?!) of professors queuing up to provide explanations as to how and why electrically-charged whirlwinds – claimed also to be a form of ball lightning – were responsible for causing crop circles. Professor John Snow's talk concerned 'vortex breakdown' and seemed to make sense to me. He was followed by a post-graduate student from Lancaster University, David Reynolds, who gave evidence of a 'swathe' type series of crop markings where flattened corn shapes radiated outwards from a central point (unlike ordinary circles where the markings are radial). Aerial photos showed this to be an extraordinary series of markings. This formation had been found in Staffordshire. The only other reporting of a similar formation had been in Kent, in 1980. This was good stuff!

Japanese professor Yoshi-Hito Ohtsuki then stunned the audience by showing film of artificial plasmas he'd created in his laboratory. Looking at these one could easily see how Meaden's theory could be applied. Indeed, Ohtsuki said he was working on reproducing the Plasma-vortex under laboratory conditions! It got better by the minute!

The next professor was Hiroshi Kikuchi who spoke rapidly and quietly. I have to confess that I didn't have the foggiest idea what he meant. As slides of mathematical formulae rapidly appeared on the screen, I glanced at Rog and Jacqui and could see that they were equally as baffled. When he had finished, the audience broke into embarrassed laughter – it seemed we weren't the only ones in this hall of Academia who hadn't the faintest idea what Kikuchi had been on about!

There was short interlude during which we roamed around trying to see Busty Taylor to find out more about his strange conversion. At one point I came across Dr Meaden talking to somebody. Eager to meet Meaden face to face, I waited until he'd finished talking, approached him and put out my hand. '...Dr Meaden – I'm Peter Rendall, I'm pleased to meet you at last...' Meaden looked right through me, saw someone in the distance he recognised and walked away! I was left standing there hand outstretched and face glowing red!

Soon, it was time for Paul Fuller and Jenny Randles to take the stage. They illustrated how Meaden's plasma-vortex could be extended to apply to many of BUFORA's UFO cases and that previously un-explained UFO reports could now be explained in the light of Meaden's findings. Randles and Fuller's talk showed how, as UFO investigators, they strove to find natural explanations for as many reports as possible.

Then it was back to Dr Meaden for 'Question Time'. The audience, a mixed bag of academics and enthusiastic followers of the circles mystery, asked a variety of questions, filmed by several camera crews present. Meaden answered them all until the point where a man stood up and, when invited by Meaden to go ahead with his question, said: '...Colin Andrews has something to ask you...'. This was new! We didn't know Andrews was there!

Andrews was by now on his feet. A camera crew were with him, filming his every word and action. He demanded to know how conventional science could explain how the formation at Bishops Cannings had 'grown' an extra ring after it had originally been measured and photographed. Andrews heatedly argued that this was proof of an 'intelligence' at work. To give Terence Meaden his due, he stood unruffled by this surprise attack. His reply was that he suspected the possible involvement of hoaxers where this case was concerned. The argument got quite heated and I think that Andrews eventually stormed out, but my memory may be incorrect. Later, Andrews was to claim that Professor Meaden '...had been undressed in public...' over the incident. Here, there's no doubting my memory; Meaden was cool, calm and collected throughout Andrews' vociferous attack. He remained the perfect gentleman even when his findings were being cast into considerable doubt.

We'd had the opportunity to chat to Randles and Fuller at length after the conference, and promised to keep in touch. We also managed to talk to Busty who, it seemed, had now formed his own group after falling out with Andrews and Delgado. He seemed to want to see us all again so we said we'd call him. We looked forward to the forthcoming cropwatch, it promised to be intriguing!

We drove home that evening in no doubt whose side we were firmly on (in spite of Meaden's apparent snub to me at the interval) and that side wasn't Colin Andrews'!

Circles now appeared thick and fast. Pat Delgado appeared in the papers explaining how the new 'dumb-bell' shapes (some of which incredibly, had 'boxes' with them) were now known as 'Pictograms' to him and his followers. The press followed suit. There was also talk of a mammoth BBC-sponsored cropwatch to take place under the auspices of *Daytime Live* and to be held somewhere in Wiltshire. More of that later.

I had a few days off in late June and so did Rog. With Jacqui in the pub one night, we decided to take a trip around the cropfields to see what other formations had occurred. It was thought that we would start the trip near Warminster, Wiltshire, where circles had been known to form in previous years, and if time permitted, perhaps go on to Winchester and Cheesefoot. But first, to make the trip worthwhile, we contacted the one person who was likely to know if any circles were there - Busty Taylor. Busty wasn't surprised to hear from us and told us that there had been a couple of circles near the punchbowl which had been investigated by some friends of his who'd just held a vigil there. We arranged to meet him in a pub outside Andover on the evening of our visit.

The day of our trip and the weather was appalling! Rain and strong winds shook the car as we went to pick up a friend of Jacqui's, a travelling musician called Nelson who'd expressed an interest in coming along. From Nelson's Bristol lodgings, we set off for Bath and from there took the A36 to Warminster. Near Warminster is the mysterious Cley Hill which dominates the landscape for miles around. The hill is well-sculpted by some unknown ancient folk and there is a round barrow on top of it. I'd been up the hill many times in the past, once with Jacqui. Rog and Nelson hadn't been up it at all. It featured not only in crop circles lore (where mystics claimed circles formed on Ley-Lines running through the hill and Dr Meaden claimed that the shape of the hill created the vortices which made circles) but also in the famous 'Warminster Thing' UFO flap of the sixties. We parked up and climbed the hill. With, I might add, some difficulty. The rain had stopped but the wind was so strong that we were bent double in order to stay on the hill. When at last we reached the top, the wind was so strong and so constant that we all were able to lean forward at 45 degrees into the wind and not fall over! But we saw no circles, only sheep.

Back at the car we went to a couple of locations mentioned in Meaden's book and at last, after passing over a railway bridge near the hamlet of Upton Scudamore, found what we were looking for. Flattened circles of crop with several rings round them! There was a big circle with fine rings round it, attended by satellite small circles, also with rings. The adjacent field had two large circles in it. Despite the wind we managed to take photos.

The next point of call then, was Cheesefoot Head. I can't recall how we got there but it was probably via Salisbury in the vain hope that we might happen across any circles on the way. We didn't. Arriving in the car park at the top of the Punchbowl in mid-afternoon we parked up and wandered to the edge of the bowl. Success! There, in the crop below us was another ringed single circle (rings seemed to be de riguer for crop circles that summer). This time, however, the central circle had been flattened down, but not completely, then a ring of standing crop surrounded it! Around all this was a much wider ring of the partially flattened crop. As we gazed in bemusement at what appeared to be nature's variation on a theme, so the sun came out and I was able to get a couple of decent pictures of the circles.

Crossing the road, we went towards the fields where, the summer before, we'd seen the 'dead' circles and the 'circle-tail'. Nothing. However, we saw people in a field next to this one and went in to investigate. Success again! Several single circles along with a patch of apparently genuine wind-damage to compare with the circles. Whilst Rog and Nelson examined one of the circles, so a man appeared with a dog. Now, legends had already started to the effect that dogs were 'sensitive' to crop circles and wouldn't go into a circle under any circumstances. Colin Andrews had claimed that when his father had tried to take the family dog into a circle, the dog had been violently sick. At Cheesefoot the dog, an Alsation, wandered into all the formations without a care or ill effect in the world. (Incidentally, over the next few years I witnessed many dogs in crop circles-none refused to enter a circle.)

We took many photos there and Jacqui took one on time exposure with the camera fixed on my tripod and held high in the air. It was a method being used by Busty Taylor and Pat Delgado involving very long poles, although I don't think we knew about their camera-poles at this stage. Leaving Cheesefoot for Winchester, we hadn't gone far when someone spotted the tell-tale 'shadow' in a cropfield (which usually signified a formation) at the bottom of the hill less than a mile from Cheesefoot Head and just before the A272 joins the A31. We put the car on the verge and set off up the slope to the 'shadow'. Much to our delight, this turned out to be the 'Dumb-bell' or 'Pictogram', which Pat Delgado had recently promoted in the press. Blue skies presented the perfect backdrop for photos of this formation. One of the circles here had three rings round it. Another formation in the field below us was nicknamed the 'Starship Enterprise' as it seemed to us to resemble Captain Kirk's ship! [2]

From there we headed off to Andover and the pub where we were to eat and later meet with Busty Taylor. After a good meal and some beer, the door opened and in walked Busty Taylor with a friend in tow. The friend was a thin man with thin hair whom he introduced as Ron Jones. Ron, apparently, also had an interest in Crop Circles. After pleasantries were exchanged, we got talking about the circles we'd seen that day. Both Busty and Ron spoke to us at some length about their firm belief that something odd was happening in the world and that the circles were the visible signs of this. Their belief was absolute: the question of hoaxing in any shape or form didn't come into it. They didn't explain why they thought this. Surprisingly, Busty was non-committal about the circles where we'd seen the dog, hinting that he thought these might be fake.

They told us of a recent crop watch, held at Cheesefoot Head, which had been held by 'friends' of theirs [3]. This watch had been significant in that no circles had been formed in view of watchers and cameras, but that they'd received strange messages instructing them to carry out certain tasks. They wouldn't elaborate but Ron told us of a strange incident, which happened one night when he and some others were in a cornfield. The clouds had formed into strange shapes, which, to Ron, resembled the 'Mirror of Hathor' or something similar. This had apparently been frightening enough, but when they heard a 'rattling' sound moving through the crop around them-they fled! 'It was just like the Rattle of Isis!' recalled Ron with a shudder.[4]

'D'you know,' said Busty, 'We'd spent ten days waiting for circles to form under the cameras and nothing happened. On the last morning of the watch we were told that a circle had formed in the field right behind us! And it was no ordinary circle-it had a tail to it![5] Another new development!'

We all looked suitably impressed whilst all thinking that they were potty. Time to change the subject, perhaps?

'How did you get to be called 'Busty'?'

Taylor smiled. 'When I was a baby, my mother took me out in the pram one day and someone peered into the pram and said "What a Busty baby!" And the name stuck. '

At 'last orders', Busty suggested we all go back to his place, which was only a couple of miles away, and continue the chat. His place turned out to be a council house on an estate on the outskirts of Andover. Sitting in front of the large TV was the same bored-looking woman we'd seen with Busty at Silbury the previous year. She still looked bored. It was assumed that she was his wife, but nothing was said by Taylor and she didn't speak. Leaving her to her TV we moved into the next room and continued the circles chat. Busty asked if we wanted to see ourselves on TV and promptly got out the video he'd taken at Silbury! We had to sit through scenes of Jacqui and myself giving our views to the people we'd met at the gate. Red faces again!

The talk got round to how circles seemed to form near ancient sites. Busty was convinced that the 'power' of these sites had a lot to do with it. Not convinced I said, 'If that was the case, then how come circles have never been seen anywhere near Glastonbury for instance?'

Busty gave me a knowing look. 'Oh, they will,' he said, 'They will. 1995. That's when Glastonbury will get circles' He then went on to describe how the circles shapes were 'evolving', getting more complicated. 'And there's more to come,' he added, 'We haven't seen a six-pointed star yet.'

What was the significance of the six-pointed star?

'Ah. You mean you don't know? That would be telling, then.'

As enigmatic as ever!

Then he went on to say that circles nearly always formed on or near Ley Lines.

'There's a ley-line running through Busty's house,' said Ron.

Oh, really?

'Yep. And we can dowse it – with our bare hands!'

Now, we'd all tried dowsing at some stage, using rods or twigs and I'd even tried using a pendulum, but *Bare Hands*? Busty nodded. 'Ron.....' he said.

Ron moved into position. They started making strange moves with their hands, supposedly detecting this line. We watched with amused looks as they 'found' the line. When they moved behind the sofa to detect the spot where the line changed course, we made our excuses and left!

Nevertheless, it had been a fairly pleasant evening and Busty and Ron seemed harmless enough. I later wrote and thanked them for meeting with us and agreeing to swop details of future circles on the basis that although believing Meadens' theory to be more likely to cause circles than mysterious unknown forces, we as a group of individuals were 'neutral'. I also expressed an interest in meeting with Ron Jones sometime in the future to talk about Glastonbury, the history of which was of particular interest to me.

On the 11th of July, Nelson was in the Winchester area when he came across a new type of formation at a place called Litchfield on the A34. Excited, he sketched the shapes and faxed it off to Jacqui's office. She brought it to show me. It was a dumb-bell, with two boxes each side of the corridor and two curved corridors above the top circle. The next afternoon we set out to investigate. We reached Litchfield by way of the A4, Newbury and through Highclere, whose Beacon Hill was the last resting-place of Lord Caernarvon, famous for excavating Tutankhamun's tomb. The A34 is no place to stop and wander across the road to take pictures of crop circles. Luckily we found a gateway to park in and climbed to the top of an old railway embankment to take a look. Later, we went a little way along the A34, turned and came back on the other carriageway, parking this time on the verge. We took some photos of the dumb-bell with boxes and rings and noted that nearby were some small circles – Busty's 'Grape-shot' – whether these had not been noticed by Nelson or had appeared overnight we didn't know. The rings around the top circle weren't really rings – they were semi-circles. They were also off-centre from the main axis and a bit 'wobbly'. Quite how a 'plasma-vortex' could make this one we couldn't see. It was labelled, if not directly as a hoax, then certainly a 'bit iffy'.

On our way back we called in at a Wiltshire pub for some sustenance. The *Black Horse* at Cherhill, near Calne, wasn't far away from that 'Celtic cross' set of circles we'd seen in 1989. While in the pub we overheard some locals talking about '...circles at Blackdown...'. We had an Ordnance Survey map of the area with us and when we'd finished our meal, went up to Blackdown to investigate. We found the formations, near Morgan's Hill, but it was getting close to dusk so we didn't go in.

When we eventually got home after a tiring day, Rog arrived with the message that Terence Meaden had phoned to say that his 1990 cropwatch was starting that week. We were to meet with him and others in the car park near Silbury Hill, the next evening! As I had to work a late shift that day, I arranged to meet the others at the *Waggon and Horses* pub at Beckhampton after work.

Friday 13th July 1990

The time of the meeting was arranged for seven that evening and Jacqui Griffiths made good time along the A4 from Bath, arriving at Silbury car park at five to seven. There were one or two people in the car park but nobody she knew, so she stayed in her car. At seven-fifteen, Roger Davis' red Fiesta pulled in and shortly behind him, a black Metro conveying Paul Fuller arrived. The three got together and Paul gave more background information about the libel case he'd been subjected to. Of Terence Meaden there was no sign.

Eventually, about 45 minutes late, the professor arrived with a camera-crew in tow. After only a few minutes disorganised milling about, a man joined the throng and asked them if they'd heard about the '...fantastic formations over the hill at a place called Adam's Grave....'. They hadn't. Where was it? Along the A4 towards Marlborough, turn right for East Kennett, follow the road to the end, turn right. It's about two miles along that road. It was, by all accounts, well worth seeing....

As they began variously to head for their cars, so Busty Taylor's Red Metro pulled in. Someone told him what was happening and the convoy began to wind its ragged way to a small place that would, within the next 24 hours, become world famous and forever associated with Crop Circles. That place was Alton Barnes.

At about ten-forty-five that evening, I arrived in Beckhampton and parked my car opposite the pub. Wandering in, I searched the place for Rog and Jacqui, finding them in a small room off the main bar. With them were an elderly man with a goatee beard, a rather large woman with a small boy, another man with a goatee and who carried a hippie-style canvas bag over his shoulder and, sitting close to Jacqui and paying her rather a lot of attention – Busty Taylor!

I got a pint and joined them. The talk was about Celtic symbolism. The large lady, whom I learned was called Isabelle Kingston was, it seemed, a medium. She had apparently predicted that a big new type of formation would occur. It had. I, of course, was ignorant of the new circles at Alton Barnes. Rog filled me in on the details.

'There's lots of circles together,' he told me. 'We went there with Terence Meaden and Busty. We couldn't see much from the edge of the road, but saw that there were over 34 people in the field! Andrews and Delgado were there and as it was also getting dark, we didn't hang around, but came back here.'

'Who found the circles – was it Condrews and Fandango (our new nicknames for the duo)?'

Rog shook his head. 'No,' he replied. 'That chap over there with the shoulder-bag who looks like William Shakespeare turned up on a Honda 50 and told us. His name is Alan Rayner'.

I joined in the chat with the others, most of whom were believers that something enormously significant was happening. Busty seemed to think that if he chatted up Jacqui enough then something significant might happen for him! Then, Terence Meaden came in and loosely briefed us on the night's watch. Were these people part of Meaden's team, then? I was surprised. I'd expected a group of academics and weather-enthusiasts (David Reynolds, the meteorologist who'd given a talk at the Oxford conference did turn up later).

The plan was basically this: choose a hill and watch out for low-flying plasma-vortices...if you can photograph one-so much the better. Meaden, Reynolds, Roger and I elected to watch over the field at Alton Barnes where the new circles were. Jacqui was coming too, and so was her new admirer. Busty was completely oblivious to the fact that Jacqui was my partner at the time!

And so we set off. Five cars, with me bringing up the rear (for some reason, Paul Fuller wasn't with us; he may have gone to watch somewhere else. We hadn't gone far along the A4 before Jacqui indicated, pulled over and turned round. She stopped and put her hazard flashers on. Rog stopped so did I. Busty soon came back. 'What's up?' he enquired.

Jacqui glared at him. 'You ran over a rabbit!' she muttered, gently cradling the stunned creature in her hands.

Busty grinned. 'So?'

At that precise moment, unknown to F.C.Taylor, his night's amorous work went up in a puff of smoke. He wasn't to know that the one thing Jacqui Griffiths cared about most in the world was – Rabbits! She collected them, photographed them and went out to watch them in the wild whenever she could. I'd nicknamed her 'The Rabbit Queen'. Busty's nonchalant attitude to running over a wild bunny put him well up on her list of people to hate! She elected to take the rabbit to a vet and without further ado, set off back towards Chippenham.

With a shrug, Busty went back to his car and we set off again for Alton Barnes.

There, we met up with Terence Meaden and Dave Reynolds. It was from Meaden that we learned of the BBC Cropwatch at Westbury, Wilts, run, as predicted, by *Daytime Live* and Andrews/Delgado. It seemed that it was fashionable to get Japanese involvement in crop circles – they also had the backing of a Japanese TV company. They had set up camp on top of Bratton castle, the Iron Age earthwork near the Westbury White Horse, and had loads of expensive technology to film circles forming.

And here we were, the *scientific side*, using ordinary cameras and binoculars! Something wrong, somewhere!

Rog and I gazed down at the dark fields where a series of circles lay. Terence Meaden and Dave Reynolds talked in low voices about how it was almost impossible to find absolute darkness anywhere on the mainland UK anymore, due to light pollution. F.C.Taylor dozed in his car. Rog and I gazed down at the dark fields where a series of circles lay – but this time Rog saw something else.

'There's a light down there…' he whispered.

I followed his pointing finger. Nothing. Then I, too, saw it. A small wavering light in the field. I drew Dr Meaden's attention to the light. We all gazed down into the field and watched the flickering light.

'It looks like a torch..' said the professor.

That's what we thought. Rog and I elected to carry out a reconnaissance. We found an old Ford Escort parked in a gateway further along the road, but decided we'd wait until first light before entering the field as once we were at the same level as the field, we couldn't see the light at all and the field was so huge we stood a fair chance of missing the circles altogether in the dark.

Back at the watch site, a film-crew had arrived. These turned out to be the crew who'd been with Meaden earlier. They were from ABC TV in the USA and wanted some more footage. Rog, Busty and I were positioned against a gate which overlooked the field, and told to act natural!

When the film crew had done their bit and gone, we resumed a silent vigil. I was looking across the field below and in the general direction of South West, when a sudden streak of light moved steadily across the sky from left to right of my vision, disappearing over nearby Stanton St Bernard. By the time I'd called Dr Meaden over. It was gone. What was it? Meaden thought a shooting star, I wasn't so sure. I'd seen many a shooting star and it was unlike any I'd seen. It wasn't a satellite either. Space debris? Maybe. But I'd seen a light like this before…

It was one evening, some time before I got involved in crop circles. Jacqui and I, with Rog (the three of us went around together a lot) were at the Rollright Stones in Oxfordshire. It was dusk when we moved across to the nearby 'King Stone'. I climbed up onto the stone just in time to witness a white light streak across the sky. And that was well outside the usual 'shooting star' period. Several have been seen since. I still don't know what they were.

Forward to 1990, that night a giant new formation appeared in the crop near Stanton St Bernard......

Back at the scientific side's cropwatch though, dawn had shoved a first tentative finger of light above the hills. Rog and I set off down the dark road to the field entrance to await enough morning light to creep our way across to the circles and find out who-or what-had made the light. Sometime after four it was light enough and we set off, silently and creeping low, through the green stems of wheat. As we drew nearer our hearts beat just that bit faster in anticipation of what we would find. Would it be hoaxers, ready to have a laugh at us? Would it be the farmer-*get orf my laand*! Would it be something connected to whatever it was that created the circles? We crept silently closer and closer. As we neared the circles, we made out a dark green shape in one of them. And our noses detected a strange smell....

As the grey light grew slowly brighter, the shape became identifiable as.....a tent! Yes, a small, one man tent. Nearby was a piece of wire attached to something in the ground. As we looked at the scene, so the tent flap opened and two figures crawled out, one tumbling over the other. They had silly grins on their faces. Who were they?

'We're Circles Phenomena Research!' said one lad, trying-and failing-to stand up. 'We're doin' work for Colin Andrews!' said the other from ground level. The strange smell pervaded the scene.

'What work?' I asked.

'We're doin' electrical experiments. Tryin' to detect any electric currents in the ground...'

He pointed towards the piece of wire in the ground. To further illustrate the point he dragged a box with a meter on it out of the tent. I recognised this piece of equipment. It was an AVO meter, commonly used by electricians to measure units of power, current and resistance-Amps Volts and Ohms. It normally operated with two probes to make a circuit.

'Uh-like-we lost the other probe...' said one of the lads. And I now recognised that strange smell...it was Ether! That explained their inability to stand up and the stupid grins. The 'team' from Circles Phenomena Research were spending the night in a tent, sniffing ether and carrying out useless experiments with a piece of equipment which was not only useless for the task in question but didn't work anyway!

In some small way, that helped redress the balance between the CPR/BBC high-tech cropwatch, and us.

Dawn had now chased night away and there was sufficient light to take in the circles. What a formation! Double dumb-bells, boxes, small circles, spurs, corridors...truly tremendous! I took several photos and we could also see some people approaching from the road. These were Dr Meaden, Dave Reynolds and the elderly man with the goatee beard who'd been in the pub the night before. Where he'd come from I don't know. Nor do I recall where Busty went. Meaden and Reynolds set about calmly measuring and drawing the formations whilst the rest of us wandered around in awe, photographing and just admiring the circles. There was just one small point though; how could a plasma-vortex make this?

'Don't worry,' said Meaden, reassuringly, 'This can all be explained by science.'

Some time after six in the morning, Rog and I climbed up to Adam's Grave to get more photos and to spend a little time admiring the amazing shapes below us in the wheat field.

It was after seven when Rog and I, in convoy, made our weary way back home, via Bratton and Westbury, just to see what was going on there. Little was apparent from the road, just a cluster of vehicles on the hilltop. I remember during that journey home, playing a new CD I'd bought. It was Mike Oldfield's *AMAROK*. Whenever I play that album, I'm instantly back at Alton Barnes in the clean cool air of the early morning light, looking in awe at the most famous Crop Circles of them all.

Chapter Six
HIGH ON A HILL
Blackbird-High Hill-Noises off-Evolution

The newspapers were full of it. *That* formation. Alton Barnes, sleepy little Wiltshire village was now national and international news. Nothing like it had ever been seen before. It was on the TV too, taking the attention away from the Condrews/Fandango set-up at Bratton. That set-up, code-named *Operation Blackbird* was confidently said to be able to capture crop circles actually being made. Whatever made them was a mystery still, but Colin Andrews, in interviews, spoke darkly about *a component*. Indeed, in an interview with the now-defunct *Today* newspaper, Andrews had said: '…..*It seems to be…created by some sort of intelligent life force as an attempt to communicate with mankind…..*'[1]

No doubt then, where his beliefs lay!

Jacqui, naturally, wanted to know all about it. She'd seen the press and TV coverage of the circles. I told her all about the lads in the tent and their useless experiments, the lights in the sky and how Dr Meaden was certain it could all be explained by science.

Dr Meaden phoned during the week, there was to be another cropwatch at Alton Barnes this coming weekend. Could we attend? We certainly could! Same place, same time, OK? In the words of a famous DJ-*Not 'Arf*!

Friday 20th July 1990

My notes seem to indicate that Jacqui didn't come along on this watch, but that her usual place was taken by Jim Crow. We all went up to Silbury in my car and met up with Terence Meaden, Paul Fuller, Alan Rayner, the old man with the goatee beard and several others. Busty wasn't there tonight. He'd become a 'Field Officer' with a new study-group the Centre for Crop Circles Studies or CCCS, of whom more later. Paul Fuller presented us with a complimentary copy of his and Jenny's new book, *Crop Circles-A Mystery Solved?* Briefly scanning the pages it looked to be full of good stuff.

The press was there this time. Reporters from the *Marlborough Times* and *The Western Daily Press* chatted to us, wrote in notebooks and took photos. During one 'photo shoot' I stood with a copy of Paul's book held surreptitiously in front of me! After all this we adjourned to the *Waggon & Horses* for beer and talk. One of the newcomers was a retired BBC sound technician, Stanley Morcomb. We discussed the various theories going around, including one of Busty Taylor's, which concentrated on comparing crop circles shapes with Celtic symbolism. We decided that it would be a good idea if someone concentrated on investigating that alone, whilst someone else could look into the make-up of crops and fertilisers used in the crop fields. It seemed like a good idea if we were all working towards a common goal. Sadly, I was deluded. On this watch, as on the last, it was to transpire that most of Meaden's team of enthusiastic watchers were seeking a paranormal solution to the riddle of the circles rather than a natural weather-based answer.

At landlord's boot time, Terence Meaden rallied his troops in the pub car park. Tonight, the cropwatch had a codename: it was to be known as *Operation High Hill* and we were to split up and watch from various places as before. Rog, Jim and I chose to watch from Alton Barnes, but this time at the opposite side of the field to our site of the previous week. Why did we choose this site? Because rumour had it that Condrews and Fandango were holding a 'vigil' at the big formation, and we intended to watch them!

We drove over to Alton Barnes but instead of the CPR duo we found a group of their 'youth movement' parked up by the gateway. We pulled up and had a chat to them, pretending to be interested passers-by. They told us that Colin and Pat were at '*Blackbird*' that night and were not expected at Alton Barnes, having been there during the day. Then we drove around to the opposite side of the field, parked up and settled down for the night. We had the windows wound down as it was a warm night and we'd be able to hear every sound. We were armed with binoculars and cameras, and a notebook. Every sight and sound, identifiable or not, was logged against the time it occurred. The following is a reproduction of that log:

00.35 .....Torches seen on Adam's Grave
02.20 .....Light breeze picks up. More comings and goings at 'camp site' (this refers to the CPR youths camp)
02.40 .....Class 59 locomotive heard
03.05 .....Wind changes. Now NNE and stronger...
03.10......False Dawn now showing up hills and tramlines (tractor lanes) nothing visible through binoculars....
03.55 .....Slight ground mist visible
04.40 .....All but daylight and nothing to be seen.
05.10 .....Left site.

On the way home we drove past Silbury Hill and saw the lone figure of Paul Fuller standing on top.

The next day, after a good sleep and dinner, I phoned Dr Meaden to report the night's events. I told him we'd seen and heard nothing.

'Nothing?' he repeated. 'Stanley Morcomb heard a strange noise, which he described as sounding like 'White Noise'. He was on Adam's Grave at the time.'

'We left him at the top car park. When did he move?'

'About one, I believe. He got bored. But the sound is interesting – it could have been a vortex....'

I cut him short. 'What time did he hear this?'

'It was around two-forty...'

I told him that we'd kept a log of everything that happened and at two-forty I'd recorded the class 59 locomotive as passing. The main railway from Westbury, Wiltshire, to Reading passed only two miles away from Alton Barnes. The class 59 was a recently-introduced American-built locomotive, which was used to haul immensely heavy stone trains from Westbury. Passing near Alton Barnes, the line was on an uphill gradient and the locomotives were working hard with up to 1000 tonnes behind them. The power unit made a loud, banshee-like wail as it roared up the hill, quite unlike any other train in Britain.[2]

I explained all this to the scientist.

'Hmm,' he said at last. 'You'd better phone Stanley and explain it to him'

I did. Stanley Morcomb had got bored and had walked up to Adam's Grave. There he'd heard the 'white noise' sound which he said seemed to come from 'somewhere above the ground and was all around him'. Questioning him further, I ascertained that he'd rarely spent a night out in the deepest countryside. I told him that I was convinced he'd heard a freight train. He was sceptical.

'I was a sound engineer-I have a pretty good idea what I hear.'

'Yes, I don't doubt you, Stanley, but the noise you heard is very much like this locomotive noise-and it was at the same time as we recorded it passing. The sound would have seemed to be all around you because of the 'bowl' effect of the landscape around.'

Stanley Morcomb eventually and reluctantly accepted what I was saying. At this stage I had no idea where his sympathies really lay, but I expect that my 'simple' explanation was eventually put down as a piece of 'Government disinformation'.

And so we come to Bratton, 25th July 1990 and *Operation Blackbird*. By this time we had massive 'Pictograms' at Alton Barnes, Stanton St Bernard and at Pepperbox Hill, near Salisbury (Terence Meaden called them 'Linear Complexes') and the people in the team at Bratton were on a high state of alert. But, as the events laid out in Chapter One tell, they weren't alert enough....

Roger Davis and I stood on Bratton castle that evening and wondered where all this was going. We stood on the edge of the escarpment and gazed down at the scene of Condrews and Fandango's humiliation. It didn't even look good. Too ragged. But who had made it? Mixing with the *Blackbird people* (they were so demoralised that they weren't even trying to guard the site anymore) we passed Pat Delgado talking to the people from ABCTV. Elsewhere we recognised the Dawn French lookalike and a youth as having been part of the CPR team at Alton Barnes the previous night. We chatted to a BBC producer and asked him why they (the Beeb) kept labelling the CPR duo as 'Scientists' when they obviously weren't. He admitted that he knew they were not scientists, but wouldn't let on why the TV people let the public believe they were. However, he did say that if Terence Meaden had sought more publicity then he might have got more coverage for his theory.

And talking of Terence Meaden, where was he? Both he and Paul Fuller had been interviewed on radio that afternoon, denouncing the *Blackbird* crowd for not verifying the hoax before announcing it to the world.

'He's gone to France!' groaned Paul Fuller when we phoned him up. 'Just when he could have the opportunity to really score over these loonies-he goes on holiday!'

This was to become a bone of contention over the next 18 months or so. Terence Meaden's delightful wife was French and every so often, the Meadens would disappear off to the Continent. No one would deny him a holiday, but it did seem to happen whenever there was adverse publicity or when he was needed most. And it was frequently at short notice.

Still, it was a perfect summer's evening at Bratton. As the sun began to go down over *Operation Blackbird* it seemed to Rog and me that it was the perfect occasion to toast the future of crop circles research with some local ale.

We retired to a nearby pub, *The Duke*.

The following evening I was unable to go up to Beckhampton. As Meaden wasn't there, presumably there would be no cropwatch. However, Roger Davis did go up and spent the evening in the *Waggon and Horses* in the company of George Wingfield (who was the 'Military Man' from the encounter at Silbury in 1988 where Jacqui and I had first met Busty Taylor). George had one of his old schoolfriends with him, 'Binning'. An interesting chap who believed that there was a mystic energy at work behind the circles and that there were fairies at the bottom of his garden. Y'know-the kind with wings. He knew. He'd seen them on his estate.

He was the Earl of Haddington. He and Wingfield had been at public school together.

Rog sat in this exalted company looking at superb photographs of crop circles and listening to the talk about the new organisation, the CCCS. Wingfield and Haddington were involved with this new group, in fact, Haddington had undertaken to be its patron. From what Rog gleaned, it seemed that the CCCS (or CCCP as we soon nicknamed it) was another group aligned to the supernatural side. Not that there was anything wrong with a belief in supernatural things as far as I, at least, was concerned. It was just that I and the others couldn't see any connection between that and crop circles.

I can't remember how we found out about the new shapes at Beckhampton. It may have been via the group in the pub that night. Anyway, Rog and I set off for Beckhampton the very next morning to investigate reports of 'Scrolls' and Triangles! Truly, if these reports were found to be true, then the weather-based theory was going to be blown away. Even a misbehaving plasma vortex couldn't make a triangle. And hadn't Pat Delgado said something about Triangles appearing next?

We duly arrived at the location and seeing no sign of any farmers and not knowing whose field it was we went in. It was true! There were a couple of formations resembling a telephone handset, which had beautiful swirling patterns and a small clump of standing crop, not unlike a corn dolly, in the middle. We photographed and measured these. Then we came to the 'Triangle'.

With some relief we found that this was really a circle, the outer edge of which had spilled over into a tractor lane, giving it a straight edge. Or so it seemed. The more we looked at it so the more it was obvious that the other sides were not as curved as a 'normal' circle. However, we were prepared to accept it as a circle. Then I found some more triangles. Long and thin, these were also rough and ready. 'Made with a plank of wood' was our verdict. This, of course, cast doubt on the other circles there....

We found some blackened and shrivelled plants in the scrolls. A rumour had gone round the pub that strange forces were leaving burnt plants behind, evidence of the tremendous energy involved in making crop circles...Cobblers! These were 'Tick Beans' –grown for cattle feed. When ripe they turned black and shrivelled up.

'We've got to find one of these plants upright and growing somewhere away from the circles' I said to Rog, 'And photograph it. That'll prove that it's nothing to do with circles or energies.'

In this, we were successful. And when the farmer came round to charge us £1 for entering his field, he confirmed that last year's crop in that field had been Tick Beans. He also told us that he always '...*phoned that Colin Andrews*...' when circles appeared on his land. I gave him Meaden's phone number and suggested he contact a *real* scientist whenever circles appeared in future. To the best of my knowledge he never did. And although I showed the resulting photographs around to all and sundry, the rumours of 'Alien Energies' burning traces in cornfields persisted. I was beginning to find out that there was nothing that people loved more than a good mystery.

That afternoon and evening I was at work. Roger and Jacqui decided to go to Bratton to see how *Blackbird* was getting on, there being no sign that without Meaden, anyone else from the scientific fraternity was organising a cropwatch. They arrived at the site at six-thirty and found a scattering of CPR 'staff' around. Amongst these they spotted Bat Fandango and asked him if they'd missed anything. He didn't realise that they were being sarcastic and told them all about his recent slot on *ABCTV*'s live satellite link-up with the USA!

Then, looking around through Jacqui's telescope –she called it a 'Bunnyscope' because she spent a lot of time watching rabbits with it- who should they see but Ron Jones. He, in turn, saw them and rapidly turned his back and moved away, ducking down behind the earth bank of the old fort. Rog and Jacqui went over to where they'd seen him and found Ron hiding behind the earthwork. When they spoke to him he sighed with relief as he recognised them.

'I thought it was someone trying to photograph me,' he said.

They assured him that they, at least, weren't and he was happy.

'I'm trying to put this tent up,' he explained, indicating a pile of canvas on the ground. 'Busty'll be along later'. Another man (whom Jacqui described to me later as 'looking like Quasimodo') stood by the tent. Leaving Ron and 'Quasi' to their efforts, Rog and Jacqui adjourned to *The Duke* to get some food.

After eating, they returned to the camp and found Busty Taylor there. He was in a funny sort of mood, 'all mysterious'-was how Jacqui recalled it. In answer to a question, Busty said Condrews and Fandango were no longer at the site and that he, Busty, was hungry!

They all adjourned to *The Duke* again where Busty consumed two pints of lager and a packet of crisps (Honest!). then, in the safe company of Ron Jones and 'Quasi', he told them of these strange letters he'd been getting.

'I've been getting them for years, ' he revealed. 'They come from this medium I know.

They're all in rhyme and....' he looked at them darkly, '...*they predict the shapes of the circles in advance!*' Ron and Quasi nodded wisely. Busty now came over all emotional. 'Sometimes...' he said, '...Sometimes the knowledge of it all and the frustration has me in tears....Tears of frustration at not being able to tell anyone about ...*The Secret*!'

Jacqui just had to say it; '*What secret?*'

Busty looked at her with puppy-dog eyes. 'Can't tell you.'

Jacqui looked at *him* with puppy-dog eyes.

Busty relented. 'Well,' he said. 'Some of it has passed, so perhaps we can, ...Ron?'

Ron Jones nodded. 'Yes, OK'. (Obviously it wasn't so secret that Busty couldn't share it with his mates...)

Busty then proceeded to recite a poem, which ended with the phrase: '*..They'll all be laughing but not at me...*' 'Then, the circles will end,' he predicted.

'What? No more crop circles?' said Jacqui.

'S'right,' muttered Busty. 'They'll go on for another couple of years then, in 1992 – STOP!'

'Stop?'

'Yep. Stop. And not return for 3,000 years!'

Jacqui and Rog looked at each other.

'C'mon,' said Busty. 'Time to go.'

Back on Bratton camp, Jacqui demanded to know what was happening next. Was there to be an all-night vigil? Ron and Busty didn't seem to know. Ron had another attempt to put up his tent and, failing to master the job, gave up. The sun had long gone down and a distinct chill was in the air. Rog, who wore only jeans and a tee-shirt, began to feel the cold.

'There's a sleeping-bag in my car-fetch it and wrap it round your shoulders,' volunteered Busty. Rog went to find Busty's car and while he was gone, Busty suggested that Jacqui should spend the night with him on the downs...

'No. I don't think that's a good idea,' she said.

'Aw, c'mon, 'cajoled Busty, 'There's plenty of room in my sleeping bag!'

'No way!' retorted Jacqui. She grabbed Rog and they left the hill.

The next evening the three us got together at my local, the *Rose and Crown* to talk. That's where I learned of the above. Busty was fast gaining a reputation as a lecher as well as a crop circles photographer!

One thing that was puzzling us, was this: Whatever happened to one group happened in a different way to the others. When one group held a vigil or cropwatch somewhere, circles formed elsewhere. For example, when we thought the CPR were watching at Alton Barnes and therefore decided to watch them, they were actually either at Bratton or (in the case of Colin and Pat) at home. On the occasion in question, a large formation formed at Pepperbox Hill, miles away from any of the watchers. When we all watched Alton Barnes for the first time, a large formation occurred at Stanton St. Bernard. No wonder some said that the phenomena was evolving and was displaying some kind of intelligence. To us, that intelligence was increasingly looking to be Human! We decided that with Andrews and Delgado effectively covered in Blackbird droppings after the hoax and Meaden in France, it could mean that the 'scroll' formations were possible hoaxes. We later learned that Busty Taylor had flown over *Blackbird* and seen some scrolls in wheat behind the site. This seemed to indicate that all the scrolls had formed on the same night. Curious!

There were other puzzles. Jacqui recalled that when they'd been with Busty at Bratton, he'd told them that the whole thing would be over by 1992, whereas on the occasion of our visit to Andover a few weeks ago, he'd said that circles would be found at Glastonbury in 1995! Something wrong. Surely?

The following Monday evening, my brother phoned with news of more circles. There were two at Olveston, near Thornbury, Gloucestershire, 1 possible at Cherhill, Wiltshire and a 'certain fake' on Rodway common, near Mangotsfield. I phoned Terence Meaden and left a message on his answerphone. The next day Jacqui and I went to Beckhampton and Cherhill, finding nothing new, and on to Olveston where we found ordinary wind damage – 'Lodging' as it's known in the agricultural world.

Other events that month included the Sunday Mirror announcing a competition to find out the cause of Crop Circles. A £10,000 reward was on offer. Professor Terence Meaden was listed as one of the judges. The Mail on Sunday ran an article in which they promoted a do-it-yourself UFO kit: a piece of rope and a pole. Using this and a team of eight or nine people they 'proved' that crop circles were hoaxes. I won a fiver for writing the 'letter of the week' to the *Western Daily Press* in which I suggested that Meaden's theory ought to get a better hearing.

Thursday 2nd August 1990

In the morning I set out to go to Wells, Somerset. I went by way of Keynsham, Marksbury and Farnborough to reach the A37 at Farrington Gurney. A mile or so outside Keynsham the B3116 meets the A39 from Bath near Stantonbury Hill, which is crowned by an old 'Iron Age' fort. The earthwork known as 'Wansdyke' crosses the road near this junction. I joined the A39 and had barely travelled a hundred yards along it when to my surprise I noticed what appeared to be a faint crop circle in a wheat field to my left. I couldn't stop because of traffic, but vowed to stop on my return a few hours later.

I did and there was no doubt; the unmistakable shape of a circle was visible. But there was something odd about this one: it wasn't completely flat. I went home and returned with binoculars and camera. Yes, it was a circular depression in a field of wheat, but it hadn't been flatted in the usual way. Instead the tops of the plants could be seen but they all seemed to be a few inches shorter than the surrounding crop. Curious.

Home again I phoned Dr Meaden. His wife answered the phone and I passed on details, including the map reference of the 'circle'. It could be, I said, that a vortex had just 'touched down' in the field but not enough to completely flatten the crop. I promised to return and enter the field and to report back.

A day or so later, I returned with Jacqui and we tried to find the farmer. No luck. The problem with cereal fields is that the farmer who owns or leases the fields often lives miles away from them. It was even worse in places like Wiltshire where unless you knew the farmer beforehand, you could spend all day trying to find out whose field it was. Anyway, on this occasion we took a chance and walked up the side of the field to a spot opposite the 'circle'. Then we trod our way carefully across to the site, finding it surprisingly easy to wend our way through the evenly planted stems without leaving a trace. At the 'circle' we found that the 'diagnosis' made from the road was correct. The stems were several inches shorter than the rest of the field, but in a circular shape and slightly 'dished'. But what had made it? Although the site fitted Meaden's theory of the eddy-vortex forming in the lee of a hill perfectly, this wasn't caused by a vortex.

No. It had to be something in the ground; some circular disturbance in the soil, such as an old barrow or filled in pond, perhaps. We took photos and left – again without leaving a trail.

I've never seen the circular depression in that field since. No 'real' crop circles formed in that field for several years until an 'all-seeing eye' or similar sort of shape was made there in the late 1990's. But this was after we'd made lists of our sites public and Stantonbury was on them. ... Besides, I am pretty sure who made *this* particular piece of 'Land Art'.

The next day being Friday, it was back to *Operation High Hill*. My notes say that Jacqui, Rog and I went to the *Waggon & Horses* where we met with Paul Fuller. Dr Meaden isn't mentioned in my notes for this day so I presume he was in France again Whilst in the pub I got talking to Paul about 'Bristol Quest' – the UFO group who'd got in the papers earlier that year claiming a UFO connection with crop circles. I'd just had a letter published in the *Bristol Journal* in reply to a recent claim by Bristol Quest that crop circles were a message left by an alien transmitter left on Mars.

'I'd be careful of them if I were you', said Fuller. 'They are part of 'Quest International' who can get a bit heavy if you question them too much. I know someone who had a threatening visitation by a couple of hairy bikers after criticising Quest,' he went on. This amazed me! Paul also mentioned the rumour that Andrews and Delgado were connected to the Freemasons, something I was to recall some weeks later when talking with Busty Taylor. After some beer, we set out to watch the fields from the top of Silbury Hill. It was a beautiful night and we began our vigil in good spirits. Shortly, a couple of German 'Hippies' appeared and opened a conversation. Soon they were passing round a flask with Mead in it -international relations certainly went well that night!

At 00.35 we were all drawn to a pin-point of light on the horizon opposite Silbury. The light was in the direction of Milk Hill where some women we'd met in the pub were going so it was possibly their torches. We saw the lights again at 1.45 am by which time Jacqui had had enough. She was bored and cold she said. She went home and the rest of us stayed.

Just before three, the blood-red moon settled into the rising ground mist and it got noticeably darker. However, the heavens were still visible and we spotted a passing satellite and a shooting star. We saw shooting stars again at 3.07 and 3.20. The people at Milk Hill were still signalling to each other with their torches. We heard dogs barking somewhere.

Daylight arrived and at 05.15 we left Silbury and went home having seen nothing of interest crop circles –wise.

'Bristol Evening Post' Wednesday 8th August 1990:

'A new crop of mystery' – Mysterious crop circles have appeared in Somerset for the first time....farmer Les Butt is convinced the seven precise shapes formed in a corner of his 25-acre wheatfield at Butleigh Wootton, near Glastonbury, are no hoax....'

Rog rang me the next morning with the news. So, it had happened; Busty's six pointed star – or very nearly- 5 years earlier than Busty had predicted. From the description, this set of circles was a central circle with six satellites around it. In the light of what Busty had said that night at his place, what on earth was to be made of this? It was almost as if somebody was listening.....

I went into the bathroom to wash. Outside someone's car radio was playing '...*Ha! Ha! Said the clown.....*'

The following Sunday, I drove to Glastonbury with my parents to look for the circles. We passed through the old town and carried on to Butleigh Wootton which is a mile or so beyond Glastonbury. I hadn't a clue which field or farm to look for and the Yellow Pages hadn't been much help. On arriving in the vicinity of Butleigh Wootton, we found that all the wheat fields had been harvested! Wandering round various fields of stubble looking for 'dead' circles got us nowhere. Then, luck! We came across a couple of farming contractors. Had they seen any crop circles?

'No, not this year. I seen 'em up near Amesbury [Wilts] last year though,' said the contractor. ''Tis the wind!' he added.

Now I hadn't mentioned any theory as to how the circles formed so I just agreed with him.

'Ah,' he continued. '..We do often come across the odd circle when harvestin', but 'tis the wind.'

'I'm sure it is,' I said.

He nodded. 'Often see hay an' straw spiral up, oh, to 300 foot. 'Tis awkward for the chap on the bailer when it 'appens, 'coz he can't do nothin' about it!'

He went to say that at a field near Godney, between Glastonbury and Wells, he'd once witnessed a hot air balloon about to land when suddenly the balloon '...shot off at 90 degrees...I reckon it was one of they vortices!'

This was good news, indeed. We talked at length about matters agricultural and when we parted he was still adamant that crop circles were made by the weather. '...they people what do think 'tis flyin' saucers an' that....*they'm a bit funny, ain't they*! '

We went home that afternoon thinking that the farm hand was probably a very wise man!

Then it was Friday again and back to *High Hill.*

We met, as usual, in the car park at Silbury Hill. This time Dr Terence Meaden was there. I'd had some photos processed, most of which were of crop circles and I wanted to show them to him. However, the good professor wasn't interested. He wanted to climb Silbury Hill to get a view of a formation which had appeared the previous week near West Kennet long barrow and had very quickly been harvested. I'd already been up to see the field and there was little to see. However, he wanted to see for himself. A couple of people he knew approached, one was a Canadian and they all went up the hill. I followed, having little else to do as nobody else had turned up yet. As predicted, there was little or nothing to be seen of the West Kennet circles. Meaden chatted to his friends and I saw Jacqui's car arrive below and also Alan Rayner on his Honda 50. I set off back down the hill followed by Meaden and co.

The group of people assembled to conduct that night's crop watch consisted, as usual, almost entirely of believers in the paranormal or UFO theories. Couldn't Meaden persuade any scientists to turn up? Anyway we all adjourned to the Waggon which was full of hippies and new age people by now. Paul Fuller arrived and we decided to put it to Meaden that he would possibly do better if the supporters of the scientific theory met elsewhere...

Meaden listened politely but was reluctant to take our advice. Whether he enjoyed the company of the 'new agers' [3] or whether he considered the watching to be almost over for that year, I don't know. Paul was in full agreement that we ought to move our meeting place with or without Meaden. He felt vulnerable in the company of so many supporters of Andrews and Delgado. We agreed to find a new location somewhere between Paul's home in Romsey and Bristol where the rest of us lived. Meaden would be invited and would be welcome should he choose to come along. Also invited was a young couple who'd spoken to us at Silbury and who seemed to be supporters of Meaden's theory. Martin and Nancy [4] lived in Beckhampton and were quite keen to know more. I promised to phone them when we'd fixed a location for the meeting.

On that note we went off to various locations for a bit of crop watching but with most of the fields now harvested it was a half-hearted affair. Most people drifted away as the night wore on and Jacqui, Paul and I had gone home by 2 o' clock.

And so *Operation High Hill* ended.

Chapter Seven
LOWS AND HIGHS
The Cropwatcher-Colin talks-Maiden Bradley-More eyewitnesses-More support

The meeting was arranged for the following Friday and was to be at the *Royal Oak* at Corsley Heath, just outside Warminster and next to Longleat. Rog wasn't going to be there as he was spending the week on the Isle of Wight. This holiday was useful because we had reports of circles at Culver Down on the Isle and Rog could investigate whilst over there. [1]

Before that, Jacqui and I went again to Butleigh Wootton in another effort to find the formation there. We drew a blank. The following Friday evening saw us heading out along the A36 from Bath to Warminster, where we turned right on to the by-pass then right again onto the A362 towards Frome. In a short while we arrived at the Royal Oak. We were there before 8.30 but it was not until 9.30 that anyone else arrived. That person was Paul Fuller. When he'd got a pint and sat down he told us that Terence Meaden wasn't coming. 'He's in France again!' muttered the Ufologist, sadly. The couple from Beckhampton didn't show up, either.

Even without Meaden, however, there was plenty to talk about. Paul had had this idea for a new magazine all about crop circles. It was to be the *'Private Eye'* of the circles world and would feature reports of circles occurring, correlations between circles and UFO reports and so on. It was provisionally to be named *'The Cropwatcher'*. Jacqui and I gave it our full and enthusiastic backing, as, apparently did Meaden, seeing it as a forum for airing his views on the Plasma Vortex. We talked about the tendency of Meaden to not recognise that most of the 'supporters' he'd recruited for High Hill were in reality not supporters of the Plasma Vortex, but just about any mystical event creating circles. They'd only latched onto Meaden because there was, at that time, no other organised cropwatch apart from *Blackbird* –and that, due to its backers, was exclusive.

Full of hope for the future and agreeing to meet in a fortnight at the same place, we left in pouring rain at ten past eleven.

The following week I went to Glastonbury where, in Gothic Image, I found that Paul Fuller's idea for a magazine about crop circles had already been thought of by the CCCS. Their offering, quite professionally produced, was *The Cereologist*. It had a distinct advantage in that it obviously had financial backing and was edited by the Grand Old Man of Earth Mysteries – John Michell. And it was full of articles backing anything except Dr Meaden's theory. I was a little surprised because the CCCS was initially supposed to be 'neutral' – or so we thought.

I next came across a poster advertising a forthcoming event at Glastonbury: a lecture by none other than Colin Andrews! Back home I phoned Paul Fuller and told him. He couldn't make it on the lecture day, so I agreed to attend and report back. 'I've had some strangers on the phone,' he said. 'Someone trying to get me to repeat my allegations about Fandango. They were probably taping the call so's they could give it to Colin!'

This was an unfortunate period for Paul. Ever since his legal battle with the CPR duo he'd felt he had to look over his shoulder all the time. There were certainly those in the circles fraternity who would have loved to shut Fuller up permanently (in a legal way, of course!) because he remained the constant voice of reason. Fuller always trod a 'middle path', taking each event on its merit and not being afraid to criticise Meaden if he felt it necessary. From early on, Paul, in company with Jenny Randles, felt that many of the 'evolving' formations were hoaxes. He never, to my knowledge, supported the 'Pictograms' with boxes, feeling that however Meaden developed the plasma-vortex theory, it couldn't supply the answers to how the boxes got there. Paul and Jenny both thought the boxes and later spurs were fake. I called Rog and he agreed to attend the Glastonbury lecture with me. Jacqui didn't go for some reason.

Sunday 26th August 1990

It was a very hot day and, by the time Rog and I arrived in Glastonbury that evening and parked in Silver Street car park it was still very warm. The audience was drifting into the building, The 'Glastonbury Experience' where the lecture was to be held. The people were a mixed bag according to their mode of dress. Inside it was almost uncomfortably warm and the windows had to be opened. This had the unfortunate disadvantage of allowing not only fresh air but traffic noise to enter the room and as I had my small dictaphone with me to record the lecture I hoped the traffic in the High Street wouldn't drown out the talk.

All around the room were photos of circles past and present. Copies of *Circular Evidence* were on sale as were copies of *The Cereologist*, the latter at £2.50 whereas in Gothic Image you could buy the magazine for £2.42. There were also tapes of Colin Andrews talking about crop circles, priced at £6 each. There was little or no mention of Pat Delgado. Then a man who called himself 'Tony' came in, apologised for the open windows and introduced Colin who came to the front of the packed room with a smile.

To describe the entire lecture would be outside the parameters of this book, so I'll just go over some of the highlights. Andrews spoke in his usual jerky manner, full of bad grammar and mispronunciations, but the audience loved it all. From his talk you wouldn't have guessed that he'd been the subject of a major hoax only weeks before. You had to hand it to him; he could bluff his way out of an awkward situation all right. He started by showing a piece from a *Daytime Live* programme in which a strange noise was heard by the sound recordist when they were filming Colin and Pat in a circle at Beckhampton. The piece ended with Colin's voice-over claiming that: '....*We really are at ten seconds to midnight. The public do know, in their* [sic] *inner selves, what a dreadful, dreadful state the planet is in. We have to face the facts, that we are destroying this planet-the very planet we need for survival. There may be some intelligence involved here. Something very mysterious is going on at the moment...*'

Colin was in his element. Here he had blended the ecology theme with the circles and added a 'thriller' element. That he would appeal to a much wider audience with this was obvious. He was to repeat the '10 seconds to midnight' phrase many times over the next year or so until the ecology/green movement began to decline and he had to take up a different theme. However, back in 1990, and Colin next gave the audience a potted history of the circles affair, being careful to mention his early collusion with Terence Meaden, albeit briefly. There were many references to 'silver discs' and 'strange lights'. And, of course, there was the '....airborne component...' ! This, said Colin, was '....*definitely in the formula*...' He claimed that he and his team had recordings of the strange noises heard and were apparently having them analysed by Sussex University. But, a word of warning to the audience:

'.....*Now I'd like, at this point, to please ask you not to follow this particular-there's nothing I'd like...at all, but Sussex University are getting very sensitive about the number of inquiries they're getting about it-uh-in fact, they're denying any association with it at all...'*

As we were to later discover through discreet enquiries of our own, there was a very good reason for Sussex denying any involvement with this-they weren't involved at all. What Colin wasn't saying was that somebody who *worked* for Sussex University was carrying out some investigations *in his spare time*! He was playing with words.

Then he came to the plasma-vortex theory.

'.....No more than half-a-dozen sane people in the world go along with that theory. I'm sorry to sound as if that's knocking, but it comes from the bottom of my heart. When we have one of this country's leading vortex experts putting forward such a theory – I worked with him for three years, myself, specifically looking at the meteorological theories......and we [The CPR] could find nothing, no correlation whatsoever, in the meteorology theories....'.

Then, just before a break, he introduced a short tape.

'....I hope you'll take this in good taste, (he said) but I just want to make the point that science is struggling with this....'

The tape opened with a shot of...Dr Terence Meaden: the caption below said: 'Dr Terry Meadows'. It was a cleverly edited piece of tape, in which Meaden was asked questions by an off-camera interviewer. He was trying to explain how the plasma vortex made circles. The interviewer then asks Colin Andrews what he thought of Meaden's explanation. Andrews replies 'Frankly, rubbish!' Then it cuts back to Meaden still trying to explain his theory. Back to Andrews: '.....We're looking at some kind of thinking. There's a thought component indicated......' then the interviewer says: '.... They [the CPR] want to experiment to capture the force behind the circles, but Dr Meaden thinks they're wasting their time...'

Dr Meaden: '.....They're not prepared to admit the real evidence...'

Interviewer: '.....And what is the real evidence as far as you're concerned?.....'

Dr Meaden: '.....The real evidence...is...is...'(pauses, sighs and looks away from the camera.)   Video ends.

The room exploded with laughter. One up for Colin.
This was wicked. The short clip was probably composed of bits of video tape, which had come off the cutting-room floor. It made a point, though. Science was struggling; - struggling to get a fair hearing from a very biased media.
There was a chink of light ahead for Terence Meaden's supporters, though. On August 17th that year, the *Bristol Evening Post*, continuing its summer theme of crop circles through the Letters to the Editor section, published a letter from a Bristol lady who had spent her early years on a farm. In her letter, Mrs. Dutton said that she knew what caused

crop circles: '.....May I offer this from personal experience...' she wrote '.....They are caused by sudden, sharp whirlwinds...' She went on to say that she, her parents and grandparents had all seen circles in crops and accepted that whirlwinds caused them.

This was just what was needed, another eye-witness account. I wrote to Mrs. Dutton, mentioning Meaden's research and asking if I might contact her by phone to ask a few more questions. I had not long to wait before I received a phone call from Mrs. Dutton. She told me that her father had worked on Perry Farm, near Maiden Bradley, Wiltshire, between 1912-1956. During that time the family had often observed circles in hay and wheat. She told me that the circles were a nuisance to farmers because the harvesting machines then used could not cut the flattened crops very well and it often had to be harvested by hand. This was useful corroborative information. What we now needed was to know what the terrain was like in order to see if Meaden's theory could be applied.

A look at the Ordnance Survey sheet for the area showed several possible hills from which an eddy-vortex could be formed. Jacqui and I set out for Maiden Bradley on the Sunday following Colin's lecture.

Maiden Bradley is on the east side of the Bruton Forest and lies to the north and west of an area whose terrain is not unlike that of the area around Alton Barnes. To the south lay White Sheet Down, to the east, Cold Kitchen Hill and Bidcombe Hill. All had their share of tumuli and earthworks. To our delight, the area around Perry Farm was dotted with a series of hills not too dissimilar in shape to that of Silbury Hill but several times larger. The shape and location of nearly all these hills fitted the vortex theory. On our return we put together a report and sent it off to Meaden, promising copies of photos as soon as these were available.

Surely then, this was the sort of thing to convince people that Professor Meaden had something here. Paul Fuller was slowly but surely adding to his list of eyewitness accounts of circles forming; most of these fitted the theory: sooner or later a wider range of people, including the press, was going to have to sit up and take notice...or so we thought.

Hardly was the first week in September over than another free paper ran a third of a page about corn circles. '*The Quest for answers in the corn circle circus*' ran the headline. Our old friends Bristol Quest were claiming that Bristol was '....having a major UFO flap....' – which was fine as far as it went. Sure, there were lights in the sky to be investigated and other odd-goings-on to boot. But the theme of the article was linking '.....balls of light in the same places as the crop formations....' – according to the 'Regional Co-ordinator' Richard Tarr. Furthermore, Quest's national Director of Research, one Tony Dodd claimed that he'd spoken to Russian and European ufologists who knew of: '....*people who were able to receive telepathic messages from aliens which were giving very strong signals that something very exciting could happen within the next two years.....*'.

Apparently it was claimed that aliens '....could well land in the West Country....' The reason for this was that the '.....corn circles and lights and objects in the sky [were] seen near ancient monuments and ley lines-which the west has in abundance....'

The rest of the article was in a similar vein. This was sad; this fledgling UFO group was only regurgitating the sort of stuff which had been written many times before and they had not the experience that people like Paul Fuller had. Even our little group had seen more circles than Bristol Quest. What was sadder was that at this stage even *they* were able to claim more space in a paper than Terence Meaden. But then, sensationalism sells papers and this *was* a free ads paper, so I suppose that the editor possibly took the view that UFO's would sell more copies than a plasma vortex.

Friday 31st August 1990

And so, after a still eventful month, we met again at the *Royal Oak*. Jacqui and I drove over to Corsley to meet Paul Fuller. Rog was also coming but had been delayed so arranged to meet us there. As it happened, all three of us were in the bar before Fuller turned up at nine. I'd phoned the couple from Beckhampton again and left a message on their answerphone. They didn't arrive for the second time so we agreed not to bother with them again. Terence Meaden had also once again been invited but he didn't attend either.

So, we talked about Meaden's attitude to the CCCS-he had been invited to one or two of their functions but had not been able to attend for one reason or another. Paul was fearful of the professor's willingness to cooperate with them and with good reason; one glance at the 'hierarchy' was enough to show that their views were not compatible to Meaden's. The Old Man of Earth Mysteries himself, John Michell, was now one of the leading members of CCCS and Busty Taylor was at work as one of their 'Field Officers' (another was George Wingfield). The Earl of Haddington was their patron. So far, anything they published had a distinctly mystical theme.

We also talked about Andrews and Delgado and speculated which direction their work might take in 1991 after the *Blackbird* fiasco, but we didn't come to any conclusion. However, Paul's new magazine, *The Cropwatcher* was coming together well and the first edition was due soon. Jacqui and I promised to do some 'fly-posting' around circles sites to publicise the mag.

All too soon it was time to go. The summer had been quite exciting overall and there was a feeling that we ought to try to keep things going – the winter was going to be quite an anti-climax – but it was not to be, for a while at least. Paul Fuller was not available to meet again for at least a month -and Terence Meaden? Nobody knew. The feeling was that if he didn't give his supporters more backing, at least by turning up once in a while, then we might (reluctantly) have to forget getting involved next year. To take on the CCCS without Meaden's backing would not be possible for Paul Fuller and *The Cropwatcher*.

My notes for September show – well, nothing much actually. Life went on without circles. We all did our bit to learn more about the subject-from all points of view. After all, how could we criticise anyone else's findings without some knowledge of what they were on about? One example was the end-of-summer 'revelation' from Condrews and Fandango that stems of crop flattened during the process of making a circle showed signs of 'molecular change'. This startling news came via research carried out at an 'Independent Laboratory' (of course). They, of course, got inches in newspapers and airtime on radio and telly programmes – all to tell us something which any plumber with an ounce of background knowledge of his subject could have confirmed.

A plumber? Yes, or any pipe-bender actually. Because in the act of bending any tube, be it metal or crop stem, the inside of the bend compresses and the outside of the bend stretches. Compare this to a 'control sample' (IE one that isn't bent) and hey presto! You have a different molecular structure in the bent sample. Basic school-level physics.[2]

Another of Colin Andrews' claims concerned crop circles near Whiteparish, a few miles from Salisbury. He had often made loose claims about 'mysterious aircraft crashes' in the same field but had never been any more specific than mentioning 1946 as a date. One of the various items I'd investigated before getting into crop circles, was aircraft accidents, mainly from around the Bristol area. This gave me contacts, so in the early part of September I wrote off to one of these asking him for any information he could supply.

After a week or so I got a reply '...*There is nothing I can find, either RAF or Naval, that fits the circumstances...*'. It wasn't a civilian plane because it would have been in local papers, which had already been searched, and you can't cover up a civilian plane crash near Salisbury! So where had Colin got his info? We never found out and this claim slipped quietly away to obscurity.

As notes for October are few, it seems probable that we didn't meet that month either. There was quite a bit of talk on the phones, though. We finally arranged to meet towards the end of the month but things got altered for reasons I can't recall and a meeting was finally planned for the 2nd of November, initially at the *Royal Oak*. Terence Meaden was actually going to attend this time! In the meantime there was some sparring with the local Bristol Newspapers and – Bristol Quest again! The good old *Bristol Journal* published an article under the 'exclusive' label in which it was claimed that two little girls playing with a Frisbee were suddenly surprised when the plastic disc 'hit a force field' and flew back at one of them. Next, the children were caught in a 'mystery yellow bubble' and 'hurled to the ground'. The mother of one of the girls was quoted as saying '...*it must have been a UFO force field...*'.

So, who did the *Journal* turn to for expert advice? Richard Tarr of Bristol Quest! Tarr was '...taking it seriously...' '...*We are getting a lot of reports about UFO's...*' he told the paper. '...*They usually fly over Downend and land at Dundry....*'

Curiously this was the holding pattern for aircraft approaching Bristol Airport from the Midlands.....

Anyway, I couldn't let them get away with such unresearched twaddle. I wrote off to the Journal pointing out that from the evidence gleaned from their article it seemed that the girls had in actual fact been caught in a plasma vortex and not a UFO force field. It certainly fitted the bill as far as Meaden's theory was concerned. The paper published my letter on October 26th. However, they edited out the last paragraph where I pointed out that the UFO's seen by Quest were more likely to be...*'flight 1763 inbound from Manchester'!*

There was some further interesting eyewitness 'evidence' during the month in the shape of a small piece I found in an article in, of all things, *Steam World* – a railway magazine. In the article a photographer mentioned that whilst out taking pictures of steam locomotives in the early 1960's, he had been surprised by a sudden 'whirlwind' which had stopped as suddenly as it had begun and '...*left a ring of flattened crop...!*' I copied this article to Paul Fuller to add to his growing list of eyewitness accounts of circles being formed.

October 1990 was the month in which rock band Led Zeppelin released an album of their 'greatest hits'. The collection of six records featured remastered tracks from the band's history. The album cover was the selling point for many however, because it featured an aerial shot of the Alton Barnes formations with the shadow of an airship passing across them, causing many folk to speculate that the band themselves were in some way responsible for the crop circles. The truth was that a Bristol design company hit on the idea after seeing the pictures of the formations. What was interesting to me, though, was that looking again at the shapes at Alton Barnes, some parts of the formation seemed remarkably similar to Met. Office weather symbols...

During the week preceding the November meeting, Paul Fuller had a call from Dr Meaden. Could we meet somewhere near Westbury? The reason was that an American, over here on a cycling holiday, had contacted the Prof. and wanted to meet him to discuss crop circles. The man would be in the Westbury area on the 2nd November, staying at *The Duke*. Paul phoned me and we agreed that the obvious place to meet was – *The Duke*!

So, on the 2nd November, I drove, with Jacqui, to Westbury and on to Bratton. Passing the White Horse in light drizzle it seemed strange to recall the events of only a few months ago. We got there at about 7.20 and found ourselves almost alone in the cold bar. Even the heaters were blowing cold air, conspiring to add to the air of gloom, which so contrasted to the hot summer. Ordering food we sat down to await the others. The waitress promised that the heaters would soon warm up. Half way through our meal Terence Meaden arrived and greeted us. Roger Davis came into the bar as well so we moved to a larger table. We'd noticed a man with a notepad at the bar shortly before and now he came over to us and cautiously asked if Dr Meaden was amongst us.

The newcomer was the man we'd been waiting for. He introduced himself as George Nehls Junior. He'd cycled in from Devon as part of his cycling tour of the Old Country. He wanted, he said, to know 'the Truth' about crop circles and as he was an engineer, he had naturally decided that Meaden was the one to ask. Terence beamed politely. Just as he began to explain the theory behind the Plasma Vortex, in came Paul Fuller so Terence had to start again. It was now over to Paul and the professor to tell the tale of their research so far. George Nehls sat and listened, fascinated.

Terence concluded by showing us all a letter and photo from another American correspondent of his who had done some research into 'vortices in a medium'. This sort of work was good because it showed that at least Meaden and his couple of Japanese colleagues were not alone in the scientific fraternity where vortices were concerned. Paul gave Nehls a copy of the new *Cropwatcher*, and Meaden gave him a copy of *The Circles Effect and its Mysteries*. Nehls waxed enthusiastic. 'Hey! This is great! I could market this back in the States!' he cried, when he'd flipped through Meaden's book.

As readers will recall, we who by now looked on ourselves as Meaden's 'Support Team' were always wary of people who claimed to be Meaden fans but had all to often been looking for the supernatural element in the circles affair. With this in mind I embarked on a series of questions about various aspects of 'New Age' interests to see where Nehls was coming from. He sounded solidly behind Terence Meaden all the way, claiming that he just wanted to know the truth. He told us that the American TV programme *'60 minutes'* had interviewed well-known author Erich Von Daniken (author of *Chariots of the Gods*) during which the more Von Daniken said, so the more he had contradicted himself. When pulled up on this, apparently the German had grinned and said '...*in my country we allow a little poetic licence...*' – or words to that effect. This cheered Paul Fuller up because Von Daniken was a thorn in the side of all serious ufologists.

Nehls brought with him a very interesting theory indeed. He'd cottoned on to the fact that sunspot activity causes all sort of problems with terrestrial communications and how, at times of maximum sunspot activity, a force known as 'ground effect EMF' [3] could cause havoc with what he called 'utility services' (computers and the like). This had happened before when US/Canadian computer networks had suffered badly during a period of sunspot activity. I could see that this made sense, especially where an electrically charged vortex was concerned. So could Terence. He glanced at me and we agreed that Nehls had a point.

We paused here to buy more drinks. The waitress was chatting to a scruffy biker. There was hardly anyone else in the pub.

Paul turned the conversation round to a book just published by the CCCS. Terence stalled him by producing a copy of it and explaining that he had a section in the book. Paul was aghast.

'Terence, they're all loonies!'

Meaden put on one of his most charming smiles.

'I infiltrated them,' he replied. 'They asked me to contribute a section on my theory- so I did.'

Paul was by now thumbing through the pages. 'They've libelled you, Terence-and Jenny and myself!' he announced, triumphantly.

Meaden grinned but said nothing. Since the Condrews/Fandango libel threat, looking for libels was one of Paul's hobbies!

Ralph Noyes, an author and ex-MOD man edited the book. The book featured photos by Busty Taylor and others. One photo showed a crop circle formation which was actually one made to advertise a car company! Just about every article in the book purported to have some evidence or other supporting a supernatural or UFO answer to the circles. Terence Meaden's piece alone supported his vortex theory.

Fuller groaned. 'They're going to make pots of money,' he said.

George Nehls predicted that those people in the UK who set out to make money out of the crop circles would suffer a similar humiliation in years to come. '.....The truth will win,' He said. '...You will be proved right in a year or so, I'm sure!'

Stirring stuff. Time would unfortunately prove just how wrong he was.
A voice called 'Time please!'

We got up to go, Nehls promising to send Meaden some papers about sunspots and EMF. We shook hands with the American and wished him a successful holiday. In the car park Meaden turned to Paul and me.

'I'm going to be very busy next summer, writing a book,' he said. 'I'd like you all to be data collectors for *CERES* – Circles Effect Research, next year. Perhaps you could come up with some plans for a cropwatch in 1991 and we'll discuss them when we next meet.'

This sounded good and of course we all agreed. We finally left the pub at 11.20, full of hope for the coming year.

Chapter Eight
REMEMBER, REMEMBER THE MONTH OF NOVEMBER
Meetings-More meetings and Chat

November 1990 was, in its way, a milestone in crop circles research. Terence Meaden began, at last, to plan for 1991; the loose group of circles fans and watchers in and around the Avebury area called a meeting to discuss the way forward and the CCCS held a meeting of all interested parties as part of its 1991 planning.

Forgetting circles for a while (well almost) Jacqui and I decided to spend an afternoon in the Wiltshire town of Bradford-on-Avon. Dr Meaden lived and worked there but that wasn't the reason for our visit. No, we went to look at the ancient Saxon church and some other old buildings. I did stop outside Meaden's place to post some mail in his letterbox. It was a copy of my letter to the *Bristol Journal* concerning the children and the 'Bubble' and some video footage of circles he wanted to see. Two days later, I had a phone call from the professor. He thanked me for the information and told me that he had received an invitation from the CCCS to a meeting that they were holding in London later that month. This was apparently because he had taken out an 'affiliation' membership with the group. This was the 'infiltration' that he'd mentioned at the meeting previously. At first, Meaden had declined the invitation but when another letter arrived suggesting he send someone in his place, he'd had second thoughts. He had considered asking Dr Derek Elsom, his co-director of *TORRO* to attend, but for some reason this was not convenient. Would I possibly be interested.....?

Yes, I would pleased to go. I'll just check my diary.... No problem. Terence promised to send me a copy of the letter.

'Who else will be going?' I asked.

'Professor Archie Roy, Ralph Noyes, and Michael Green of the CCCS amongst others. There are about thirteen or fourteen names on the letter.'

There were, I thought, a few names which I would have supposed to be going and whom I knew by now that Terence Meaden wouldn't want to meet. So I asked him, 'What about Andrews and Delgado?'

The answer surprised me. 'Not apparently invited,' replied Terence.

Further talk led to the idea that Roger Davis should go as well. Terence said he would write to the CCCS advising them of this. Meaden had also had a note from the William Shakespeare lookalike, Alan Rayner (whom you will recall was one of the goatee beards in the crop watches earlier that summer). Rayner was thinking of organising the various factions interested in circles into one cohesive group for the coming season. To this end he was holding a meeting at the *Waggon and Horses* at Beckhampton on the 16th of November. Terence was invited. He couldn't go (or didn't want to...) so Rog and I were deputed to go instead. It was beginning to be a busy month.....

That evening Jacqui and I went to the *Carpenters Arms* at Stanton Wick, Somerset, not far from the Stanton Drew stone circles. We took Jim Crow along and spent the evening talking about Andy Collins and the *Black Alchemist*. Somehow I felt that we were soon going to be once again immersed in crop circles so a little diversion was necessary.

16th November 1990

Jacqui and I arrived at Beckhampton at around 8pm and parked opposite the pub. Rog had called earlier to say he was running late and hoped to see us there later. We walked into the almost empty bar and bought our drinks. The handful of people there on that rainy evening weren't familiar to us. We ventured into the side-room where we'd often gathered during the summer cropwatches and found people we recognised: Steven Verner (the other goatee beard) and Stanley Morcomb. Verner obviously mistook me for somebody else because when I greeted him with '...Hi, long time no see...' he replied, 'About a month, I'd say,' When I replied that it was the beginning of August since we'd last met, he looked strangely surprised. 'Oh...as long ago as that.....?' I don't think he was convinced. Anyway, we sat down at a table in the window and waited. We waited 20 minutes before anyone else arrived. Someone commented that it was probably too wet for Alan Rayner to turn up on his Honda.

By quarter to nine I was getting impatient. 'How long do we give them?' I asked Jacqui.

'Nine-thirty,' she replied. 'If Rayner hasn't arrived by then, we'll shove off.'

Fifteen minutes later she grabbed my sleeve. 'There's an E-reg Metro with 'L'-plates on just arrived.....'

Lusty Busty!

Sure enough, the familiar small figure ran across the busy road to the pub followed by his henchman, Ron Jones. Busty didn't go to the bar immediately but came straight to the small room, stood in the doorway with the brighter lights of the main bar behind him and glanced around. I squinted at him and raised my hand. He came over.

'Doesn't he ever smile?' he grinned at Jacqui, indicating me. He sat next to me.

'I've got some photos you might be interested in,' he said, pulling out a wallet of pictures. The first ones he showed were of a circle near Winterbourne Stoke, off the A303 in Wiltshire. It was a large single circle with the crop flattened in quarter segments; each segment so flattened lay a different way. We'd seen this one before in one of the books on circles. Furthermore I believed it to be a hoax. Why? Because a few months before I'd been driving through Devizes and had come to a stand at a road junction. Whilst waiting for the road to clear I glanced around and, having an interest in house building styles, I'd looked at a 1930's house and to my surprise, on the gable end was a circular design with four segments, each laid with bricks and each laid a different way! Just like the Winterbourne Stoke circle! It was as old as the house so hadn't been inspired by the circle of the 1980's.

So, looking at the photo I commented, 'Just like Andover Road...'

'Andover Road?' said Busty, nonchalantly.

'Yes,' I replied, 'The design on the house.'

'Oh,' said Busty and glanced towards the door. His attitude was one of almost disinterest. But it was false. He was trying to appear disinterested whilst really wanting to know more. It was so transparent.

I carried on. 'That's the shape on the gable end of that 1930's house in Andover Road, Devizes – y'know, near the *Moonraker* pub!'

'Oh, really?' muttered Busty, lightly.

'Yes. It's the same design as this circle.'

Busty suddenly seemed none too keen on pursuing this line of conversation.
His feigned lack of interest was saved by the arrival of Ron Jones with a pint for Busty and a brandy for himself. Ron was wearing specs-I'd not seen him wear these before and said so. 'My second best pair!' grinned Ron.
We carried on the small talk until Rog arrived. Shortly after Alan Rayner walked in with his (then) lady friend whom he introduced as Pam Price. Rayner had had a haircut since the summer and his resemblance to William Shakespeare was not as good as before. Whilst he and Pam sorted themselves out, I tried to bait Busty over his apparent falling-out with Condrews/Fandango. Busty was very dark about his involvement with the CPR duo. I knew through Meaden and Fuller that Busty still talked to Colin and Pat but in conversation he denied having anything to do with them nowadays. I tried a different tactic.

'Why is it that you seem to have trouble with Colin and Pat? Is it because of the Masons?' (This was based on a rumour going round that Colin had lately joined the Freemasons.) To my surprise, Busty looked startled. He looked at Ron Jones.

'He's got it right first time-right on the button!'

Warming to the subject, I said, 'Are Andrews and Delgado Masons?'

Busty's reply didn't really make sense in the light of his last comment.

'No-I don't think so,' he said.

I changed the subject. 'You're now a Field Officer with the CCCS, do you have any more power with them than you did with CPR?'

Busty looked mysterious. 'That?' he replied, 'Oh, *that's* going down the same road as before…..'

That surprised me. 'You mean you're being put upon as you were before?'

'Something like that,' said Busty, looking at the table. Then it was his turn to change the subject. 'I was in Berlin last week and I'll be in Cairo in 48 hours,' he said.

'D'you want another drink?' –it was Rog. I replied in the affirmative and Rog wandered off to the bar. Followed by Busty. At the bar, the following conversation took place:

Busty: 'What's Pete's involvement with the Masons?'

Rog: 'Oh, passing interest, like most of us.'

Busty: 'Colin and Pat are not Masons – but it is sure that the local Masons are giving them full backing...'

Rog: 'Oh, really?'

Back in the small room it was now twenty to ten and someone suggested that we ought to start the meeting! He asked for a show of hands to find out how we viewed the circles phenomenon-natural, supernatural etc. The result was 50 percent believing the circles to be the result of UFO's and the other 50 percent being split between the Supernatural and the Natural. We were already in the minority. Busty was talking to Jacqui who was trying to wheedle a copy of the CCCS book out of him. A chap with glasses stood up and said that everyone should state their name, job and what their interest in the circles was. As each took his or her turn to answer, I noted that we had present a Roman Baths tour guide; a Postman; the Portsmouth town Deputy Architect and his wife; a plumber; a writer and a part-time systems analyst (Alan Rayner). Ron Jones stood up.

'I'm Ron Jones and I'm a travel agent from the Planet Zork!' He was by now pissed and slurring his words, having been knocking back the brandy at a tremendous rate.

'I'm Busty Taylor, I'm a driving instructor. My hobbies are flying planes and maintaining planes and gliders. And trying to find out what's causing this phenomenon.' Busty's timely statement saved Ron from further embarrassment.

'What do we say?' I hissed at Rog. 'Whatever we think of first...' he hissed back.

Then it was his turn: 'I'm Roger Davis and I'm a self-employed computer consultant. I've been following this phenomenon for – what – three years?' he looked at me. I nodded. He continued: 'Everyone likes a good mystery and this is the best one for years!'

Everyone laughed.

It was my turn. 'I'm Pete and I agree with Rog!'

Jacqui said, 'I'm Jacqui and I do too!'

More laughs and we were through without having revealed that we were working with Terence Meaden. Even Busty didn't know that.
All present had now introduced themselves so Alan Rayner stood and started the meeting proper.

'Since we were last here,' he said, ' The consensus of the group known as the Marlborough and Swindon Crop Circles Group, was that we would become the Beckhampton and District Pictogram Monitoring Group, but would stay an informal gathering.' He sat down again. Nobody else moved to say anything so I stood up.

'I feel that everyone ought to state their religion...I'll go first – I'm a Pagan.'

'And so am I,' – the Portsmouth Architect's wife. Alan Rayner said he was a 'non-Christian but believed in a Supreme Power' as did a couple of others. The Plumber was a committed Christian. After him the subject petered out in a general hubbub of conversation. A ginger girl tried to keep it going by confessing to being non-Christian and Ron Jones slurred out that he was a Christian.

'How can you be when you believe in earth-bound intelligence and reincarnation?' I argued. Ron said something unintelligible before hastily sitting down.

'It's quite possible that reincarnation of spirits is in some sense responsible for this phenomenon,' Pam Price was trying hard to get people's attention. Not easy. She went on, 'We might have built Stonehenge-perhaps it got so...too...powerful and had to be dismantled......'

Ron Jones got unsteadily to his feet again.

'It dates back to the Egyptians...'

'*What, Stonehenge?*' called someone.

'No, no. *The Circles*. They're over 5000 years old. Date back to the Egyptians and beyond....' Nobody was really listening to him. Busty was in deep conversation with Jacqui who was still trying to persuade him to part with a free copy of that book. Another girl stood up.

'It's very possible that there have been civilisations rise and fall before this one. It could be a warning about the state of the planet....'
Obviously a convert from the Colin Andrews school of Green theories.
Pam Price again: 'The circles are possibly a warning, y'know, by whoever's out there, warning us to take better care of our planet. Warning us that we're out of control - what with all the wars and threats of nuclear war...'
Admirable sentiments, but no one was listening in the pub either.

People were drifting off to the bar. Jacqui had gone somewhere or other so I tackled

Busty about something I'd read.

'Here, Busty, y'know the words that appeared in the crop at Cheesefoot the other year....'

'*WEARENOTALONE*-yeah?'

'Yeah. Who found it?'

'I did. I was on a flight with Pat Delgado when we flew over it'.

'Pat believed it, didn't he?'

'Yes.'

'He must have been potty, believing that! It's straight out of '*Close Encounters*'!

Jacqui came back at this point. 'That's right,' she said. 'If it was done by Aliens it would have read <u>YOU</u>ARENOTALONE!'

Busty smirked. 'I went into the field before the farmer cut it down ...I don't know...it *looked* right...the lay of the corn was right....'

'But surely,' I argued, 'You don't believe it was an alien intelligence...?'

Busty shrugged. 'Who knows?'

The evening wore on. The rain and wind outside had got worse. A strong gust of wind blew some pot plants off the window ledge outside the bar. Rain clattered against the windows. By about eleven, Alan Rayner decided to try and bring it all together again.

'I propose,' he called, above the hubbub of voices, 'That we have a meeting sometime where Busty Taylor can instruct people in how to look for circles. A sort of 'Crop Circles workshop. Do we want it to be big or small? Big would be about 200 people like Michael Green (CCCS) had at one of his lectures.'

'If you let it get that big, 'I said, 'It'll be un-manageable. CCCS was formed to do the big stuff and let the small groups feed info into it. Keep it small.'

To my surprise there was a murmur of general agreement with this. Alan Rayner went on to suggest a small, local meeting with all Busty's expenses being paid by the group. Someone else suggested that it might be an idea to rent a room in a pub in Marlborough. Rayner said that he couldn't arrange that as he was '...only a part-time resident in the area...' The woman who'd suggested it said that she would try and do the arranging on Rayner's behalf. Possibly January or February? There was a lot of muttering, but the group could not agree a date for Busty's talk!

A barmaid appeared in the doorway and stood patiently waiting to collect the glasses. The meeting broke up with no agreement and no plans. It was a shame because Alan Rayner had the right ideas and was tactfully neutral but at that stage he hadn't the strength of character to push things through. We all moved out of the pub in a loose throng. Alan Rayner promised to send me a newsletter advising of the next meeting. Outside, Rog had to go so he made for his car. I looked round for Jacqui and found her sitting in Busty's car with the door open, flirting heavily with the lecherous pilot-still trying to get a copy of the book! Ron Jones was standing around in the rain, shivering!

I tapped on the window. 'Busty! Let Ron in -he's soaked!'
Busty let his sidekick in but Jacqui didn't get out....I strode off to my car in disgust! Five minutes later she scampered over. 'Got one!' she said, leaping into the car.

'What was the price?' I asked, sarcastically.

Not cottoning on she said, 'He said he'd settle up next time we met.'

'I bet he will! Lecherous old sod!'

A slight domestic dispute followed and the rest of the journey home was in silence!

Tuesday 20th November 1990
That evening I phoned Terence Meaden. Firstly, he told me that he agreed with the idea that both Rog and I should go to the CCCS meeting representing *CERES*. He had advised Ralph Noyes of this. What had happened at the Beckhampton meeting? I told him. When I got to the bit about Busty not really believing that the words *WEARENOTALONE* were fakes, the professor said, 'Well, when I looked at the formation at Pepperbox earlier this year, there were words faintly visible there.'

'Really?' I exclaimed. 'What were they?'

Meaden consulted his notebook. 'Ah, let me see.... Ah yes, the words were 'Skins Up'. I laughed much to the professor's surprise.
'Sorry, Terence, but that is the cannabis user's phrase for 'Dope's ready!'

'Oh, dear. I didn't know that. I suppose that casts some doubt on the formation?'

'Possibly. Unless some travellers got there before you did and trampled the words into the corn. Perhaps we had better label that one as 'doubtful'-it wasn't as good as the Alton Barnes and Stanton St Bernard ones, was it?' Terence reluctantly agreed. He went on to tell me that there was good news in the pipeline. The Bristol United Press group had been in touch and were interested in running a cropwatch in 1991. Tentative plans were that they would arrange to fund equipment if *CERES* would supply manpower. I suggested to Terence that if he accepted the offer, it might be an idea to contact some of his landowner friends and see if we could use their land for the site, in return for a promise to keep the site a secret. These were times when New Age Travellers were the bane of every farmer's life, often turning up without warning and camping on or near their land. We knew that any request to mount a cropwatch on land in Wiltshire or Hampshire would be met with opposition from farmers who would be afraid that the subject would attract travellers who wished to 'worship' the circles. Terence said that he'd see what he could do.

Saturday 24th November 1990

This was the day of the CCCS meeting. The venue was at chairman Michael Green's house on Clapham Common, London. I picked Rog up and we set off up the M4. As we joined the M4 at junction 18, snow was already falling and turning the grass verges and fields white. The road was OK though and we made good time to Chiswick where we left the motorway and headed through the streets to Clapham Common. We found the address without too many problems and parked. Green lived in an elegant house facing the common. We walked up the steps to the front door and pressed the bell marked 'Green-CCCS'.

The door was opened by a pleasant, short plump woman who introduced herself as 'Christine' and ushered us into the house. 'We've already started,' she explained, showing us into a darkened room where a slide show was taking place. The slides were of crop circles and the projectionist was none other than.....Busty Taylor! This was a turn-up for the book! He was busy and didn't see us. We sat down next to a slim, middle-aged woman wearing a 'hippie' dress. She whispered that her name was Diana Clift. We introduced ourselves and watched the show.

When the slide show was over, the lights were switched on and a man stood up at the front. He was tall, balding and probably in his late 50's. He introduced himself as Richard Andrews and he was to talk about the Dowsing effects found in crop circles. Apparently there were 'Energy Lines' involved in the formation of crop circles. Tractor drivers, said Andrews, unconsciously aligned themselves with Ley lines when ploughing and spraying fields. Dowsing these lines, he said, was an important part of circles research. In fact, by dowsing, one could discover where circles would arrive up to two years before they formed! Andrews went on to say that many people acknowledged dowsing as a subject nowadays and even Dr Meaden accepted it (news to me).

When Andrews had finished, I turned round and sitting behind me was F.C.Taylor. 'Surprise, surprise!' smirked Busty.

'Yes, and there's more to come!' I grinned back.

Ralph Noyes leaned across and gave us a plastic folder containing a list of all those attending and a couple of CCCS fact sheets. I noticed that Rog and I were listed as *CERES* representatives-something that must have puzzled Busty, as he didn't know that we were involved with Meaden.

Ralph Noyes now read a section from the CCCS book, *The Crop Circle Enigma*. The section was that written by Terence Meaden. When he'd finished, Noyes invited me to comment, with a twinkle in his eye! Luckily I had noticed that there was a tape-recorder running at the front of the room, so I wasn't going to say too much!

'Thanks, Ralph. *CERES* still believes that Crop Circles are caused by a weather-based factor. This is probably caused by a wind-vortex. Dr Meaden believes that even this year's Pictograms can be explained by this....'

Ralph Noyes' eyebrows shot up at this.

I went on,'…..You must appreciate that this year, the phenomenon has accelerated at a tremendous rate and we still have much to do evaluating all we have seen. This is mainly because much of the summer time was spent measuring and photographing circles. Winter is the time to evaluate all that information and prepare for 1991. I'm not at liberty to comment any further on Dr Meaden's work as it is not yet complete'.

There was a murmur of agreement with this and I sat down, feeling that I'd done fairly well.

Michael Green moved to the front and gave his theory on the origin of circles. My notes are a bit thin here, but Green gave us the benefit of his theory that the circles were based way back in prehistory. He showed lots of examples of figurines and the like, whose shapes he claimed he could recognise in that summer's crop circles. It was all a bit far-fetched, especially as Green worked for English Heritage! But more was to come. Green explained that earlier that year he and a group of friends had climbed Silbury Hill. On the top they sat in a circle and, with a portable tape-recorder running a short distance away, communally invited the Earth Goddess to get in contact. Apparently, she had….

Green set up the tape-recorder and put a cassette in. Asking for quiet, he pressed 'play'. We all listened.

What *I* heard was a lot of distant road noise from the A4, wind, a jet aircraft passing overhead and the faint whine of the recorder's motor.

What *Green* heard was the Goddess talking or something like that. There was no aircraft anywhere, he claimed. The whine came from deep within Silbury…..

I glanced at Rog. We both had difficulty in keeping straight faces. What a load of Bollocks! We both knew that with a portable cassette recorder, the built-in microphone with automatic recording level would pick up any noise which dominated more than others. There was little doubt that there had been a plane overhead and although Green and co weren't aware of it (who is in this day and age? Ask yourself how many times you actually notice a plane flying overhead. It happens all the time so it doesn't register in your mind)-the noise was louder than any other noise and the microphone pulled it to the front of the recording. As for the whine, we'd conducted experiments earlier that summer in some circles at Beckhampton, in order to see if we could replicate the noises apparently recorded by the BBC when they were filming Andrews and Delgado. In the company of Jim Crow, we'd set up a tape-recorder in the circles and left it running. It recorded nothing of interest at all, but the faint whine of the motor was present. This was what Michael Green had recorded.[1]

Next, Professor Archie Roy of Glasgow University spoke a little about the 1989 *Operation White Crow*, run by Andrews and Delgado and which he, Archie Roy, had been involved with. Nothing new here.

The next speaker was George Wingfield. He had a bit to say on the subject of the changing of the molecular structure claimed by Colin Andrews to be present in bent stems. George himself had tried this, submitting for analysis three sample; one bent stem from a circle, one straight stem from outside a circle and one stem he had bent himself. The results? After six months, the lab had not come back with any results.

I said, 'George, surely the change in molecular structure is as a result of the stem being bent, not the cause of its bending?'

Wingfield looked at me as if I was spoiling his game.

'I think, ' said Archie Roy, 'That that is quite likely.'

'I've tried an experiment whereby I put a sample of crop stem in a microwave oven and it bent!' put in Richard Andrews.

'It could be that microwaves are causing the circles to appear, then,' ventured another man. I was fascinated by this as for a while I'd had a theory that microwaves might be affecting plasma-vortices and intended to put it to Meaden at some opportunity. Wingfield gave up at this stage, and the subject returned to dowsing, with someone saying that he could provide the CCCS dowsers with a meter to carry in their hands whilst dowsing. This meter could detect whether the brain or the energies was moving the dowsing rods.

This brought us neatly to one – thirty when Michael Green announced that lunch was ready. We all trooped upstairs to a room where Michael Green enthusiastically handed out glasses of sherry to all and sundry. Lunch was Game pie (one of my favourites!) and ravioli. The Greens did us proud. The tall, almost skeletal Ralph Noyes buttonholed me and spoke at length about Terence Meaden and his work so far and how they all appreciated his contribution to the subject. Noyes was a gentleman of the old school and I always enjoyed talking with him. Rog, meanwhile, had got talking to a young lady called Clair Appleby who was connected in some way with Archie Roy and was a computer adviser to the CCCS.

'By the way, Ralph,' I said, 'Where's John Michell?' The Grand Old Man of Earth Mysteries was nowhere to be seen. As editor of the Cerealogist I would have expected him to be there.

'Ah, he couldn't be here today,' answered Noyes, 'But he'll be at the CCCS 'Inner Council' meeting tomorrow'.

CCCS' Lucy Pringle came round to ensure we all had our plates full. Ralph excused himself and went off for some more game pie. I now found myself next to Busty Taylor.

'Surprised to see us?' I asked.

'No, no. You told me you were coming,' He replied.

I had to hide my surprise. I certainly hadn't told him anything of the sort! How could I when our attendance had only been finalised on the preceding Tuesday and we hadn't seen or spoken to Busty since the Friday before that.

'I most certainly didn't!' I eventually said. Busty smiled one of his enigmatic Mona-Lisa smiles.

'Don't you remember?' he said. ' I said I hadn't been invited when you said you were going…..'

Now this was not true. The bloke was definitely wrong here. Why, I had no idea. I hadn't told him we were going; Terence Meaden wouldn't have told him we were going – so who had? Jacqui? I smiled back at Busty but I was grimacing inside.

'You know that's not the case, Busty. I didn't tell you anything.'

'How did I know then?' Busty had the upper hand. I had no idea. But how did he know? I changed tactics.

'Anyway,' I said. 'Do you still think that this is 'going down the same road as before'?'

'Possibly,' said Taylor, helping himself to a glass of Michael Green's best claret. I did likewise.

'D'you reckon this is a good idea-setting up a central database here?' (This had been mentioned by Michael Green with the claim that Glasgow University was to supply the software-a claim denied straight away by Professor Roy)

Busty grimaced. 'I don't really like the idea. The idea of all our info going to a central database is ok in itself-but all these people (he indicated Green et al) are armchair researchers. We'll end up giving them all our info and they'll take all the credit.'

I couldn't disagree with him there. Then a thought struck me. 'By the way, Busty, what does Ron Jones do for a living?'

'Ron? He's a hairdresser!'

Archie Roy appeared on the scene and wanted Busty for something or other. I discovered Rog now chatting to another 'gentleman'- Richard Andrews. Andrews was saying that Condrews and Fandango were '...on a loser now...' It seemed that after the *Blackbird* fiasco, when the press were interviewing Colin and Pat, Richard, who'd been a loose part of the CPR team, had also been on the interview list. When he eventually enquired when he was to be interviewed, the producer had said that they didn't need him now as they were only interested in '... the losers...'. And Richard it seemed, wasn't thought to be one of them. It looked very much as if Colin and Pat's bandwagon was wobbling a bit.

Richard Andrews agreed with this observation. 'Oh, yes,' he said. ' They've attracted too much publicity!'

'Quite,' I said, 'Especially with that *WEARENOTALONE* picture...'

Andrews put on a wry look. 'Yes, we pleaded with them not to publish that one...but they insisted. It'll do them no good at all.'

You couldn't dislike Richard Andrews. He was a one-time farmer and a gentleman. Always polite. I could not disagree with his enthusiasm for dowsing, being interested in the subject myself, but I felt it had nothing whatever to do with crop circles.

He went on to praise Terence Meaden for his work on the subject of circles. In this, he was one of several of the CCCS 'Top Brass' who fell over themselves that day in order to praise Meaden's contributions. Almost all of them made some comment or other about *CERES* data and information that Meaden possessed concerning circles he'd researched before any of them became interested in the subject. Andrews and Delgado had similar info of course, as they and Meaden had worked together in the early 1980's. But they were not giving anything away to anyone. Ralph Noyes had been overheard telling someone that....'some researchers are not revealing all they know....'- I was getting the distinct impression that the CCCS wanted access to *CERES* data....

Richard Andrews seemed to confirm that idea when he said, 'Scientists and Mystics ought to work together, y'know.'

Lunch over, we all trooped back downstairs to the chilly, sparsely-furnished room again. The first topic of the afternoon session was '.... Do we think that there is some intelligence behind the phenomenon?' It was led by Professor Archie Roy. He took a straw poll and, to my surprise, almost everyone present indicated that they thought some sort of unknown intelligence was behind the crop circles. And this from a group who claimed to be neutral.

George Wingfield then told a tale of how '......*Six of us, for the want of anything better to do, went and sat in a circle after dark....*' He described how a strange noise appeared to 'lead' them across the field......

I interrupted. 'Pardon me, George, but in an esoteric magazine-I forget the title-I read an article by Colin Andrews in which he claimed that *Seven* of you, one of whom was a medium, sat in the circle at midnight. This was apparently as the result of a letter that Colin had received.'

Wingfield looked a little taken aback by this. I noticed the ghost of a smile appear on Archie Roy's lips. George recovered his composure.

'It was SIX of us, ' he repeated. 'As for the letter, well...' he reached under his chair and pulled out a copy of.... UFO Report 1990! He read out an extract from a childish poem.

'It's obviously in doggerel,' observed Archie Roy.

It was certainly in something! I spoke again.

'But, six or seven of you went into a circle, at *midnight*, with a *medium*, sent there by a *lette*r with a *poem* in it-I put it to you, George, that you were *expecting* something to happen! You were all in an expectant frame of mind! And, ' I went on, 'It's not a good indicator for Joe Public when the whole incident is written up in UFO Report 1990!'

Wingfield, now in some discomfort was rescued by Archie Roy. Astonishingly the Professor said, '......*If the noise you heard moved, it shows some signs of intelligence...*' George relaxed again. There was, it seemed, little room for unbiased investigation within the CCCS.

The next speaker was an agriculturist, Montague Keen. He was to speak on his specialist subject-crops. He obviously knew his subject thoroughly and gave a very interesting, if short, talk. When he'd finished, Michael Green stood up said, '.... We ought to give people specific tasks to do, before next season. There's not that much time before summer comes round again....'

There was a general rumble of agreement and I expected him to allocate tasks to people there and then. Instead, the meeting dissolved into small groups chatting amongst themselves-much as Alan Rayner's meeting had. As Rog and I wondered what, if anything, was coming next, Michael Green called out: '...Tea and biscuits will be shortly available. After tea we'll have half-an-hour's talk then close.'

Over tea and biccies, I put it to Rog that I didn't think we were going to get much more out of the meeting. After tea, I said, I thought we should leave. My Capri also had a lighting fault and I would rather get out of the capital and onto the M4 before it got too dark. Rog reluctantly agreed.

According to my notes, I next had a conversation with George Wingfield on the subject of a horse mutilation, which apparently happened at Bratton. George ventured the opinion that Jenny Randles was wrong to write about it in the *Cropwatcher*. I said that the incident was not true as far as I was aware. Richard Andrews chipped in with the news that he'd spoken to the Police and it was true! After 10 years I still haven't the faintest idea whether it happened or not.

Anyway, we announced our impending departure. Archie Roy came over and shook our hands, saying how pleased he was that *CERES* had been represented after all. Michael Green shook hands and wished us well. I didn't shake hands with Busty, saying '...We're bound to meet again soon, Busty-our paths will cross.....' Richard Andrews came to the door with us. There, he shook hands, clapped us both on the shoulders and said, '.....I'm on your side, chaps!' –Which was odd.

The journey home was uneventful; Rog falling asleep for most of the journey so there was little talk about the day's events. However, we met up with Jacqui later at the *Bull*, where the three of us had dinner and talked it all over.

So, what did we make of it all? The idea that the CCCS was to be a 'cross-party' group to investigate crop circles from a neutral standpoint seemed to be a non-starter. We couldn't get over how many educated, intelligent people were accepting things at face value and ploughing ahead with a group belief in 'something unknown and intelligent but not human' [my words]. There was little doubt that they wanted to believe it was all caused by something supernatural.

At 11 o' clock the following morning Paul Fuller rang me to find out how the meeting had gone. When I told him all about it he just groaned. 'I knew it,' he said. 'They are all as bad as Colin and Pat. And as for Busty Taylor, he's running with the hare and hunting with the hounds! He ought to make up his mind whose side he's on! Are you going to tell Terence?'

I said I was and that we ought to meet with him to work out the way ahead. Paul couldn't make a meeting that week due to commitments, so I arranged to travel down to Romsey, where he lived, by train on the following Friday.

The next day I rang Terence Meaden and arranged to meet him at his office in Bradford-on-Avon the following day.

I arrived at Bradford-on-Avon at two-thirty five and parked at the side of Meaden's motor-showroom after being warned by him that parking on the road opposite was not a good idea because of a keen local traffic-warden. Entering the showroom I noticed an Austin-Healy sports car and an E-type Jaguar before A delightful French lady, who was obviously Mrs. Meaden, came out to guide me upstairs to Terence's small, cramped office. The office had a lovely polished desk and on the packed bookcase were photos of crop circles. Terence Meaden welcomed me and invited me to sit down and tell him all about the meeting with the CCCS.

I told him the entire story, including the bits about Michael Green and the tape-recorder and Busty Taylor's opinion that the CCCS were '...Armchair researchers...' and were only after others to get the information for them. I ventured the opinion that with the likes of John Michell being involved there was a good chance of a 'crop circles cult' springing up (and how right I was!!). I told him about Archie Roy. He was shocked. '...What's a man with his qualifications doing mixed up with a bunch like that? What a nincompoop!'

I also told him of Busty's change of spots.

The professor looked concerned. He rubbed his chin and sank into deep thought for a few minutes. Eventually he spoke:

'...Hmm. Well. My affiliation membership of the CCCS worked. It got me the chance to put my views in the Taylor/Noyes book so it was worth it for that. When renewal becomes due-I shan't bother again. It looks as though you and Paul were right about Busty. I'm not sure if he can be trusted. You and I, Peter, must work closer together in future. You are one of the few people I can trust. There is a lot more information which I have about crop circles and which I cannot yet divulge, let alone publish.'

'That's fine, Terence,' I said, 'Keep it quiet until you are ready to tell people.'

Meaden smiled a wan smile. He indicated the pictures on the bookshelf. 'This is my life, now.....the circles.' He said. Mrs. Meaden entered the office with tea and biscuits.

'Do you know, ' said Terence, pouring the tea, 'That during the summer my wife was receiving an average of 92 phone calls a day –all concerning circles..'

'Yes,' said his wife. '...So many calls, so much work. Terry was so busy.'

I could imagine that. This was obviously why the professor wanted to offload some of the data collection for 1991 onto Paul Fuller and myself. Mrs. Meaden left and we continued to chat about theories, including the microwave/plasma vortex theory that I had. Meaden had a theory that the criss-crossing of fields by tractors whilst ploughing/sowing created a grid and may be responsible for some sort of moisture retention. He postulated that this might be the reason behind Richard Andrews' dowsing effects.

I explained that Rog had a plan whereby we all put data onto floppy disks and swapped disks on a regular basis. This would ensure that we all had the same info (e-mails weren't generally available in 1990). Unfortunately it appeared that Terence Meaden had a different type of computer to Rog, who had the same as me, and Paul's was different again. The plan collapsed at this point.

'We must meet in January,' said Meaden. 'Once the Xmas break is over we need to start planning for 1991.'

I agreed with that. And so, at five-fifteen I left, travelling back to Pucklechurch via Farleigh, Colerne and Marshfield to avoid the rush hour. I had with me a package of information from Terence to give to Paul Fuller when I saw him on Friday.

Friday 30th November 1990

I drove to Bath, parked and caught the 09.38 train to Portsmouth Harbour. After an uneventful journey I arrived in Romsey station at 10.54. Paul had said he'd pick me up at 11.00 so I wasn't surprised to find nobody there when I walked out of the station entrance. Dead on time Paul Fuller drove up in his little black Metro. After greetings were exchanged we moved off out of the station and through the streets of Romsey to where Paul had a flat in a small, private block on the edge of town.

Once inside the flat, I handed over the package from Meaden and Paul put the kettle on. Over coffee and biscuits we studied Paul's collection of over 500 press cuttings of crop circles. After lunch, provided by Paul, he suggested a drive out to Cheesefoot and the site of another 1990 circle, Farley Mount. Off we set in Fuller's Metro and shortly arrived in the country park in which Farley Mount, a circular mound topped with a 'church'-like building. From a distance it was impressive. However, when we walked up to it I was surprised to find that the 'church' was only about twenty feet tall! It was a memorial to a landowner's horse! We agreed that the summer's circle, which was a large ring with a small circle in the middle, was 'suspicious', as it was, in effect, a schematic view of the mound.

Leaving Farley Mount we headed out to Cheesefoot, passing on the way a collection of microwave aerials. I briefly explained my theory of microwaves and plasma vortices to Fuller.

'The theory is this,' I explained, '...Microwave activity may be responsible for interacting with a plasma vortex, thus causing it to 'misbehave' and resulting in not only circles and rings but perhaps some of the lights and noises seen in conjunction with circles forming. It's only a theory, but there do seem to be microwave towers and dishes in many places where circles have been found. Then again, putting them on top of hills and escarpments where they have better range is a logical thing to do.'

'You may have something there, Pete-does Terence know?'

'Yes. He's also looking into the sunspot activity theory as well.'

We had now arrived at Cheesefoot Head. We parked in a gateway and Paul showed me where the CPR *'White Crow'* site had been. We crossed the busy road and walked to the edge of the punchbowl where so many circles had been seen. Hundreds of rabbits scattered on our arrival. We also went to the Longwood Warren part of Cheesefoot where circles had been found. It was good to get to know the lay of the land with someone who knew it well. I got out my binoculars and studied the area to commit landmarks to memory.

Back at Paul's flat, Paul brewed more coffee and we discussed future issues of the *Cropwatcher*. Paul showed me some photos, which he planned to accompany a future article. They were of a site in Devon where a key-shaped circle had appeared. Someone obviously wanted to perpetuate the myth that where a circle had been, no future crops would grow. The area had been doused with weedkiller in a rough imitation of the key shape. Irresponsible.

I was to catch the 17.48 train home so Paul ran me to the station, on the way passing the council offices so he could point out where Colin Andrews worked. We parted at Romsey station with promises to meet again in the New Year. I went onto the platform and Paul drove off to the launderette to do his washing!

There was little of 1990 left. On the first of December, Jacqui and I went off for a tour of the summer's crop fields. This was partly to check that there were no weedkiller-type attacks to add to the myths. We went to Alton Barnes and East Kennet. To reach the latter site involved driving through narrow lanes and pools of mud. My Capri was plastered! We found the site and also a power cable route along the side of the field which might be responsible for dowsing effects. Jacqui chatted up a horse before we headed off to the *Waggon and Horses*, there to satisfy my hunger before I resorted to eating said beast! After a good lunch, we went home.

As the old year drew to a close and Christmas approached, I set to work to draw up a ghost of a plan for the 1991 season. Paul sent through a series of press cuttings all about Colin Andrews, and Terence Meaden sent some copies of literature concerning a ground electrical effect known as TESLA.

Then crop circles were forgotten as the festive season got under way. Forgotten except for the (by now) usual exchange of silly cards with Busty Taylor!

The Circles which started it all for me – Silbury Hill July 24th 1988

The circular traces found in a field at Pucklechurch, Gloucestershire, during the summer of 1989 after a 'Land-Devil' whirlwind had been seen in the same field.

The circle which appeared at Cheesefoot Head behind the 'Operation White Crow' caravan. Doug Bower claimed this as one of his solo efforts.

Roger Davis (left) and Nelson investigate a crop circle at Cheesefoot Head in 1990

At the beginning of 1990, Pat Delgado remarked that: '...All we need to lay to rest the meteorological theory are triangles and squares...' Somebody obliged with this. It was a triangle formed out of circular motion. Beckhampton July 1990

Often found in the centre of crop circles – a standing twist of crop, resembling a corn dolly. This one was at Beckhampton, 1990.

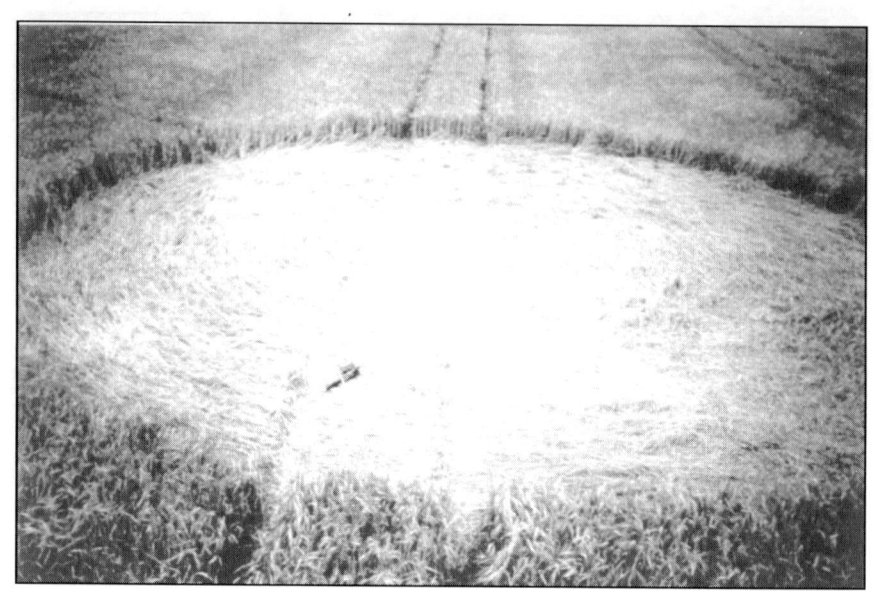

Another 1990 circle. Photographed in July 1990, this was the centre circle of a 'dice' formation found near the golf course at Blacklands, not too far from Morgan's Hill.

'Ring and Ditch' at Cheesefoot Bowl 1990. Another formation claimed by Doug Bower and Dave Chorley.

The most famous Crop Circles of them all. Alton Barnes 1990 in its setting of the now-equally-famous East Field.

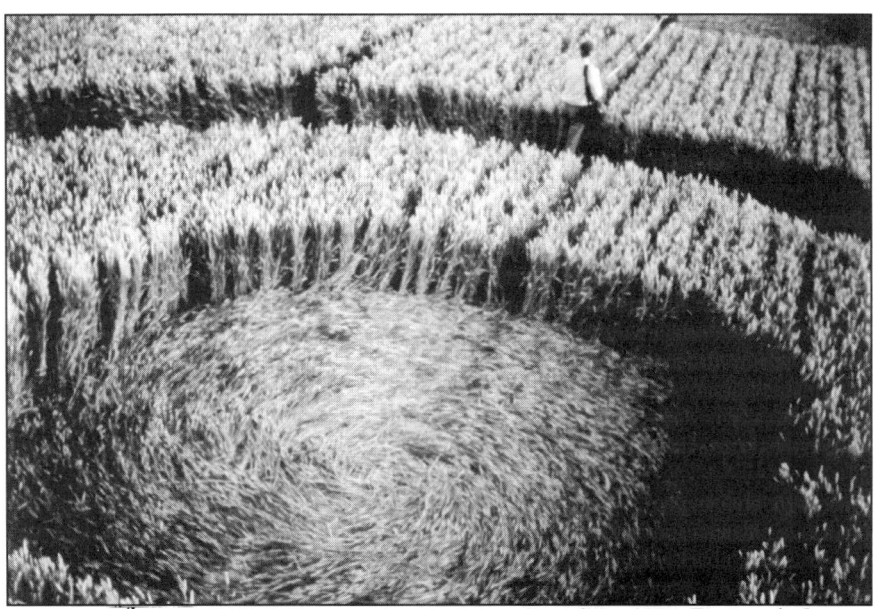

July 14th 1990; 05.15 in the morning. A closer view of the Alton Barnes circles. The figure in white is Dr.Terence Meaden with his tape-measure

Butleigh Wootton, April 20th 1991.(L-R) Pat Delgado, Colin Andrews, Busty Taylor, Richard Andrews. On the car roof is Busty's camera pole.

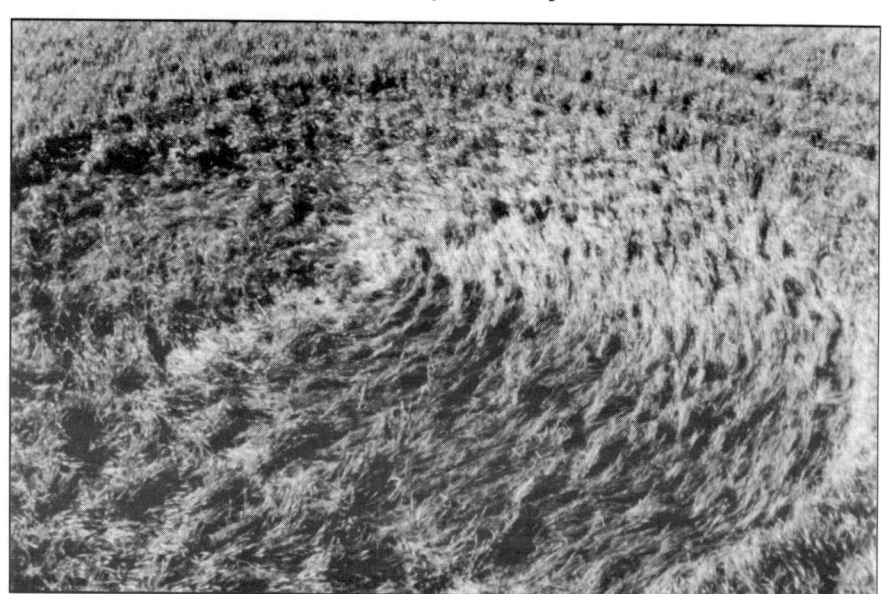

Butleigh Wootton 1991. This picture, taken from our camera pole, shows just how rough the circle was.

The *CERES* HQ at 'Operation Blue Hill' 1991. The scaffolding tower awaits the arrival of the radar scanner. Compare this with……….

….The motorhomes of 'Operation Chameleon', the David Morgernstern/John Macnish setup. The netting was quite ineffectual as it did not cover the entire vehicle. Our original site was to have been in the trees behind these vans.

Roadside conference at Lurkeley Hill, 1991. Alan Rayner – Dr.Terence Meaden – Jacqui Griffiths

'Jim Schnabel – Washington Post!' Jim Schnabel (far right) confronts the National Geographic crew. Who was he kidding?

Chapter Nine
THE BEST LAID PLANS
1991-Our Plans, Their Plans-promises of help-the first circles of 1991

January 1991

The New Year celebrations over, it was time to return to the subject of the Circles. Terence Meaden had spent the Christmas/New Year period in France, but lost no time in continuing the evaluation of 1990 evidence on his return to Bradford-on-Avon. Wishing to conclude evidence on the Butleigh Wootton formation of the previous summer, Meaden wrote to me, asking: '...did you visit this site? The circles look good...so far as I can tell...' and enclosing a copy of an article from the Shepton Mallet Journal of December 27th 1990.

However, when I next spoke to the physicist, I had to confess that I hadn't visited the site before the harvest; after that, without knowing the approximate map reference, it had been like looking for a needle in a haystack. I explained what I had been told by the farm workers when I had been out looking for the site. Not only that, but I viewed the appearance of these circles with some suspicion after the meeting with Busty Taylor in June of 1990. I also pointed out that there had been a hippie camp at Butleigh that Summer. The doubts were enough; I was not prepared to accept those Butleigh Wootton circles as being anything but a hoax. Terence hummed and hah'd a bit. '...It would have helped if you'd been able to find the circles,' he said at last.

Ok, I had to accept the criticism, but don't forget the odd circumstances surrounding the appearance of the formation, after my asking Busty why nothing had yet appeared at Glastonbury. Terence sounded puzzled. 'Y-e-s,' he said at last, ' But, you know, Busty has never told me these things he told you. I've known him for four or five years now.'

This was awkward. I didn't want to seem as if I was trying to darken Busty Taylor's character, but it was pretty obvious that whilst he was in Terence's presence he always said he '..didn't know..' what caused the circles, and when he was with mystics and Ufologists he spoke about his strange dreams and his 'horsemen of the apocalypse' idea. I reminded Terence of Busty's contributions to *'Flying Saucer Review'* as a 'consultant'.

'Perhaps you are right,' sighed the meteorologist. 'These people must be treated with caution in future. Now, to business. The reason I phoned you was to say that I may be going to France on the nineteenth for the weekend. If I decide not to go, we'll arrange a meeting for that weekend, if you could tell Paul Fuller.'

Yes, that would be fine by me. Just then, Terence's wife came into his office and they had a short conversation. After a moment or so, Terence came back to the phone and confirmed that he was definitely going to France on the nineteenth. That meant the meeting would possibly be on the 26th. Meaden advised me to phone him on the 21st to remind him about the meeting.

I agreed. After Terence Meaden had rung off, I dialled Paul Fuller's number. After the phone had rung for a short time, a quiet voice said 'hullo?'

'Hello, Paul, it's Peter'.

'Hi, Pete,' said the beleaguered ufologist. 'Have you spoken to Terence about a meeting?'

'Yes, just. It's provisionally arranged for the 26th of Jan. He can't make it any sooner, as he's off to France for the weekend on the 19th.'

'That's typical of Terence,' groaned Paul. 'He is always going on holiday: he should be here, helping to fight his corner!'

I suggested that perhaps the meteorologist was taking the opportunity to have some time away with his wife before what looked like being a busy season began.

'I suppose you're right. I've had a nasty letter from George Wingfield,' he went on. 'He says my denunciation of an article of his in the *Independent* was highly biased! He also states that Terence's theory is now 'discredited".

George Wingfield was rapidly becoming the most vociferous of the fledgling Centre for Crop Circle Studies. We didn't want to upset them, even though it was plain that our ideas were worlds apart. What had Paul done to invoke such a response?

'I sent him a copy of an article I intend to publish in the next '*Cropwatcher*'. He got most stroppy, and is demanding the right of reply.'

It struck me as odd that a magazine which was intended to be the "*Private Eye*" of the crop circles world, should send copies of forthcoming articles to the very people it intended to surprise when the article was published. However, Paul knew more about that sort of thing than I did, so I didn't argue. We arranged that Paul would phone me on the 21st, after I'd spoken to Terence Meaden, and we would finalise the meeting details. Paul promised to bring a copy of Wingfield's letter with him, for me to see. The business of the evening being over, I retired to the '*Bull*' where I met Rog and filled him in on the latest plans.

On the 21st, I phoned Terence and it was confirmed that we would all meet in his office, at Bradford-on-Avon, on the evening of the 26th January. Paul Fuller would be given the option of staying at my place overnight if he wished to avoid the long journey back to Romsey the same night and we'd adjourn, with Rog, to the '*Bull*' for lunch on the Sunday

26th January 1991

Saturday morning and I was at work behind my desk in the signalling centre at Bristol. All trains were running more or less smoothly, and there was not a lot for me to do. One of my staff brought me in a cup of tea, just as the telephone rang. Noting an 'outside' line, I answered it swiftly. It was Paul Fuller. He had a transport problem. He'd taken his car to a local garage to have a broken wheel stud repaired. Not only could the garage not get a spare stud until Monday, but also when the mechanic tried to refit the wheel he broke another stud! 'I'll have to come up by train,' concluded Paul.

I grabbed my timetable and found a Portsmouth to Cardiff service that afternoon, which called at Romsey and arrived in Bath at 15.30. I related the details to the ufologist, and said I'd see him later, outside Bath Spa station.

As I finished the early shift at 15.00, I drove straight to Bath. Traffic was fairly heavy for a winter Saturday, due in some part to extensive roadworks in the city. However, I reached Bath station in time, and parked outside the station. I was listening to the Rolling Stones *'Brown Sugar'* on the car stereo, when I saw a thin figure weighed down with rucksack and sleeping bag stagger from the station entrance. I switched off the tape, and sounded the car's horn.

We exchanged greetings, Paul dumped his burdens in the back of my Capri and we headed out of Bath via the A4 and A46, thus avoiding the roadworks.

'Jacqui is going to cook us all a Chinese meal,' I told Paul. 'Rog will come over for dinner, then we'll all head for Bradford-on-Avon afterwards.'

'Sounds OK to me,' said Paul. "I've brought a copy of Dear George's letter for you. He's really upset!'

'I've got a few things to bring up tonight," I told him as we crawled up the A46 behind a huge articulated lorry. 'There was a Dr Blackmore in the local paper the other day-she's into circles and wants to know what it's all about. I was thinking of contacting her.'

Paul frowned. 'I've never heard of her. I think it's best not to tell her anything, Pete. The CCCS will only end up finding out what we're up to, and get there first. It may even end up that the CCCS get exclusive rights to the circles, and we don't get in at all until it's too late to glean any information at all. And remember, Terence started researching circles in 1980, before any of these people!'

Now there was a possibility I hadn't thought of. What if the Beckhampton group negotiated with farmers for their members to visit circles first? What if the farmers would only allow limited numbers of investigators onto their land? What I also didn't know, was that some members of the CCCS were thinking along the same lines! They were afraid that the scientists might get in first and, as one member put it,:…'fence off the fields to carry out their research - stopping us from visiting OUR circles ever again…' - or very similar to that.

When we arrived at my house, Jacqui was already preparing dinner. I put the kettle on, and, whilst the tea brewed and Paul Fuller made himself comfy on the sofa, I nipped upstairs to change out of my uniform. Rog arrived at 17.00 and we all chatted over more tea, until Jacqui announced that the meal was ready. An hilarious time was had by all as we tried to eat our dinner using chopsticks! After dinner, Rog and I demonstrated the circles program Rog had written for my Amstrad. Paul was impressed.

'I had no idea your work was this far advanced,' he exclaimed.

'We've got the background in Earth Mysteries, as well. With your BUFORA stuff and Terence's scientific work, we have a good cross section of knowledge to put up against the New Age folk,' I said.

'If they'll take any notice,' muttered Paul.

Later, on the way to the little Wiltshire town of Bradford-on-Avon we spoke at length about the *'Cropwatcher'* and what Paul would put in the next issue.

'We must persuade Terence to stop co-operating with the mystics,' said Paul. 'He just doesn't realise that all these people are not supporters of his vortex! They only want to make him look small and discredit him, but he can't see that. Sometimes he can be so naive,' he added.

'I don't see that we can tell him what to do,' I replied as we arrived outside Terence Meaden's workshops. 'He's been in this for a lot longer than we have.'

'Yes, but someone's got to tell him. If he'd sued Andrews and Delgado ages ago, none of this would be necessary!'

'Where's the meeting taking place?' asked Rog.
In the office above the showroom. We pushed open the showroom door and made our way to the stairs, passing several restored Jensen-Healy sports cars and an E-Type Jaguar - all for sale. At the foot of the stairs were a couple of piles of Terence's book *'The Circles Effect and its Mysteries'*, presumably for sale to visitors to the showroom.
The meteorologist appeared at the top of the stairs.

'Hello, come up to the office everyone,' he beamed.

We trooped up the stairs and into the office. Once inside, we shuffled around to make space, eventually all finding a chair to sit on. Terence spoke first.

'Well, welcome everyone, to our first 1991 meeting. I expect you are all aware of the situation with the CCCS. Peter and Roger went to a meeting at Michael Green's house last November, and from what they told me, the CCCS sound as if they are following the same tracks as Andrews and Delgado. What Archie Roy is doing mixed up with a bunch of paranormal enthusiasts, I just don't know!'

'Before we go any further, Terence,' I said, 'I'd just like to clarify a few things...' I wanted to know what we could and could not say, really. With the bulk of the 1990 findings not yet analysed, and only a few ideas from Terence concerning what might have caused the Linear Complexes at Alton Barnes, Stanton St Bernard and East Kennett, I didn't want us to put our foot in it.

'The theory is still the same for single circles and ringed circles,' replied the professor. 'That's all in my book. These new formations have many similarities, and will take a lot of looking into. It may be that a series of vortices were attracted to the fields and touched down together...'

It was obvious that a lot of work remained to be done on these formations, so we agreed to limit our reply to any questions on the subject to '...work is still progressing on analysing the 1990 data, but first indications are that science CAN explain the Linear Complex...'

Then Paul Fuller launched into a series of questions he wanted to ask Terence Meaden in order to clarify some points he wanted to raise in future issues of the *'Cropwatcher'*. These were questions on behalf of Jenny Randles as well as Fuller and took up some considerable time, which was galling as I was keen to get on to strategy for 1991, but couldn't stop Paul once he was in full flow! Roger and Jacqui said little. After about an hour, Terence suggested that we break for a drink, and disappeared off to his house to fetch some liquid refreshment. I persuaded Paul to let me get a word in and discuss 1991.

Terence soon returned with some cans of beer and a carton of orange juice. The beer was almost all lager, except for one can of Ruddles County, which swiftly found its way into the hands of Rog! Whilst he opened the can with a contented look on his face, Paul and myself settled for lager. Jacqui and Terence had orange juice.

'You will recall I told you about a possible watch organised by the Bristol United Press,' said Terence. 'It was to be secret and would provide press releases for the *'Bristol Evening Post'* and the *'Western Daily Press'*.'

Yes, we all remembered. What was the latest on that front?

Terence shrugged and sighed. 'I've heard nothing at all from the editor. I've tried phoning and writing, but no response, so it looks as if the project is off.'

That was a disappointment, as the paper was going to find a radar set for *CERES* to use, if the plans had come to fruition. What equipment did we have if the BUP watch didn't happen?

'I've got a barometer, a barograph, magnetometer and a selection of meteorological equipment,' said Terence, 'But that radar would really be very useful if we could get hold of a set somehow.'

Big time stuff. I had a camera and a pair of binoculars and the others had similar: this was hardly going to be a high-tech affair at this rate.

'Do you know who was going to supply the radar?' I asked.

'I believe it was Marconi. I suppose I could get in touch with them and see if they'd lend it to us - it would be far too expensive to buy,' he added, pre-empting my next question! It transpired that a radar set would cost in the region of £4,000 so buying one was definitely out!

I moved on to mention Dr Blackmore. Terence knew of her!

'There was a small group of people that the *'Evening Post'* was getting together to form a team which would comment on the circles events as they happened. This would then be printed in the *'Evening Post'* and the *'Western Daily Press'*, ' he told us. 'Dr Blackmore was to be one of that team.'

I told him I'd thought about sending her a note. Terence shrugged and explained that apparently she knew Ralph Noyes 'well'. After some deliberation, we all agreed that we wouldn't contact the skeptical doctor for the foreseeable future, in case she was seconded to the CCCS.

'There is something else,' said Terence. 'This summer, a film crew from *National Geographic* magazine is coming over from America. They will be following me around for much of the summer. In addition, a film crew on behalf of Channel 4 will be in the area, making a film to show as part of the '*Equinox*' series. I will have to spend some time with them. This is why it's vital that the three of you, Peter, Roger and Paul, handle the data collection. I'm going to be busy.'

Over to Rog. Rog explained all about the circles programme he'd produced and how the circles data was stored and retrieved.

'Of course,' he said, 'If Terence and Paul had IBM compatible machines, it would make the whole thing easier. There could be a weekly exchange of data disks. This would mean everyone was up-to-date at the end of each week.'

'I can't afford to change my word-processor,' muttered Paul. 'I'm broke!' By now the ufologist was noticeably shivering. It was a little chilly in the office, but it didn't seem that cold to me.

'How much would it cost to provide me with the right sort of machine?' asked Terence. 'My daughters are always using the two machines I have.'

'You've got the same as Paul, I take it?' said Rog. Terence agreed. Both he and Paul Fuller used the older Amstrad model, which wasn't IBM compatible. Rog, of course, being in the computer business, had the latest model. Mine, although not quite as up-to-date as Rog's, was nevertheless compatible with all his machines. We were split down the middle. Terence and Paul could exchange info (as they had been doing for a while) and so could Rog and I. When Rog told Terence that he'd have to spend around £600 to get a computer and printer, from the look on the professor's face, it seemed we'd stay split!

As time was getting on, I produced some of my photographs of the 1989 and 1990 seasons, and Terence brought out a selection of his pictures. Almost before we knew it, the time was well after 11. It was time for us to move on. Especially as Paul was now shivering uncontrollably! We swiftly wound up the proceedings, promising to meet again as soon as time allowed.

Back at my place, Paul swiftly wrapped himself in his sleeping bag on the sofa and I retired to my bed. I left the central heating on all night in order to keep Paul warm, as he was still shivering!

The next morning dawned dull and cold. I had a thick head due entirely to the stifling heat of the room. Opening the bedroom window, I dressed and crept downstairs. On the sofa was a bundle with a pillow over its head! Leaving him to sleep on, I moved into the kitchen and made a pot of tea. At about 10.15 I heard groaning from the living room.

Paul had woken and complained of a headache!

I offered him a cup of tea. 'Oh, no thanks - I feel sick!' Paul was in a bad way! However, after washing and dressing he felt much improved, and when Rog arrived at 11 o' clock, the ufologist was back to his usual self.

We set off in Rog's car and made the short journey to the field on the far side of the village of Pucklechurch where Jacqui had seen the land-devil in 1989. Paul was most impressed with the location and took a few photos. By now the weather had turned nasty and some snow was beginning to fall, so we hopped back into the car and sped off to the next site Paul wished to visit: Kelston, near Bath, the site of the 1989 ringed circle. It took us about a quarter of an hour to reach the site just off the A431 where the circle had appeared in August 1989. Paul took more photos, then, with the weather worsening, it was off to the '*Bull*' for food! At the pub, the landlord had provided us with a corner table in the dining room. We drank real ale in front of the roaring log fire in the lounge until called for dinner. During a splendid meal of roast pork, we discussed the coming summer. Paul was keen not to take on too much.

'It's alright for Terence,' he said, 'he has a lot more time and money than we do. He can spend most of the summer looking for circles, whereas I've got to work. Then there's the car loan - I really haven't that much money to spare.'

I agreed that we were all in similar positions, though without the burden of the loan.

'We'll just have to ensure that we don't put more money into this than we can afford,' I said, between mouthfuls of roast pork. 'We would be spending petrol money chasing circles anyway, even if we were not involved with *CERES*. That has been part of our lives now for the last two or three summers. If we can work out a plan where we each cover a separate district, then we might be able to keep the travelling to a minimum. What d'you think, Rog?'

Rog swigged at his second pint of 6X and nodded slowly.

'Sounds OK,' he agreed

During the week that followed, there wasn't much chance to discuss plans, as Rog went down with some bug or other, and was out of circulation for most of the week. Jacqui went to Glastonbury, and, calling in at 'Gothic Image', bought the latest copy of the '*Cereologist*'. In it, George Wingfield had an article in which he 'revealed' to all and sundry his theory that the Government and the Army were responsible for the hoax played on Andrews and Delgado during the previous summer. Jacqui summed up the article with a short statement: 'What a load of cobblers!'

Sometime during the week, someone handed me a cutting from a local free newspaper. It was an item called "*Close Encounters -Fact or Fiction*" and displayed a large photo of a dumb-bell circle formation with four boxes! It seemed that a woman driving near Shepton Mallet the previous month, had been 'followed' by a brightly-lit flying saucer! There were other UFO sightings mentioned, and comments by Bristol Quest's co-ordinator, Richard Tarr. The UFO investigator claimed that they had received many reports of UFO's over the past month, and were holding a major conference on the subject at a school in Patchway, Bristol, during the coming March. Speakers would include - here my eyes popped out of my head – '..*George Wingfield, author and principal field officer for the Centre for Crop Circle Studies; Britain's leading UFO authority*' !!

The way the article was set out, it seemed to give the impression that the CCCS was 'Britain's leading UFO authority' - although it was presumably meant to indicate that George was given that dubious title. I'd certainly never heard that George Wingfield was a UFO expert so, after consulting with Terence, I decided to send a note to Ralph Noyes. This was to 'test the water' and to see what the CCCS would say when I pointed out that *CERES* was a little disappointed to see that the Centre was apparently allowing its principal field officer to make a UFO connection with the Circles. A reply was not long in coming. On official CCCS notepaper. Ralph wrote that he considered the article '...*probably intends to say that George Wingfield rather than CCCS is 'Britain's leading UFO authority'*...and that CCCS '..*remains committed to no collective view...*' He added that he'd sent a copy of my letter to George in case he wanted to add anything.

This was all very useful; we'd now got the CCCS policy in writing from its secretary and this statement might prove useful in time to come. Why? Because it was obvious from the attitudes and beliefs of the CCCS leaders and council members that their underlying feeling was that some form of 'superior intelligence' was at work in the crop fields. And don't forget that tape recording Michael Green had played us back in November of 1990. It was still amazing to me that a group of intelligent, educated people could sit around and be puzzled and excited by nothing more than a recording of a distant aircraft and the motor-whine of the 'ghetto-blaster'!

Meanwhile, Alan Rayner, the unofficial 'convener' of the Beckhampton group, had been busy with is latest newsletter, a copy of which dropped through my letterbox on the morning of 12th January. Alan welcomed the new decade and outlined his plans for the coming year. For a start, he set out the Beckhampton group's relationship with the CCCS. It had been decided at a meeting of the group in the previous September not to align themselves with the fledgling CCCS, and this decision it seemed, still stood. Alan recommended, however, that individual members join the CCCS 'as a way to keep in touch with national and international events'. He went on to say that the Beckhampton group would keep on good terms with both the CCCS and the Andrews/Delgado Circles Phenomenon Research (CPR), reporting circles events not just to both of them but also to Dr Meaden. Rayner also stated that he and his group would not support the transformation of their group into the Wiltshire Branch of the CCCS.

From the newsletter I learnt that Una Dawood, a short, plump, middle-aged woman, whom I recalled speaking to on the subject of Isis when we were all meeting at Silbury the previous summer, had taken on the role of contacting local farmers. As she lived reasonably close to the Avebury area, this would be a relatively easy task for her. How were we at *CERES* to do the same? I would bring this up when we met with Terence.

There was a short piece by Pam Price (who, at the November meeting we'd attended, supported a theory that UFO's were responsible for the circles - a feeling shared by Stanley Morcomb and several others). Ms Price commented that perhaps '...planet Earth is a turning point for humankind, or a battleground between spiritual and material forces...' and went on to suggest that there may be a '...New Age; a Second Coming...' – no problem then in working out where her sympathies lay!

However, if the circles business was to bring all types of folk together to puzzle over the formations, each with his or her own views, but all happy to co-operate and exchange information - well, so be it. I wouldn't knock that idea: but, there were already signs that it wasn't going to be like that at all. The manic ravings of George Wingfield, for example, in his 'It's all a Government cover-up' theory to explain the *'Operation Blackbird'* hoax in summer 1990, was not helping at all. He was already talking in terms of an 'official de-bunking campaign' by the Army! It was getting just like the Warminster 'Thing' craze of the mid-1960's. In fact, reading Arthur Shuttlewood's first book on the famous 'UFO' flap, one could see that the same script seemed to be being used; only the characters were different.

And people's awareness was becoming greater. There was now much more of a commercial side waiting to be exploited. Already it was rumoured that Colin Andrews and Pat Delgado had made more than £10,000 EACH from *'Circular Evidence'* (If this was true, it was galling. *'Circular Evidence'* was full of inaccuracies and mis-representations: whether inserted knowingly or otherwise was not my place to suggest; however, the pair of them had shut poor old Paul Fuller up for two years, just for telling the truth in private correspondence!). It remained to be seen just what would happen during 1991, and whether or not reason would prevail. In the event, what was to transpire surprised all of us.

On February 2nd there was an article printed in *'TODAY'* newspaper in which one of *CERES*' Japanese allies, Professor Hiroshi Kikuchi (who'd spoken at the Oxford conference the previous summer) voiced his opinion that dust-laden winds passing over hills created friction which electrically charged the dust particles and created the plasma vortex. He also added that most circles could be explained scientifically although he agreed that some circles '...were the work of pranksters.'. This was good news. Kikuchi was a respected authority, and the publication of his paper could only do *CERES* and Terence a lot of good. The only criticism I could think of lay in the name: 'ELECTROMAGNETOHYDRODYNAMIC VORTICES'! Hardly a name to trip lightly off one's tongue!

On the morning of the 13th February 1991 the expected letter from George Wingfield arrived. One and a half pages of it. As expected, Wingfield: '.... *could not see what you...are objecting to....*' He agreed with Ralph Noyes that the title of 'Britain's leading UFO authority ' in the *Bristol Observer* was most likely intended for him and not the CCCS. '*.....I cannot think that I deserve this appellation, but I must say, I'm flattered....*' he wrote.

If he'd left it at that he would have lost no respect from us. But he had to take up the rest of the letter slagging off Jenny Randles and Paul Fuller, and calling Terence's plasma vortex theory '*...as much a fairy tale as 'alien spaceships'...*' and concluding: '*...Enough of my views of this phenomenon, which are not necessarily the collective view of CCCS. Our understanding of the Crop Circle phenomenon will only come through **careful observation, application of the scientific method, and consideration of all the evidence rather than that which suits particular theories. It is to this goal that CCCS aspires....*' (the enhancement is mine, PDR)

These rather interesting views were to contrast strongly with George's later statements, and those of other leading members of CCCS: especially when the camera crews came round later that summer; that was when these folk stood up and championed their cause, confident that the complexity of the 1991 formations had successfully seen off the challenge of Terence Meaden's vortex. Or so they thought.

Further notice of the way the CCCS was going was given by the sending out, in February, of the ballot forms for the centre's first 'democratically elected council'. Twelve candidates were to be chosen from fifteen men and women. As CERES was still at that time 'affiliated' to the CCCS, and as CCCS wished to '.... express no collective view....', it was reasonable to expect Terence Meaden to be asked to stand. Not a bit of it! The fifteen names on the ballot paper were a collection of UFOlogists, dowsers, 'metaphysicists', holistic teachers and mystics. There was no way that a 'balanced' council could be elected: it would comprise entirely of people of similar persuasion. So much for 'no collective view'; it would not be possible for CCCS to express anything but the 'New Age' view. To save the centre money, it was also decided not to use the Electoral Reform Society to deal with the ballot; papers instead were to be sent to the CCCS' patron, the Earl of Haddington (who later appeared in a Sunday colour supplement article in which he admitted he believed in Fairies...).

CERES had by now been receiving support from other scientists and physicists, as well as promises of help from Dr John Graham, an Agronomist (crop expert) from Cranfield Institute of Technology. John Graham had been down to the Wiltshire crop fields the previous summer, and had carried out some experiments in the company of Terence Meaden and Paul Fuller. More technical support came from a scientist who sent a letter with complicated equations that I couldn't begin to understand, and suggesting various lines of investigation we might travel down in our quest to understand the plasma vortex.

Nature intervened during February. Snow fell heavily over the country and meetings were inevitably postponed. The capital was badly affected and a CCCS meeting was cancelled. Poor George Wingfield couldn't speak to the CCCS faithful, but the promise of a forthcoming circles lecture tour of the States in the company of his old school chum John Haddington must have cheered him up no end. The weather prevented me from attending the Beckhampton group-organised 'workshop' run by Busty Taylor. In the event it seemed that the snow and ice didn't put too many people off going. Twenty-odd folk turned up at the *'Bear Hotel'* in Marlborough to hear Busty talk and to see some of his magnificent slides of crop circles. To the delight of his audience, Busty revealed details of his trip to Cairo and the pyramids which he'd undertaken with Ron Jones during the preceding November. It seemed that there were 'similar measurements and dowsing patterns' to be found in the pyramids and at the Sphinx as there were to be found in and around crop circles. Busty likened the mystery to a *'....cipher or cryptogram, where knowledge of the key word allows all to become clear....'*. Later that year we were all to learn what the 1991 'keyword' was, and it was a four-letter word beginning with H.....

Alan Rayner kept himself busy with the season approaching and in his February newsletter, he speculated as to whether "pictograms" would appear in the snow.[1] We later heard that a group of CCCS members spent several chilly hours up on the Wansdyke, hoping to see circles forming in the snow. They weren't successful....Rayner was also in contact with Terence Meaden and had promised to include *CERES* contact numbers in a group newsletter that summer.

Around this time the group of people who were now coming together as the *CERES* team for 1991 were invited to lunch one Sunday at the Meaden household. Jacqui and I made our way to Bradford-on-Avon with Rog. Arriving at the Meaden's place we were greeted warmly by the Professor and shown into the house. Now, Terence Meaden was often criticised by the 'New Age' brigade as being a 'Christian Scientist' and having no time for 'alternative' doctrines. It has to be said that the Meadens were probably more 'Green' and 'New Age' than their critics, (and Terence in particular was definitely *not* a Christian). That day, Mrs. Meaden came in from a short walk along the canal bank where she had been collecting fresh herbs. We were delighted to find the family not averse to 'alternative' things.

Paul Fuller and David Reynolds also turned up and, after a superb meal, Terence took us into his confidence. It seemed that there was more behind his 'circles effect' than met the eye. He explained that he had been developing a theory for some years now in which he believed that Stone Age man and his predecessors worshipped the trace marks left by whirlwinds, tornados and plasma-vortices. Terence thought that these circular marks were thought to be signs from the Gods and were outlined with stones set upright in the ground. To assist with his research he had amassed an amazing collection of pictures and paintings of stone circles and other ancient sites.

'There's such a lot of work still to be done,' he said to an enthralled audience. 'I'm finishing off one book of what will probably be a trilogy. It should be published this summer. I'm afraid it will upset a lot of people, both in conventional archaeology and religion.' He showed us some of the photos he'd taken and some of the diagrams drawn. It certainly all made sense. Terence pleaded with us to keep all this secret. 'Nothing must get out before publication date,' he said.

The secret was safe with us!

It was agreed that we needed to find a suitable site to base our 1991 cropwatch at. We also decided it would be a good idea to buy a decent secondhand caravan between us to use as 'HQ'. Paul was busy and Dave Reynolds lived in Wolverhampton so it was down to Jacqui, Rog and myself to sort something out.

Later the following week, Roger and I set about planning the 1991 season. First off, a site had to be chosen for the Cropwatch. This site had to match a number of criteria set down at the *CERES* meeting early in the year. Firstly, it had to be relatively central to the area where the circles appeared. Next there had to be road access, but at the same time the site had to be 'off the beaten track' enough so that several cars and (we hoped) the caravan could be parked without being too obvious. Then, the site had to be in such a position as to give a good vantage point over a fair part of the area we wished to survey. As if these were not difficult enough to match, the site also need to be in a position whereby the quality of radio and car-phone reception was high. We planned to make use of CB radio sets. Additionally, we had decided that it would be desirable to have the use of a radar set and IF we were able to, then the chosen site had to be able to allow the installation of this vital piece of equipment and allow the scanner an uninterrupted sweep over the areas of Yatesbury/Beckhampton/Alton Barnes. Pretty stiff criteria.

The OS map of the area was produced, and all the main Wiltshire circles sites of the previous 5 years or so marked on it. Then a box was drawn round these and we had the 'boundaries' of the area to search for the site. Several places were tentatively marked as 'possible', amongst these were East Field at Alton Barnes, a site on the Wansdyke overlooking Stanton St. Bernard and Morgan's Hill, near Bishops Cannings. After several trips to the district by car, and a couple of mountain-bike rides across the Marlborough Downs, most of the possible sites were crossed off the list for one reason or another. However, one particular site appeared to match most of the criteria: Morgan's Hill.

The hill, crowned with a distinctive clump of trees, even had road access from the Bishops Cannings to Calne road, and as it could be seen from almost every place we went to in the area (except East Field), reason said that most of the places we wanted to watch would be visible from the hill. A trip up the hill revealed this to be the case; the hill next to Adams Grave, which overlooked East Field at Alton Barnes, could be seen, so, provided someone was looking in the right direction, any 'vortex' which might descend over East Field should be spotted. There was even an old, empty water tank on the brow of the hill facing Devizes. This would be an ideal observation post; a watcher could stand in the tank and peer out over the edge without being seen. And with Devizes just down the road, surely this was the ideal spot?

One, or rather two, things were against the site: the two tall masts, which stood on the top of the hill, a field away from the clump of trees. These masts we knew to broadcast radio beacon signals for aircraft, would these signals interfere with the CB radio links, the telephones or the radar? The radio beacon signals were certainly able to be picked up on an ordinary car radio, so there was every chance that the signals might 'bleed across' the CB channels. We would have to carry out tests.

Before that however, there was a talk to do. Terence had been invited to give a talk on Crop Circles at the Central Veterinary Laboratory in Weybridge, Surrey. Being busy or in France he deputised this to Paul Fuller and myself. The talk was on the 28th February and we duly turned up at the CVL. Paul was introduced and got onto the podium. Whilst he gave the audience the background to the phenomenon and Meaden's vortex, I showed the slides. After Paul, Rog got up to give the latest on the 1990 season and how CERES and BUFORA believed there to be a certain percentage of hoaxing going on. After Rog it was question time. I joined the other two on the stage for this. Disappointingly, there was little asked about the vortex or Paul's work with Meaden. Instead we were asked such questions as whether we thought that the '....*fact that the St. Michael ley line and the St. Mary ley line crossed somewhere near Silbury had anything to do with the large proportion of crop circles being found near there.....*'

There were quite a few other questions on a similar theme. Although we afterwards felt that we'd given a good account of ourselves, it was yet again a surprise to find that a group of educated people was not taking the scientific solution seriously and instead seeking the answer in the paranormal.

We'd now sorted out a plan for the coming season's watch. The plan was this: Four sites were chosen-Wansdyke, near to Alton Barnes; Scratchbury Hill, near Warminster (this watcher would cover Maiden Bradley as well); Pepperbox Hill, near Salisbury and a site near Cherhill. The following groups were identified as being essential to our plans:

Mobile watchers: would cover each site and be able to be summoned to go to any nearby location if a circle was found or a vortex reported.

Walkers: Individuals who would be dropped off by car at various locations and would walk set routes, looking for circles.

Mobile teams: Different from watchers, these would be on 'standby' to be called out and directed to locations by Terence Meaden whenever weather conditions were right for circles to form. As many teams as possible to be equipped with CB radio or mobile phones.

All of the above would report to and be controlled from the central watch site.

And so it came to pass that one evening in early March, two cars arrived at the foot of Morgan's Hill. One, a Fiesta, sported a thin 'whip' aerial on its roof, while the other car, a Capri, was carrying a four-foot semi-rigid fibre glass aerial. The idea was that I would stay parked at the foot of the hill in the Capri, while Roger, in the other car, would set off towards Devizes. With the aid of a map and using the radio link, I would give Roger his directions and 'guide' him past various circles sites. Places with poor reception would be marked on the map, as would areas where there was a radio 'blackout'. At the same time we'd listen for any sign of the aircraft beacons interfering with the radio. The test was a complete success. The beacons were not heard, and Roger was guided over a wide area with only one blackout area being noted. It was found that climbing up from Alton Barnes to Knap Hill the radio reception was fairly good, but from Knap Hill along the road to the junction with the East Kennet road, the transmissions could not be picked up from Morgan's Hill. A week later, another trial took place, this time with Jacqui Griffiths being sent to Bratton, whilst Roger was sent out through Devizes, Potterne, Urchfont, Woodborough and thence via Alton Barnes, Stanton St Bernard and back towards the A361 at Bishops Cannings.

Jacqui was guided from Bratton to Devizes via Urchfont and then onto the A361. By careful planning, I brought the two vehicles together on the A361 at Bishops Cannings, waited for them to appear, then drove out behind them. The success of the operation was toasted in the *'Waggon & Horses'* at Beckhampton! On another occasion I acted as 'control' and positioned Rog out on the Devizes Road to watch for Paul Fuller, whilst I sat up in a layby. As Roger reported Paul's approach so I drove out onto the main road as Fuller drove up behind. Rog was soon behind the UFOlogist and he was 'escorted' to the hill in this fashion!

So, Morgan's Hill was the choice for the site of the CERES 1991 cropwatch. There remained one small but significant problem: who owned the hill and would they let us use it. The results of the search and the radio tests were put to Terence Meaden for the final decision.

On the evening of Saturday 5th April I came home to find a message on my answerphone; it was Terence Meaden: 'I have been back from France 2 days. There's a large mailbag. Some matters which we have to attend to straight away'. I wasn't going to ring him at 11.30 at night, so left it until the next morning. However, the phone was busy each time I tried so it was late in the day before I got through. After a brief chat, it was arranged that I would visit the Professor on Monday morning.

Monday 7th April 1990

I drove over to the professor's place. There, I was shown a letter from Alan Rayner. The gist of the letter was that the CCCS seemed to be too busy holding committee meetings to take action in respect of preparing for the 1991 season. As a result of this, a group letter, which Rayner had been proposing to send out to local farmers on behalf of the Beckhampton Group and selected others, was being withheld until after a CCCS meeting in the coming May. Crucially, Rayner also said that the letter to farmers might not include as much about *CERES* as Terence would have liked. Also, he was '....*reluctant to include too many CERES phone numbers....*' as this '.....*might be affected by a CCCS Embargo....*' The CCCS were apparently setting up a 'Hotline' phone number and it appeared that they wanted this exclusively on the Beckhampton Group letter to farmers, to the exclusion of all others.

'They've got a cheek!' I exclaimed. Terence Meaden looked sad. Although a respected physicist, professor and amateur archaeologist and having worked in various places across the world, it had to be admitted that Meaden was a little naïve when it came to dealing with the likes of Colin Andrews and the CCCS. The Press did not help either, giving as much publicity to the mystics as they could. As I've said before, the truth doesn't often make a good story. What was even more surprising was the attitude of the farmers themselves. Most of them seemed to prefer to contact first the CPR and later the CCCS rather than a REAL scientist with connections to an agronomist. Odd.

Anyhow, Meaden seemed to be a little miffed that the CCCS should muscle in on the circles game. We put our heads together and came up with an obvious solution and one which would begin a long battle with the CCCS and their hangers-on and to some extent isolate *CERES* amongst the crop-circles fraternity: We decided to send our own letter to as many farmers as we could find addresses for. This was to be a questionnaire based in parts on a BUFORA/TORRO survey of 1987, and asked a variety of questions. Some were obvious questions, such as when was a circle first spotted, who spotted it, what it looked like, etc. Another asked for the farmer to indicate the stage of growth of the crop when it was flattened. These were to be compiled by me, approved by Terence and printed off by Rog. The same team was to produce posters and fact sheets to distribute throughout the year including a list of *CERES* contacts. This would, we hoped, take advantage of the time being wasted by the CCCS.

Back home that night I was working on the drafts when, at ten-o'-clock, the phone rang. It was Terence. He'd been in contact with Dr John Graham of the Shuttleworth college and the *CERES* watch of 1991 will be held in conjunction with them. This was good news! '....Please include a stamped, addressed envelope addressed to Dr Graham, with every one of the letters you send to farmers...' said Terence. What a move! Any farmer worth his salt would surely cooperate with a leading agronomist from an agricultural college? The letters would speak the same language as any cereal farmer and Dr Graham's name should add the final seal of approval. This was surely a coup d'etat over the mystics and UFO believers! How naïve we all were! We failed to recognise that one thing speaks louder than anything else-*Money.*

The next day, Tuesday 8th April, I decided to visit Glastonbury market. On the way back I took a trip around the area of Butleigh Wootton, collecting a couple of farm addresses on the way. Negative. I made sure that my route also took me past Stantonbury Hill-also negative. Later that day I gave Rog a disk with the draft list of farmers on it. He said he'd see what he could add and print the lot off as stick-on labels, plus the return labels to Dr Graham.

The following evening, Jacqui and I were in the '*Bull*' with my brother and his girlfriend. My brother was still sceptical about circles. Although he had seen the 1990 Pepperbox Hill shapes from the road, he was still not convinced that most circles are genuine. I was trying to explain Meaden's theory when Rog hurried in. He carried a folder. When he'd bought a pint, he joined us and handed me the folder. In it were the completed questionnaires and contact sheets. Excellent!

Thursday 10th April

That evening I began the task of putting the letters, contact sheets and report sheets into envelopes with the SAE's. It took quite a while as there were nearly a hundred. Later still I went out and posted them.

Friday 11th April

I decided that a trip to Avebury was called for. I often went there alone, finding it a good place to lose oneself amongst the stones and meditate. I spent a while there and returned home via Alton Barnes, Stanton St. Bernard, Cherhill and Blacklands. Apart from a ring of green grass near the golf course at the latter location (which was nothing out of the ordinary when checked) all was clear.

Sunday 14th April

I spent most of the day indoors, writing up my diary for the week and mused over the fact that 98 people should have received their questionnaires by now! The first barrage in the 1991 battle of the cornfields had been fired, with the 'shells' landing at farms across Wiltshire, Hampshire, Somerset, Surrey, Avon and even the Isle of Wight! What would the CCCS do in reply?

Friday 19th April

Jacqui and I were spending a quiet evening in when, at approx. Nine-o'-clock, the phone rang. It was the professor. Excitedly he announced that the first circle of 1991 had been reported! He gave a map reference: ST 345515.

'That can't be far from Glastonbury with that OS reference,' I said.

'Butleigh Wootton!' was the reply.

I was astonished. Why? Because I'd been out the previous night with Jacqui and Rog and we'd gone to one of our North Somerset watering holes, the *Carpenter's Arms* at Stanton Wick. Over a beer or two I had told the others about a series of coincidences which were arising during the course of my writing a novel. The pattern was that several of the fictional incidents were being mirrored by real-life events. And I'd only recently written a section involving Butleigh Wootton! I didn't tell Terence this, however.

'I'm very busy at present,' went on the Prof. 'Could you and the others possibly.....'

I was happy to agree to go to Glaston with the others to investigate the report but it would have to wait until the following morning. 'By the way, Terence, where did the report come from?'

'Richard Andrews of the CCCS phoned me and told me all about it. He will be going to Butleigh with Busty Taylor first thing tomorrow. Perhaps you can tie up with them.' He went on to give me Richard Andrews' phone number. 'Oh, by the way,' he continued, 'I'm trying to set up a meeting between ourselves and a couple of farmers who own the land around Morgan's Hill. I'll try to make it for one morning this coming week.'

I said that would be fine by me and rang off. I made two swift phone calls. One to Richard Andrews' answerphone to say that a *CERES* team would meet Busty and him in the Abbey car park at Glastonbury at nine the next morning. The second was to Rog and, within half an hour, Rog, Jacqui and myself were all in a pub on the A46 excitedly discussing the coming day!

Saturday 20th April 1991

A weak spring sun rose over the hills and shed its light on Pucklechurch. Today was my birthday and would be spent looking for the first crop circle of the year. I got up at just after seven, breakfasted and waited for Rog to arrive. He drew up outside at 07.40 and soon, with Jacqui, we set off in my Capri to meet Busty Taylor and Richard Andrews. It took about an hour to reach Glastonbury and when we arrived in the car park adjacent to Glastonbury Abbey, at around 09.30, Busty and Richard were waiting. After friendly greetings were exchanged we studied the OS map and agreed on the location.

We set off in short convoy to Butleigh Wootton. Our route took us out of Glastonbury towards Street. From Street we took the Butleigh road and after about a mile, arrived at a junction where a road joined us from the left. According to the map reference, the circle was here somewhere. We parked up at the roadside and got out. A swift look around and –there it was! In the corner of a field, adjacent to an avenue of cedar trees.

First impressions of the circle were that it was a fake. Even seen from the road it exhibited none of the usual swirl effect noted in apparently 'genuine' circles. The young, green crop was badly trampled. As was usual with modern cereal farming, there was no farm anywhere in sight. Nonetheless, after a brief attempt to discover who the farmer was, we all agreed to nip into the field to do a quick job of measuring. Whilst Jacqui shot off some video footage for us, Rog and I helped Richard Andrews with the measuring. Busty wandered up and down the road, dowsing.

After the measuring, and after having taken some still photos, my next move was to set about examining the edges of the field for any evidence of underground pipelines or cables. This was done as a means of ascertaining if there was any underground influence, which might result in a dowsing effect being registered by a dowser, and was just one of many similar experiments carried out by *CERES* during the last year or so. At that time several dowsers claimed to have found some disturbance of their rods in or around circles. I'd done a similar search at Cheesefoot the previous year. Finding nothing around the field boundary I went out into the road to see if there were any markers to indicate a pipe or cable route. As I left the field, so Busty came into the field with his long camera-pole. 'I got an effect!' he grinned. 'There's an apparent line from Glastonbury Tor running right through this field!' I just grinned back.

Wandering along the roadside I found no evidence of any pipeline markers and was about to head back into the field when I noticed a farm worker approaching on his tractor. I turned and noticed that the others were still in the field. Busty was just dismantling his camera pole. Quickly I shouted a warning to them, but against a stiff breeze, they didn't hear me.

The farm worker drove his tractor into the lane and came to a halt. He leapt from the machine and yelled at the four people in the field to 'get out' (or words to that effect!). Busty, Richard, Jacqui and Rog shuffled out of the field and joined the rustic at the roadside. Understandably, the farmhand was somewhat annoyed. Richard Andrews tried to pacify him by explaining that they had tried to contact the farmer, but without success, and that they were trying to find out the cause of the circles.

At this, the rustic swore loudly. '....*I seen they ******* 'Ippies do that!*' he exclaimed, pointing to the circle. '....*An' they used a ******pole!*'

Ah. Ok, then. We all apologised profusely and promised to leave the area. All the information being gathered in, there was no need to stay any longer anyway. As we got back to our cars the general consensus of opinion was that the circle was definitely 'A Fake'. 'Let's go and have a cup of tea,' suggested Busty. We all of set off to nearby Street for a cup of tea. We found a café on a corner and were soon enjoying a cuppa. Whilst the *CERES* team were happy that the circle was fake and that the farmhand's evidence was conclusive, Busty seemed edgy. Conversation was stunted and he kept looking over his shoulder. It soon became apparent that Busty and Richard had arranged to meet someone else that morning and were waiting for a phone call on Busty's mobile. Taylor's unease became such that eventually Richard Andrews excused himself and left the café to find a phone box. Busty tried to joke about this, saying that it would '…save the expense of an outward call on his mobile…'

We thought that it was more likely that he didn't want us to know who else he'd arranged to meet…..

When Richard returned, seemingly successful, we agreed to go our separate ways. Leaving the café, both cars set off, with me leading, along the road which would take us back past the circle site for one more look before we left the area. Halfway between Street and Butleigh Wootton, Jacqui noticed Busty suddenly stop and turn back. Thinking he might have car trouble, I turned back also.

By the time we'd caught up with Busty again, he'd turned his car round once more and was parked in a farm gateway. As we pulled up, Busty and Richard were chatting amicably with….. Colin Andrews and Pat Delgado! I parked up and we all got out of the Capri. Joining the small group we all shook hands. Not having a clue who we were, Pat was quite friendly. He remarked that he and Colin just seen the circle and agreed that it '…looked a bit rough…' Whilst we spoke with Pat and I took photos of the group, Busty and Colin chatted amicably, but it was apparent that they were still waiting for someone else…..

Then a red Triumph Stag drove up pulled over and stopped. The driver and his companion got out and I recognised the shortish fair-haired man as John Macnish, one of the BBC's *Daytime Live* camera people. He had been heavily involved with *Operation Blackbird*. His female companion we discovered later, was his wife, Jayne. From the way they all greeted each other, it was obvious that these were the people that Busty, Richard, Colin and Pat were waiting for. They spoke briefly and in hushed tones, then got back into their cars. '...We're going back to the circle...see you...' called Busty. We called our 'good-bye's and got back into the Capri.

As we were going to go home via Street and Glastonbury, it meant that I had to turn the car round as I was facing the wrong way. The others had disappeared by now so I drove along the road towards the circle with the intention of turning the car round at the first opportunity. We'd only gone a short way along the road when we were passed by a police car. I had a feeling that this would be significant so kept going. By the time we reached the circle site, the police car was stopped by the entrance to the field and behind the cars belonging to Busty, Colin and Macnish. Two policemen were chatting to the six other circles enthusiasts and the farmhand, who was preparing to spray the crop.

'Drive by slowly and I'll video them!' cried Jacqui. I slowed right down and she poked the camcorder out of the window. Then we beat a hasty retreat![2]

A year or so later, John Macnish wrote a book called '*Cropcircle Apocalypse*' and in it he claimed that the 'Meadenites' as we were apparently known, said that Butleigh Wootton was a hoax only after the farmhand said so. Not so, John. We said it was hoaxed from the moment we saw it.

George Wingfield accepted it as genuine though......

Later that day, I rang Terence Meaden. He was most surprised to hear that Busty was apparently still on good terms with Condrews and Fandango. 'I thought they had all fallen out,' he said. 'Yet you say Busty was talking to them as if they were still friends?'

I agreed that this was so.

'That's odd, Busty gives me the impression that Colin and Pat had cheated him in some way and that he has nothing to do with them.'

Not so. We had the proof on film and video. What now?

Meaden sighed. 'We'll just have to be careful what we say to Busty. Colin and Pat are not inclined to mix with *CERES* or myself and we don't want them finding out about our cropwatch.'

The rest of April passed without incident and the Butleigh Wootton hoax remained the only circles report on the *CERES* database for a while. Towards the end of the month Terence phoned to say he'd received a fax from a group calling themselves the 'Wessex Skeptics'. These people wanted to meet Terence to talk about his work. As usual, he deputised me to contact them. This I did, writing to their contact, one Robin Allen, offering to arrange a meeting and giving various dates when we were free. I told Paul Fuller about this when I next spoke to him. Fuller reacted with horror.

'Oh, God, Pete! The Skeptics are dreadful people! They don't believe anything-hence their name!' He went on to tell me that they were post-graduates based at Southampton University who set out to 'prove' that everything had a simple explanation. Apparently a couple of them were quite reasonable but the rest were renowned for being belligerent. Nevertheless, Fuller agreed that we should meet them, even though the chances were high that they were out to prove that the plasma-vortex didn't exist! We waited for a reply.

By now, Alan Rayner had got the Beckhampton Group guidelines for cropwatchers sorted out. It consisted of a general letter which would be given to every cropwatcher connected with the group or who attended one of their meetings. In it were sensible guidelines for cropwatching including instructions for anyone finding a circle to avoid entering the formation until it had been photographed; Beckhampton Group contact telephone numbers were given. In the event of no answer on these numbers, Rayner gave the CCCS 'National Report Line' number and at the end, a *CERES* contact number! Interestingly, the newsletter gave details of the CCCS National Cropwatch, This was to run between June 22nd and July 7th and was to be coordinated by Stanley Morcomb. During the two- week watch, Morcomb and his wife would be staying at a caravan sited near Beckhampton in order to run the watch. The Beckhampton Group was to run a series of local watches along the lines of the 1990 meetings up to and after the CCCS watch. They were, it seemed, getting quite well organised.

It was May 13th when I had an early phone call from the professor.

'Peter, there's been a circle sighting in Wiltshire. It's at Yarnbury Castle.'

Where?

'Yarnbury Castle. It's an Iron Age hill fort just off the A303 between Winterbourne Stoke and Wylye. Actually, the formation is opposite the castle, on the south side of the A303.'

'Could this be the first 'real' circle?' I asked, excited.

'Very possibly,' returned the professor. ' First reports are that it is a dumb-bell shape, similar to some of the dumb-bells from last year.'

'Who found it?'

The meteorologist was silent for a minute. 'Well, I suppose you ought to know...it was Busty Taylor.'

How?

'He flew over it. When he landed, he phoned me. He says he hasn't told anyone else yet.'

Terence was, of course, busy that day preparing for the forthcoming publication of his new book to be entitled *The Goddess of the Stones.* I gave Rog a ring and he was soon outside my place in his Fiesta. We set off straight away armed with cameras and tape-measures. It took us a good hour to reach Yarnbury and a further fifteen minutes to find a gateway to park in, the A303 being short of parking places! It was a lovely warm spring day and one could see for miles across the plain. Walking along the side of the motorway-standard main route to the West, we found the field in which Meaden had told us the circles lay. It was a crop of oilseed rape. We could see nothing. Eventually, by standing precariously on a barbed wire fence, supported by Rog, I could see a vague shadow in the yellow crop, way out in the middle of the field. We tried to walk through the crop but it was so interwoven, plant to plant, that this was not possible. We tried crawling along the tractor-lanes beneath the crop but this too was impossible. Not only that but the flies were buzzing round us in clouds! We withdrew to the comfort of the verge.

'What now?' Asked Rog. 'We daren't go into the field because it's impossible not to leave a trace.'

'Give Terence a ring,' I suggested. 'See if he knows who the farmer is.'

Rog wandered off to his carphone whilst I set up our latest piece of equipment-a camera pole. Camera-poles were invented by Busty Taylor. His consisted of a length of what seemed to be scaffolding-tube to which he fitted his camera. He would hoist this into the air and take an 'aerial' photo. It was carried on his car roof-rack when not in use. Others copied his idea. Mine was made from a telescopic aluminium television aerial post. Into the smallest section was fitted a four-foot pole to which was attached a camera tripod top. To use this piece of equipment, one first attached a camera to the tripod mounting in the normal way. Then the camera was set to operate on its timer. One then had about thirty seconds to undo the securing wingnuts, slide the two extensions out to their limit (marked by a red line), do the nuts up again and hoist the pole (now at about 18 feet long) and camera into the air and point it at the circle. After much practice I had got this down to a slick operation which took little time to do. I directed the pole towards the centre of the crop and shortly heard the shutter operate. Lowering the pole I reset the timer and took another shot. Rog returned. 'Terence doesn't know who farms the land. He suggests we try asking at local shops.'

I had another idea. 'Why not phone Busty?'

'Good thinking,' replied Rog. We rang the little man's mobile number. After a few rings, Busty answered.

'Hi, Busty,' I said. 'It's Pete-from *CERES*. We're at the Yarnbury circles site but can't get into the field. Do you know who owns the land?'

'Hello, Pete,' said the familiar voice. ' *Things are happening!*'

'What?'

'Things are happening. Can't tell you much but its good stuff....'

I didn't have a clue what he was on about so repeated my original question. After a short pause, Busty said '....I don't know whose field it is...'
Thanking him I rang off.

Rog looked at me quizzically. 'Well?'

'He hasn't a clue,' I said.

Rog grunted. 'Nothing new there, then.'

What now? We had (we hoped) photos for Meaden so decided to set off around local shops to see if we could trace the owner of the field. The A303 is not noted for having shops along its length and so we tried local villages. No luck. Just where the locals got their shopping we didn't know. There was a clue in that there was only one place where it seemed likely that the owner might live. Steeple Langford was the village on the south side of the area where the circles were. We found a register of electors in the church there and chose the only 'farm' likely and wrote down the address with the idea in mind that we'd write to the landowner, enquiring if it was his land and asking if we could enter the circles. That done, we headed home.

Early sketches of the Yarnbury formation showed a strange dumb-bell. The central 'corridor' was topped and tailed by circles which were off-centre to the corridor. Did this mean that the plasma-vortex was unstable when it touched down in the crop? Hoaxing *must* be out of the question as there was no doubt that anyone trying to get into that field would have left an unmistakable trail. Alan Rayner had ideas about this formation as he set out in the Beckhampton Group's May newsletter:

'.....*The "out of balance" effect [Hopi word Koyaanisquatsi] contrasts with the beautiful symmetry of the late 1990 formations.....The Yarnbury formation may be yet another reminder of how much our way of being on this planet has become out of balance.....*'

Other things mentioned were that the CCCS were considering appointing a Public Relations Officer to deal with the Press and that they had sent letters out to 105 farmers. And a film company called Juniper Films was apparently going to make a documentary about the circles, with CCCS cooperation and also that of the farmers. Oh, and Terence Meaden asserted that the lack of circles so far that year was entirely consistent with his theory.

On the 19th May, Jacqui and I set off in her Cortina Estate with our mountain bikes in the back. Destination: Morgan's Hill. We wanted to check that the hill would indeed afford the protection from passers-by and the all-round vision that we needed for the cropwatch. Arriving at the bottom of the hill we parked up and got our bikes out. The road up to the hill was very steep so we didn't bother trying to pedal up it, especially as there were gates to open and close. If we were able to obtain a caravan for the HQ would we be able to get it up the hill?

On top of Morgan's Hill is a copse and it was to one side of this copse that we planned to park the caravan, just out of view to anyone passing along the road. This was a necessary precaution as not only did we not want to publicise the cropwatch for fear of hoaxing, but also the farmers were understandably paranoid about New Age Travellers at that time. The site of an old caravan on a hill was enough to bring hordes of the 'consciously aware' types to join it with the resulting noise and mess many Wiltshire and

Hampshire farmers knew only too well. At the rear of the copse was a field and a gateway here led out onto the Wansdyke, that long, ancient earthwork which stretched for miles across several counties. From here, with the aid of binoculars, we could see the planned site of the CCCS 'base' – in a metal barn owned by Beckhampton farmer Stephen Horton (the man who we'd spoken to in 1990 and who usually preferred to contact Colin Andrews rather than Terence Meaden when circles appeared on his land.)

We cycled from the Wansdyke to join the old coaching road to Bath, leaving this near the golf course and using the road to return to the car. Putting the bikes away we returned home via Alton Barnes and were able to later report to Dr Meaden that the hill was the perfect site for the *CERES* cropwatch-as long as we could get a caravan up the hill.

Later that evening I had two phone calls. The first was from a Chris Nash of the Wessex Skeptics. He sounded quite a pleasant bloke and agreed that a meeting, at Terence's place, on the following Wednesday was acceptable to his group. There would be three of them attending. I said I'd tell Terence. The second call was from Paul Fuller. I told him about the meeting but he would not be able to make it. A pity. He had news of a couple of setbacks; on a lecture tour in Germany to promote the book written by Paul and Jenny Randles, Pat Delgado was set to appear to promote his and Colin's books and, it seems, wouldn't if Jenny was on the same bill. The promoters bowed to his argument and Jenny Randles was pushed out. The other setback was that Randles and Fuller's publishers, putting out a German edition of *Crop Circles-A mystery solved?* had commissioned a foreword from the last person on Earth Randles and Fuller would have wanted to appear in the same book as them: Erich Von Daniken! They protested that Von Daniken was from a completely different standpoint, but to no avail!

So, Good news and Bad news.

Later that week (I didn't note the exact date) Terence rang to say that he'd set up the meeting with the farmers. We were to meet with Dr Graham at Avebury for lunch and then go on to Baltic Farm to meet farmer David Shepherd who farmed the northern side of Morgan's Hill. After that we would go on to Bishop's Cannings to meet Farmer David Brown who farmed the south side of the hill.

The next day I met Terence Meaden and John Graham at '*Stones*' restaurant where we had a splendid lunch marred only by my knocking over a bottle of Perrier water and nearly soaking the agronomist! We arrived at Baltic Farm in the early afternoon. Farmer David Shepherd was waiting and we all piled into his Range-Rover and set off along tracks and up impossible slopes to the top of Morgan's Hill. Here we stopped and got out. Terence and I explained to the farmer what we intended to do. The farmer scratched his head.

'Seems ok to me,' he said. 'I've got oilseed rape in this field, but if I understand you rightly, you will be based on David Brown's land,'

I nodded. 'We'll need to come onto your land to watch over the fields below the hill-where you've had circles before.'

That was ok with the farmer. We promised that we would not publicise our cropwatch so as to keep people away.

'Ah, well,' said the farmer. 'There's a footpath that comes up to the Wansdyke, so you'll get a few walkers I expect.'

That was fine. Next it was off to Farmer Brown.
Farmer Brown lived in a splendid old house on the edge of the village of Bishops Cannings. He welcomed us and showed us into the kitchen where it swiftly became obvious that the farmer was taking advantage of having a tame agronomist on the premises. A good hour was spent with the farmer and farm scientist poring over crop yields, planting plans and computer programs. Eventually we got out to Morgan's Hill. Here, as with the other farmer, we explained what we wished to do.

'If you are in agreement,' said Meaden, 'We will set up our caravan on the top of the hill, well under cover of the edge of the copse. We will camouflage it. In addition, we'd like to use that disused water tank on the front of the hill as an observation post. We might, if all works out to our advantage, set up a radar scanner somewhere on the hill.'

Farmer Brown raised his eyebrows at this.

'It'll only be a small scanner,' soothed the professor. 'From the road it wouldn't be visible except through binoculars.'

The farmer wasn't too keen on this but the promise of a good donation to the village church funds won him over. He gave us permission to not only site our cropwatch on the hill and use the old water tank, but gave us permission to use his manager's farmyard to charge radar batteries (should we get a radar set, which was still 'pie in the sky' at this time) and draw fresh water. We went down to the manager's house and were introduced to the man who would be our 'keeper' over the next few months. Andrew Woolley was an amiable man and quite interested in our project. It turned out that he and Meaden had met before when the Prof. was researching circles on land farmed by him.
We finally left the area late that afternoon, happy that we had a site for the cropwatch which met all our specifications and the cooperation of both the farmers concerned and their staff. All seemed to be on course.
And more Good news. Rog had news of a caravan for sale! It belonged to the father of a work colleague and was for sale at a very reasonable price. The only snag was that it was in Honiton, Devon! Some quick phone calls and a four-way split was agreed with Rog, Terence, Jacqui and myself being shareholders. Paul Fuller later joined the 'consortium'. All we now needed to do was go down to Honiton and look over the caravan. Rog said he'd arrange this.
Before that, Terence and I had our evening meeting with Robin Allen, Chris Nash and Martin Hempstead of the Wessex Skeptics. The substance of their argument was that they could not see how science could explain crop circles. Terence put forward his theories but they disagreed. Vehemently. Martin Hempstead appeared to little or no respect for Meaden and was quite unbearably rude. Chris Nash was the only one of the trio who seemed to be able to keep his cool. It was not a pleasant evening.

What with all this and their conspicuous absence, Crop Circles had been pushed into the background. Just after the Spring bank holiday, Rog and I set out on a 'Grand Tour' of circles sites. From Pucklechurch we went up the A420 to Chippenham and from there took the A4 through Calne. Just after Calne we turned right for Blacklands and Morgans Hill. Nothing seen. The crop was growing nicely but no circles. From Morgan's Hill we went through Devizes and Potterne, heading for Salisbury. Travelling through Tilshead we arrived eventually at the small lay-by opposite Yarnbury Castle. I took a couple more speculative shots with the camera-pole.

'Why not try to see if we get a better view from the ramparts of Yarnbury?' suggested Rog. Good idea. It meant driving a few miles along the A303 to Deptford, turning round and coming back on the opposite carriageway. Twenty minutes later saw us parked on a dusty chalk track by the ancient monument. We trudged along this track towards the castle. '...The things we do for the Goddess!' said Rog. I echoed his sentiment. As we drew closer to the gate leading to the ramparts I could see a notice there. We arrived at the gate and stopped.

Private Land. No Entry.

Bugger! There was nothing for it but to return to the car, drive home and go to the pub!

The weekend that followed was a Bank Holiday weekend. Paul, Jacqui, Rog and I decided that the *CERES* cropwatch ought to start. It was arranged that we'd all meet at the bottom of Morgan's Hill at six-o'-clock on the evening of Saturday 25th May, bringing sleeping bags and camping gear. The intention was to spend the weekend on the hill, roaming around different locations and looking out for circles.

We all arrived at the base of the hill and made our way up to the copse where we parked the cars. Whilst I got the camping stove going, Rog and Jacqui tried to put up a tent in the shelter of the old water tank. We 'signed in' in the Duty Site Operations Officer's Log for what was to become known as '*Operation Blue Hill*' – a name Dr Meaden had coined from an observatory. We were full of enthusiasm. The weather though was typical of Spring Bank Holiday weather – overcast. As the evening wore on the wind began to increase and it got colder and colder. We retreated to our cars. As darkness fell it became obvious that staying on the hill was not a good idea; the wind seemed to be nearing gale-force and we mutually decided to call it a day. Two cars made their way forlornly down the hill at ten-thirty and made their way to the '*Waggon and Horses*'.

28th May 1991

I had a day off and was wallpapering one of the bedrooms when the phone rang. It was Rog.

'I've had a circle report!' he announced.

Where?

'Newquay-Cornwall. It's a single circle, near Porth and RAF St.Mawgan.'

He went on to say that a workmate had spotted it whilst on holiday. The man had been given a *CERES* report form by Rog. I took down the details for the *CERES* database and looked up the site on a map. It was a bloody long drive and equally as tedious a journey by train! Perhaps this was one we wouldn't visit personally!

However, there was soon one reported that we *could* see.

Over the bank holiday it seems, a circle had been found in Wiltshire, at a place called Chirton. Not one of the usual sites, it was just off the A342 between Devizes and

Upavon. I arranged to meet Paul Fuller at Chirton church on the evening of the 30th May. The plan was to find out which farmer owned the land on which the circle was, obtain permission to enter the field and measure the formation and take photos. I had a nightmare journey, being stuck behind a learner army driver in a camouflaged truck for mile after mile across Salisbury plain; the roads were too narrow to overtake. Eventually I did manage to get past the truck and arrived outside Chirton church at about six-twenty.

Paul was already there. 'I came past the circle-it's just back along the A342 and looks like a definite fake,' he said. We set off towards the field with the circle, not knowing quite what to do, as we were reluctant to go in without permission but didn't know who the farmer was-the usual position! As luck would have it, just as we arrived at the lane leading to the field, so a tractor approached. I flagged down the machine and asked the driver whose field it was. The farm-worker, a genial man, said it wasn't his land but belonged to a farmer who lived in the village. He pointed out the farmhouse.

'I'll go and ask him for permission to enter the circle,' I said. 'At worst, he can tell us to shove off.'

'No. Mark wouldn't do that, he's all right, is Mark,' said the tractor-driver.

He was right. After a short trip to the farmhouse the door was opened in answer to our knocking by a pleasant young man. We handed him our *CERES* investigator's calling cards and explained the reason for our visit and asking if we could enter the circle to measure and photograph it.

'Yes, OK,' said the farmer. 'It appeared overnight on the 25th-26th. I've already had a visit from a man who took pictures-he reckons it's a fake.'

'We're of the same opinion,' I replied. 'Who was this chap?'

'Oh...Buzzy...or something like that.'

Paul shot me a glance. '...Busty?' he suggested.

The farmer smiled. 'Yes. That's him. Busty.'
So the lecherous aviator had been there before us!
There was another surprise in store. The farmer, looking at our cards, said, 'Ah...Peter Rendall...the Germans mentioned you.'
Germans? *What Germans*? I didn't know any Germans!

The farmer smiled again. 'They came round the other day,' he said.

'We'd better get along to the circle,' interrupted Paul. 'It'll be dusk soon.'

He was right. I'd ponder over the Germans later.
Up at the circle we unloaded our notepads, measures and camera-gear. The circle was rough. The stems had been roughly trodden down and there was no 'swirl' effect present

in either the circle or its ring. Not only that but there was a hole at the centre. Dead giveaway, really.

I looked around at the terrain. 'Well, it's obviously a fake, but the problem is that the site matches Meaden's theory pretty well.'

'The trouble with Terence,' said Paul, looking up from his notepad where he was jotting down measurements, '…is that he too easily accepts fakes as being genuine.'

This was something we would have to deal with several times over the coming months. There was more than one occasion when Paul, Roger or myself declared a formation to be 'Fake' only for Terence Meaden to accept it as real, often on the flimsiest evidence.

Our work finished, we adjourned to the local pub for a swift pint and, I hoped, some food, as I hadn't eaten since breakfast. I was out of luck. There was no food available so I had to make do with a pint of the elixir of life – 6X! - and a bag of crisps. Over the beer, Paul told me that Busty had apparently reported to Terence that there were some 'fakes' in the field below Pepperbox Hill; the same field that had had a 'pictogram' in it in 1990. We pondered over the new improved Busty. He seemed to be reporting circles to *CERES* rather than (we supposed) the CCCS. Would it last?

The beer finished, we left the pub and parted company. Paul to Romsey and me to Pucklechurch via any chip-shop I could find open! Again, I was out of luck. My route home didn't pass any chippy and I had to make do with an omelette before bed.

Chapter Ten
REALITY IS AN ILLUSION
Fake?-No. Duplicity? Yes!

Friday 31st May 1991

Finding myself at a loose end today, I decided that the reported formation at Pepperbox Hill ought to be looked at. Rog and Jacqui were at their respective work so I set out alone for Salisbury, arriving in the city of the Spire an hour and twenty minutes after leaving home. Then I had to battle my way through the busy streets and out on the Southampton Road. Leaving Salisbury behind me I took the Capri along the A36 for about five miles before turning off left at Witherington Down and following the sign for 'The Pepperbox'. I drove a few hundred yards along the chalk track and parked in sight of the old hunting lodge shaped like a pepperbox and from which the hill took its name.

Locking the Capri I carried my camera, fitted with a long lens, with me and climbed over the barbed-wire perimeter fence. Standing on the very edge of the hill I had a good view over the fields towards Salisbury, the magnificent spire of Salisbury cathedral just visible through the gloom of the overcast day. I also had my binoculars with me and focussed these on the fields below. No apparent crop circles formation was readily visible. This was unusual because a good formation, even if seen from ground level, appeared as a 'shadow' on the crop. Seen from a few hundred feet above the field the formation should have been obvious. Then, through the gloom, I noticed a line of disturbed crop in the right-hand corner of the field. I concentrated the binoculars on it. Yes, this must be it! But it was very tatty and seemed to be a straggling series of circles and corridors-nothing like the 1990 shapes. I took a couple of long shots and looked again with the bins. No. This was too much of a mess. I wasn't happy with this one at all. Fake.

Back over the fence and back to the car. Driving out onto the A36, I thought long and hard about this formation. I made up my mind to go down to the lane, which ran alongside the field and have a look from there. Ten minutes later I was parked at the edge of the field. I got out of the car and looked towards the formation. I couldn't see it from the road. No tell-tale 'shadow' on the wheat. I was tempted to go into the field and look closer but I knew that the farmer who owned the field was very anti-circles researchers. In the early days, when Meaden, Fuller, Andrews and Delgado were all friends and circles research was in its infancy, these four had had some trouble with the farmer here. He'd blocked their cars in with his and sent for the police. I didn't intend to get *CERES* bad publicity, however much I was itching to go into the formation. Reluctantly, I headed for home.

The next morning, Rog rang.

'Could I borrow the camera-pole?' he asked. 'Terence rang me last night – he tried to get you but there was no answer – he wants me to go to Pepperbox Hill and photograph the formation there.' I knew why Meaden hadn't been able to get me-I'd gone out and forgotten to leave the answerphone on! But why did Meaden want the formation photographed?

'Apparently some Germans went into it the other day...' (Those Germans again!) '...And have declared it genuine.'

'No. That can't be right. I went there yesterday morning-it's crap! Anyway, you can't see it from the lane so it can't be 'poled' and you can hardly see it from the hill.' I was puzzled.

So was Rog. 'You'd better tell Terence, then,' he suggested. 'He's happy to accept it as real. I was going to photograph it on my way to Honiton to look over this caravan.'

'Fine. Look over the caravan by all means. But don't waste time on the circles!'

'Good. That's saved me a long diversion!' Rog rang off and I was about to ring the professor when the telephone shrilled. It was Paul Fuller.

'Hi, Pete. It's Paul. Look, Terence has been on to me – he reckons Pepperbox is definitely genuine. I think we ought to go there as soon as possible. Busty has been on to him and says that a 'friend of a friend of a friend' reckons that Farmer Sparkes doesn't farm there any more so it's ok to go into the field.'

Sparkes was the farmer Andrews *et al* had had the trouble with. I told Paul what I'd seen and what I'd told Rog. There was a brief silence.

'Oh,' said Fuller at last. 'In that case you were right not to go in. Just in case Farmer Sparkes *is* still the owner - he gets mighty angry!'

'He trapped Andrews and Delgado, didn't he?'

'Yes – and me!' replied the UFOlogist. 'That was the only time in my life that I've been arrested!'

'What shall we do about the formation?' I asked.

Paul thought for a moment. 'I'll go to the hill on Monday and have a look. If I agree with you that it's most likely a fake, we'll stay out. If it looks OK we'll have to try and go in to confirm it.'

OK. I said I'd speak to him next week. I put the phone down and then dialled Meaden's number. The professor answered.

'Hello, Terence. It's Peter. I thought I'd let you know that I went to Pepperbox Hill today to look over the new complex there'.

His reply took me by surprise; 'Pepperbox?' he said, in a shocked tone. 'Who told you about that?'

Puzzled, I said, 'You did – or rather you told Paul Fuller that Busty had flown over it and reported it to you. Still...' I tried a joke here, '...Professors are supposed to be a bit absent-minded....'

That went down like a cup of cold sick. There was a brief silence before Meaden said, '...Yes, well we are a bit forgetful and I do have a lot on. I've been trying to contact Professor Ohtsuki.'

I quickly explained my morning's expedition to him.

'Did you actually go into the circles?' he demanded.

'No. In the light of previous experiences which people have had with Farmer Sparkes I thought it wouldn't be good publicity if I went in and got caught.'

'Hmmm. The Germans went in...' (who *were* these bloody Germans?)[1]'...They are from good connections and they have taken photos and declared it absolutely genuine.'

Personally, I didn't care if they were directly related to the Kaiser – those circles were fakes. However, I didn't relay this thought to Terence! I tried a gentle approach.

'...Have they much experience in this sort of thing?' I inquired.

'They've been reading the *Journal of Meteorology* for the past two years – about the same time as you have,' came back the answer.
I wasn't sure how to take this. Surely being able to spot a fake circle from a 'genuine' one wasn't just dependent on how long one had been reading *J.Met*?

'I've spoken to Paul and Roger,' I said, conciliatory. '..And we've agreed that Paul will go to see the formation in the next day or so. If he is certain that it looks genuine-we'll go there and have a quick dash into the field.'

The professor wasn't very amused. 'I see. By then the CCCS will have been in there. They're having a conference at Ely and Busty is giving a talk. He's bound to tell them and they'll come swarming into the circles.'

'W-e-ell...If it's any help, the circles can't be seen from the road and can hardly be seen from the Pepperbox.' I was trying to win some ground. But it was difficult.

'The Germans reckoned that with a camera on a pole one could photograph the circles.' Terence was so reluctant to accept that these could be fakes.

'From what I saw,' I said, 'You would need a 60 or 70 foot pole to see anything. Anyway, the weather conditions weren't right for circles to form....'

'Oh, ah....well....One shouldn't take the weather criteria too rigidly,' said Terence. 'Any moving mass of air will do.'
Oh, hell. This was moving the goalposts a pretty big bit! However, I said nothing to this. Why? I was too surprised. The Meaden theory was moving around as much as the vortex itself. Firstly, we'd had the highly-believable Plasma-Vortex, the swirling mass of

air caused by warm wind passing over a small hill such as Silbury or a 'Punchbowl' such as those at Cheesefoot or Alton Barnes. Then, as the 1990 circles developed into fantastic shapes, so the theory was modified. It now became similar to a fast-flowing stream where the water swirled round pebbles and stones, causing vortices to occur in various places downstream of the obstruction. A mass of air doing this, Meaden argued, would cause several vortices to form and when they touched down in the field, the regimented and orderly-sown crop would fall down in round shapes, lines and boxes.

Still plausible. But still reliant on the right weather conditions. To change the conditions to suit the formation was a little like desperation. And of course there *was* an element of desperation in our work. The CCCS were rapidly growing in numbers and, like Andrews and Delgado before them, seemed to be grabbing the interest of the farmers, public and press with their wacky theories. Through Alan Rayner, they'd just sent out a very comprehensive set of cropwatching guidelines indeed. Real-time science was in danger of losing out again.

Nevertheless, Paul, Roger and I were all agreed that declaring a fake to be a fake was equally as important as identifying a 'real' circle. We just had to convince Professor Meaden of this.

Terence said, 'Busty Taylor will be going to inspect the Pepperbox formation on Sunday morning, early. If you like we will agree that we will wait until Busty has reported back before coming to a conclusion.'

I said I thought this was a good idea. Before ringing off, I asked Terence: 'By the way, did you ring me last night?'

'Yes, I let it ring for a minute or so and realised you weren't in.'

'Sorry about that. I went out and forgot to switch the answerphone on.'

'Ah, so it isn't just me who is forgetful, then!'

I had to laugh. 'Touche!'

In the absence of anyone else being available, Roger had taken Jacqui along with him when he'd gone to Honiton to inspect the caravan which was for sale. They reported back that the van was in 'good nick' and would be ideal for the summer's cropwatch HQ. Having left Meaden alone for the majority of the weekend I took a chance and phoned him on Sunday, only to find out that he was '...Out flying...' Mrs. Meaden promised to get her husband to call me later that evening.

Sure enough, later that day, just as I was about to phone Rog to see if he was interested in a pint, the phone rang. It was Terence, returning my earlier call.

'Hello, Peter, what can I do for you?' The scientist sounded very upbeat.

'It's about the caravan, Terence. Jacqui and Rog have been down to Honiton, looked at it and reckon it's OK. Paul is interested, as is Jacqui so it's a five way split.'

'Yes, yes, that sounds fine to me. Go ahead and arrange it. Let me know when we can pick it up and we'll fetch it with my Peugeot. Now, let me tell you what I've been up to. I went flying over circles with Busty Taylor. We took a cameraman from *National Geographic* with us and flew over Pepperbox Hill. The circles look quite good from the air and there's more! A dumb-bell has arrived in the adjacent field and also a formation shaped a little like a letter "A".'

Alarm bells began to ring. Surely he didn't believe......

'...After landing, we all went by road to Pepperbox and took a chance on going into the field. I am certain that the circles are genuine. There is quite a bit of new growth after the initial flattening took place and very little damage. The "A" and Dumb-bell are not so good. They all look as if they were made at roughly the same time.'

Oh, God! He DID believe the circles to be genuine! I wasn't giving up, though.

'Terence,' I said as carefully as I could, 'Don't you think that the circles must at least be classed as 'suspect ' if there is a letter "A" nearby. Even allowing for all sorts of alterations to the vortex theory, the wind cannot make an "A"!'

This short couple of sentences was cut even shorter on three occasions by incoming calls which Meaden found it necessary to answer, keeping me hanging on the line.

'Well, I'll admit to the "A" being suspect, but I want the others put on the database as 'Genuine', please.' The professor was adamant. I was compiling the *CERES* database but the final classification of circles was Terence's. Talk got back to caravans and it was arranged that I'd call him if I could sort out collection for the following Friday.

Later that evening, in the Bull over a pint and a game of darts, I explained it all to Rog. He just shrugged at Terence's acceptance of the Pepperbox circles on the grounds that he hadn't seen it and that put him in no position to take sides. He also wasn't around on Friday.

Later still, the Pepperbox formations went onto the database as 'genuine'....

Over the next couple of days, more circles were reported, but this time there was no doubt as to their origins. A hoax was reported north of Gloucester, near the A46 to Stratford-on-Avon. According to the 'Gloucester Echo' a couple of lads were arrested after being caught making the circle. The odd fake popped up in other places too. It seemed that after the *Blackbird* fiasco and the Butleigh Wootton fake, everyone (except, perhaps, Terence Meaden) was being cautious....

Friday 7th June 1991

Jacqui had declared herself 'not available' to come to Honiton, so it was up to me and the Prof. When I'd told him that the others were not available he was keen for me to go by myself and even offered to lend me his Peugeot estate so I could fetch the caravan! I politely refused this offer, mainly because I'd never towed anything bigger than a trailer before but also because caravans need a certain amount of manual work to hitch and unhitch them. This normally needed another person to help. Also I wasn't insured to drive Meaden's car. So it was that I arrived at Terence's place in Bradford-on-Avon at 09.35 that morning. I found the professor upstairs in his office, photocopying documents. He left the machine and took me down to the yard behind the workshop where his Peugeot stood.

'I won't be long.' He said, vanishing into the house. He emerged over five minutes later.

'Things are happening!' he said.

'That's what Busty always tells me,' I retorted, wondering what was coming next.

We got into the car and Terence started the engine. As he shot off out of the yard and onto the main road he explained that it had been Busty on the phone which delayed him. We tore along the road towards Melksham (Terence may have been a gentle sort of character but his driving certainly didn't fall into the same category!)

'Busty tells me that he flew over Hampshire yesterday and there are new formations!'

'Where?' I asked, hanging on to the roof strap for dear life as Terence negotiated a roundabout in a fashion guaranteed to make a racing driver go pale.

'There's a couple of circles at Cheesefoot-opposite the 1990 Telegraph Hill site- and a three-in-line at a place called Upham, near Big Path Farm,' he pulled out a map and indicated the latter site whilst driving at speed along the road. 'There were a few areas of stable air over Hampshire last night. I'm booked on the 21.00 ferry to France tonight, so I can't visit these circles....'

France again. Oh, well, 'That's OK Terence. Rog and I will go and see them.' Meaden beamed.

We went to Honiton via some circles sites. At Bratton, Upton Scudamore and White Sheet Down there were no circles to be seen and soon we were speeding along the A303 to Honiton. We arrived at 11.30 and were soon looking at a smart, if elderly, caravan. It was a deal and for £375 we had our HQ. The deal was sealed over tea and slices of 'Unclebuncle' cake – apparently a local speciality – and we left a happy ex-owner with a cheque and hitched up the caravan. On our way back up the A303 Terence mused that we would need a different means of getting power to the van; 'This type of caravan runs off a car supply. We'll have to modify that,' he said. It seemed simple but if only we'd known what a problem it would be!

We arrived back in Bradford-on-Avon a couple of hours later (even Terence Meaden had to drive slower with a caravan on the towbar) and manouevred the caravan into a parking place outside the workshops. Once we'd unhitched it, we stood and looked at the van.

'It will look good with "*CERES-Circles Effect Research*" painted on the side,' said the professor. I agreed; it certainly would.

So, that afternoon I went home with two free copies of Terence's latest book on crop circles "*Circles from the Sky*" – and Terence and family went off to France.

But, even with the professor away, *CERES* work went on. Not only were Rog and I going to go down into Hampshire the following day, but after returning home from the caravan trip, Jacqui and I were off to Beckhampton to meet Alan Rayner.

Alan Rayner? Yes. The reason was this; in conversation with Rayner at some meeting earlier in the year, one of us had mentioned that we intended using CB radio during the cropwatch. Now, Alan had decided to use CB and written to me asking for advice on how to obtain/use the device. Whilst we wanted to keep details of our cropwatch secret, there was no harm in assisting Alan's group with the radio. After all, even if we were on different sides, so to speak, Rayner was always most polite and helpful where he could.

Jacqui and I arrived at the '*Waggon and Horses*' at around eight and went straight to the bar to order drinks and food. We knew that Rayner and others of the Beckhampton Group were meeting in the 'Tack Room' so decided to sit outside in the main bar to eat. We were half way through our meal when Rog arrived and shortly after Alan Rayner came out into the bar. Seeing us he made his way through the tourists, locals and jockeys who crowded the popular pub. I apologised for not coming into their small gathering but indicated our food.

Rayner nodded his acknowledgement and sat down with us.

'It's very g-good of you to travel here to s-see us,' he said, his slight stammer betraying a slight nervousness. 'But we need help to get started with CB radio and are willing to cooperate with *CERES* in return.'

'That's no problem,' I replied. 'We have been using CB on and off for years so know a bit about it. As for cooperation, well that's good news, but will it extend to having *CERES* contact numbers put in front of CPR in newsletters?'

Rayner coughed slightly. 'M-my contact with Andrews and Delgado is currently virtually non-existent,' he said. This was a surprise. I thought that all these groups were together and against the scientists. Thinking back, though, there had been no one from CPR at Michael Green's meeting the previous December. Rayner continued, '..In fact, my offers of help were refused by Andrews, to the point of bluntness.'

Blimey! Were the circular twosome being ultra-careful of whom they associated with after the *Blackbird* fiasco?

'How about the CCCS?' asked Jacqui.

Rayner shrugged. 'They seem to be in some disarray. Richard Andrews has been openly challenging some of the high-level decisions they've made. Busty Taylor has been so fed up with them that he's been cooperating with Terence Meaden and has flown him over fields looking for circles.'

We knew this, and it seemed that the CCCS had little or no knowledge of the formations found so far that year. Meaden needn't worry about CCCS members trampling all over the Pepperbox formation, then! Just then, Stanley Morcomb came into the bar and sat down with us. Greetings were exchanged. He obviously knew the purpose of our being there because he told us that he had an old CB radio but didn't know how to use it.

'I think one other CCCS member has one as well,' he said.

'What happened to all the CCCS resources,' I asked. 'Where's all the equipment they should be supplying?'

Morcomb snorted a wry laugh. 'What equipment? They put me in charge of finding a suitable site. I found one and negotiated with the farmer. Then I asked the CCCS what equipment they were going to supply. D'you know what they said?'

I hadn't a clue.

Morcomb went on, '...They said that they thought *I* was supplying all the equipment!'

'That's a bit of a cheek,' I said. 'What about all their funds?'

Morcomb shook his head. 'That's mostly gone on producing *The Circular* (the CCCS magazine-PR)...Three and a half thousand quid!' he said. 'Which still leaves another one and a half grand in the kitty-but they don't want to spend it. At least, not without yet another committee meeting to decide what to do. That's all they seem to do, have meetings.' He looked at the ceiling.

'They haven't yet decided who will be the Wiltshire area organiser,' put in Rayner.

'And all I've got is an old caravan plus Busty's equally ancient one, a tape recorder and mike-supplied by me-and a CB radio. That's the sum total of the CCCS cropwatch equipment!'

Stanley Morcomb was obviously quite pissed off with the CCCS hierarchy.

'F-farmer Shepherd tells me that *CERES* will be using his land to site their cropwatch on,' said Rayner

What! We were desperately trying to keep all that a secret! I denied it. 'We've looked at many sites, and Baltic Farm was just one of those we looked at,' I replied, not lying but trying not to give anything away. Much as we were willing to cooperate with Rayner and co, we still wanted to conduct a proper, scientific cropwatch with the minimum of interference. Also, the fewer people knew, then the less chance there was of someone pulling off a *Blackbird* stunt under our noses.

'...In fact, I can tell you that we have no plans at all to mount a cropwatch on Baltic Farm. Terence is, this week, going to talk to Farmer Carson, who owns the land around Alton Barnes; we may end up over that way somewhere.'

OK, this was deliberate dis-information. Yes, Terence *was* seeing Carson, but on an unconnected matter. We had no intention of watching over the famous fields of Alton Barnes.

I decided that more drinks were called for and while Jacqui assisted me at the bar, Rog explained the workings of CB radio to Rayner and Morcomb. When I returned, there were wry faces. Alan had listened intently but thought he would 'look into' the possibility of buying a second-hand set first before committing himself to CB. Stanley Morcomb was not sure if it was worth the expense.

I sat down with a pint of 6X. 'Tell me,' I said. 'What would happen if the CCCS came down and found you two cooperating with *CERES*?'

Stanley grinned. 'They've put me in charge, with little or no equipment and little or no cooperation. I'll cooperate with who I want!'

'But what if the CCCS say No?'

Morcomb shrugged. 'Michael Green has always encouraged cooperation with Terence Meaden. He says he's a gentleman. Most of the rest of the CCCS committee are against it, though.'

Well, this was a turn up for the book. We left that evening with promises to find out where CB radios could be bought and the cost of that and things like aerials. We'd all meet again the following Friday. Driving back home, Jacqui and I pondered over the fact that the CCCS seemed to be in a state of disarray.

8th June 1991

I picked Rog up at 09.40 and we set off to find Upham and the circles reported to Terence by Busty. We went via Bishops Cannings and Devizes, thence to Chirton where the hoax was still clearly visible from the road. Just after Chirton we got stuck behind a couple of slow-moving army trucks and it was twenty minutes before we could overtake. From there we made good time and after passing through the outskirts of Winchester, got onto the A272 after which it was not long before we arrived at Cheesefoot Head. We followed the A272 as it climbed round the bends which skirted the Punchbowl and soon, on the left, we could see the familiar 'shadow' on the crop which indicated a circles formation in a field up on Chilcomb Down. We'd visit this once we'd turned round. Turning necessitated going past Cheesefoot to the car park. On arriving here we found it full of Traveller's vehicles; old army lorries and buses with small wind-generators and wobbly stovepipes on their roofs.

'That puts an element of suspicion on the circles, then,' observed Rog, eyeing up the travellers camp as I waited for a gap in the traffic.

Seeing a gap I swiftly accelerated the Capri across the road and back down the hill.

'Yes,' I agreed. 'It certainly does. They've obviously been there for a week or two, judging by the semi-permanence of the camp. And,' I went on, 'Wasn't there a major conjunction of some planets the other night?'

Rog nodded. 'That's right. Plenty of mystics have put a lot of faith in that.'

We pulled up on the verge opposite the Chilcomb formation. A man sat quietly sketching the circles. From the road, through binoculars, it looked like a circle with a dumb-bell in it. It looked quite rough and 'ropey' and the outer ring seemed somehow 'offset'. Not too dissimilar to the elusive Yarnbury formation. This one too, was elusive as the land belonged to the notorious Farmer Bruce; even Andrews and Delgado shrank from entering his fields. He was rumoured to shoot first and ask questions later.

Whilst we pondered over what to do, another car pulled up behind us and a young man got out. He came over to us and started chatting about the circles. They had, he said, been formed on the night of the 6th June-the night of the planetary conjunction. His name was Robert Trevalyan and he was a CCCS researcher. He and Rog swapped business cards (we carried *CERES* cards). He too, was cautious about entering the field. Minds made up, we bade him farewell and got back into the car to go off to Upham.

On the way, Rog and I came to the conclusion that the planetary conjunction of 6/6/91 and the presence of the travellers, coupled with the apparent roughness of the Chilcomb formation, classified it (in our minds at least) as a definite 'Hoax'.

To find Upham involved turning the car yet again and following the A272 back past Cheesefoot and continuing for another mile or so towards Petersfield. Turning right we travelled for another couple of miles through Lane End and at a crossroads turned right. Two miles through the delightful Hampshire countryside and eventually we turned right towards Bigpath Farm. Without the OS map we'd never have found the place.

According to the map we had to continue up a footpath so I parked the Capri up in a pull-in and we hoofed it through a wood and, ten or fifteen minutes later, came out of the woods overlooking a sort of small valley. The fields in this vale were full of cereal crop and there, on a slope facing us, in a field of barley, was our formation. I got the binoculars out.

A minute or so later, Rog said, 'Well, what do you think of it?'

Wordlessly I handed him the bins. He scanned the crop for a while, then lowered the bins and looked at me.

'I know,' I said. 'It's a bit....rough...Let's sketch it anyway.'

Rog got out the pad and I wandered off with the compass to find the formation's orientation. When I returned with the compass point of 30 degrees North, North East, Rog handed me the sketch. It showed a small ring with two corridors emanating from it, each with small circle at the end. In the ring was a smaller circle. This ring, in turn, 'sat on' a much larger ring of flattened crop which had a corridor running through it. At the 'base' of this ring was a smaller circle and on a tangent to this latter circle was a harp-shaped formation which looked like two letters 'D' joined side by side.[1]

Underneath the sketch, Rog had written, 'Hoax if ever I saw one!'

Which was what I feared. There had been no doubt in my mind when I'd first set eyes of the formation that it was fake fake fake. Why? Because it resembled nothing less than an insect or cartoon alien! We agreed that it wasn't even worth the effort going into the circle to measure. Surely, from the sketch, Terence Meaden would see it was a joke; even the name of the location gave the game away – *Upham*!

Hunger now took over and we left the scene. Back at the car a swift look at the map showed that there was a pub in Upham village so we headed there.

The '*Brushmakers Arms*' was a typical little Hampshire village pub, quaint and red-brick. Inside a small knot of locals was enjoying lunchtime drinks and, by the tantalising smells coming from the kitchen, good food also. The menu confirmed this and it wasn't long before we were supping Morland's bitter and enjoying a lamb curry. It was whilst eating this meal that we overheard talk about ...crop circles. We listened for a while as the small group of lunchtime drinkers discussed the arrival of the phenomenon in their village. When I'd finished my meal, I joined the knot of well-spoken people at the bar. They were very interested to learn who we represented and I handed a *CERES* card and report form to the pub landlady who promised to pass it on to the farmer who owned the land on which the 'insect' had appeared. Apparently the farmer, who used the pub as his local, was 'furious' at being the recipient of the formation and wouldn't let anyone near it. Another woman said that the circles had appeared overnight on the 1st June.

The locals were very friendly and even told us that we weren't the first researchers to pass that way in the past few days; a couple of Canadians had been there before us.

And then it was time to go. We bade farewell to the locals at the '*Brushmakers Arms*' before wending our way back to Bristol and hoped that we'd hear from the farmer in due course (we never did...).

The following day it rained on and off for most of the daylight hours. I stayed firmly indoors, entering the latest crop of circles onto the *CERES* database. The total for 1991 so far was 13, of which we had listed at least seven as hoaxes. Of the remaining six, there were a couple of suspected hoaxes but we hadn't had them visited by *CERES* or anyone whom we knew, so they were classed as 'probably genuine'. Paul Fuller rang and I filled him in on the latest news. He promised to take a look at the Chilcomb formation as soon as he could. From my description, he didn't think the Upham 'insect' worth another look.

That afternoon, the *Western Daily Press* rang me. The reporter was due to fly over Chilcomb later that day and wanted to know what our impression of the circles was. I told him that the circles appeared rough and that we thought they were hoaxes. And no, we hadn't gone into the field because we were aware of Farmer Bruce's antagonistic attitude towards circles researchers. Did I think that the lack of good weather was responsible for the lack of circles so far?

Yes. I did. The Meaden theory was not applicable to most of the circles so far. I didn't tell him about Terence's widening of the Pepperbox goalposts. The following day the *Press* published a short item wherein they confirmed that the Chilcomb and Upham formations were thought to be fakes.

Tuesday 11th June and Terence Meaden was due back from France, so I rang to report our findings of the weekend. Once again, Terence didn't seem too happy to accept that we found both formations to be fakes, but admitted that Paul Fuller had been in touch and voiced his opinions that Chilcomb was doubtful.

'However,' said the Prof., 'I have heard from some Americans who have been into the formation at Chilcomb and they are pretty keen on it.'

I could feel the hairs of doubt start to stand up on my neck.

'They were a father and son visiting their other son who is at Marlborough College,' went on the professor. (Not *more* well-connected people!). '...They were apparently sent to the circles by Colin Andrews, who didn't warn them about Major Bruce. Nevertheless, they went into the circles and reported that they are beautiful, with lovely swirls and are, in their opinion, absolutely genuine.'

Cautiously I asked; 'How many other formations have they seen?'

Terence Meaden cleared his throat before replying: '..Uh..well, this is the first one they have ever seen.....'

'But you accept that it is genuine?'

'Why not? At least they went into the circles....'

Oh, shit! He had us by the proverbial short and curlies there. Rog, Paul and I, who'd all seen loads of circles and thought we could tell Stork from Butter, were sure it was fake just by looking at it from the road. Terence was prepared to accept the findings of a couple of Yanks who'd never seen a circle for real before.

'We aren't doing too well, are we?' I groaned, mainly to myself and referring to the efforts of Rog, Paul and myself in trying to convince Meaden not to accept everything as genuine. It just didn't seem right that Chilcomb was natural. I fought on.

'If – *if* – that formation is genuine, then the mystics will have a field day. There was a major planetary conjunction the other day and that is the day on which Chilcomb was formed.....'

'I know nothing of all that rubbish!' snapped the professor.

I sighed. Let him have it his own way. If he wasn't prepared to accept our findings then perhaps he'd better stop buggering off to France at every available opportunity. I didn't say so, of course. I just accepted what he said and promised to keep in touch. When I returned to the computer though, Chilcomb stayed on the database as 'Hoax'.

Another annoying episode occurred later the same day. Rog rang to say that a large area of crop 'lodging' had been reported in the *Bristol Evening Post*. So what? Lodging was a well-known problem with cereal crops. It usually happened in wet and/or windy weather; large patches of crop became top heavy and fell down. Trouble was, that in this case, at Tortworth, Gloucestershire, one Richard Tarr of our old friends Quest, had got involved and was apparently puzzling over the first occurrence of square crop circles!

Another 'letter to the Editor' followed. I also wrote to the *Bristol Journal* and the *Winchester Gazette* appealing for anyone finding circles to report them to CERES. As an indication of what we were up against, these appeals proved fruitless.

Chapter Eleven
JUST FOR THE RECORD
Blue Hill gets under way-Terence and The Press-Farmer Brown-NTV-Out in the cold

Circles now began to be reported from all over the country. Soon we had reports not just from Hampshire and Cornwall but from Leicestershire, Shropshire and Nottinghamshire as well. Most were hoaxes. Work continued 'behind the scenes' as *CERES* got ready for the coming high season. I made out a blank calendar of June and July and sent copies out to everyone who we had promises of help from, indicating that they might like to fill in those dates on which they were available to attend the cropwatch and return the sheets to me. This produced the grand total of one phone call and one letter. Neither was available to assist.

So far, by the end of the first week in June, it looked like the *CERES* cropwatch 1991 was going to be manned by Terence Meaden, Paul Fuller, Roger Davis, Jacqui and myself. Terence would be taking some time out of this to promote his new book whilst Paul, Rog and I all had full-time jobs. Jacqui was going to be very busy indeed if things didn't change! As it turned out, we ended up with plenty of others on site but they were not always those we would have chosen.

On the 15th June Terence rang me with some brilliant news. The Bristol United Press group, publishers of the *Western Daily Press* were going to back the *CERES* cropwatch on condition that they had exclusive press coverage. They were also supplying us with a radar set! This was indeed excellent news. With radar, we could keep an eye on the area surrounding Morgan's Hill and hopefully spot a vortex in action. All we needed was a site for the radar set. All being well, this would be on top of that disused water tank on the side of the hill. Terence would work on the farm manager. The professor also said that the film cameraman who had been part of Operation Blackbird had contacted him. Apparently John Macnish was interested in some sort of collusion with Meaden. He also told Terence of a report of some circles at a place called Frampton Mansell, in Gloucestershire. These were a fantastic array of shapes. Guess where Rog, Jacqui and myself went that same evening?

From the start, everything was wrong. The map reference showed the site of these circles to be in a river valley and in an area not known for cereal crops. When we arrived at Frampton Mansell we found a small cluster of cottages and a pub. Parking at the pub we set off along a path and soon found ourselves on the towpath of a weed-choked canal. Thick trees and bushes clogged the banks and by the time we arrived at the mouth of a dis-used tunnel it was obvious that there weren't any crop circles here. We retraced our steps and tried the opposite direction. Eventually, after pushing through bushes and undergrowth, we came out into an area of grass bordering the river. Here at last we found what we were looking for. A series of shapes ranging from circles, arches, triangles and squares had been flattened into the grass. We reckoned they'd been there at least a month from the way in which the grass was growing up straight again in places. It was obvious that they were nothing to do with crop circles, but what were they? A pyramid of sticks stood over the remains of a small fire, leading us to conclude that this was a camp of some sort-travellers or Boy Scouts we didn't know which. It was growing dark and beginning to drizzle as I took out my camera and flashgun and took a few shots

By the time we got back to the pub car park we were all wet through. This didn't stop us from going in for a swift pint, though! It was twenty past ten by now - we just made it.

I tried to find out more about the grass markings from the pub staff but nobody seemed to know or care what they were. Circles mania had not reached Gloucestershire!

The next day was a Sunday. I telephoned Farmer Brown's manager, Andrew Woolley and asked if we could meet him later that morning to set out just what we wanted to do on Morgan's Hill. He was happy with that and we arranged to meet at his house near the hill later that afternoon.

Next I phoned Terence, told him of the meeting with Woolley and our findings of the previous night. This time he did not hesitate to accept my word that there was nothing for us at Frampton Mansell. Even he could see that the place didn't fit. There was some talk as to whether this had been a bit of 'mis-information' from Macnish, designed to send us out of the area for some reason. After all, he was firmly on the side of Condrews and Fandango. We decided that the cameraman had no reason to do such a thing, but we decided that *all* suspect or known fake circles would henceforth be called Hoaxes.

Strangely enough, during the afternoon, I received a phone call from Alan Rayner, who told me that at a CCCS meeting at Beckhampton on the previous Friday, only three people turned up! He also told me of a new formation at Yatesbury, just west of Avebury. It was a dumb-bell in a field of barley.

Early evening and Rog, Jacqui and I turned up in the farmyard. Andrew Woolley was waiting for us. He indicated his Range-Rover and said 'Hop in, we'll go up the hill and you can tell me what you want to do.'

We piled in and drove across the fields and straight up the steep slopes to the water tank. It was raining again by now as we inspected the tank and told Andrew that we could roof the tank with planks and set the radar scanner on top of it. We would also like to use the tank as an observation post. Woolley thought for a moment.

'That will probably be ok, just as long as you camouflage the scanner and the caravan. I don't want travellers seeing the caravan and thinking that they have mates up here.'

This was understandable. We promised to do as he said. Terence had been contacted by a man called Eddie Brown, the owner of a Militaria shop who was interested in joining the watch. Eddie had access to a camouflage net or two, which we would cover the caravan with. All was Go!

Leaving Andrew Woolley at the farm we set off, full of enthusiasm, for Yatesbury as the rain fell.

After a bit of searching we found the circles. From the road it looked like a three-in-line set. We got out the notepad, surveyors tape and cameras and set off carefully into the barley to where we could see two men in the circles. These latter turned out to be CCCS members and were quite chatty. Independently we got on with the measuring. The circles were very wet and muddy but quite good. We all thought 'possibly genuine'. The CCCS said that they had information that the circles had formed on Saturday night. This raised an eyebrow or two, as that was when we'd been wandering around Gloucestershire. Hmmm.

The work done, we struggled out of the wet field, discovering just how wet one can get from a young cereal crop! Back at the car and again cold and wet, we put the measuring gear in the car and got in. We were using Jacqui's Cortina estate that day and the damp had got into the car as well as its occupants. The car proved difficult to start but luckily it eventually did, and we moved off in fits and starts back through the lanes towards Avebury Trusloe. Suddenly a red Triumph Stag came round the corner, passing us and heading towards the circles field.

'Y'know who that looked like?' murmured Jacqui. 'Macnish!'

'Good grief!' I exclaimed. 'You don't think he did have anything to do with those Frampton Mansell circles after all and had this made to catch us out?'

'Dunno,' was the reply; Paranoid the thought may have been, but we had to be very careful that *CERES* wasn't set up in the same way that CPR had been at Bratton last year. Whilst there was no evidence that the BBC people had been involved in any deception, we felt that we couldn't take chances. Bearing that in mind we headed for Chippenham and food! It being Sunday there was only one chipper we could find that was open. We bought our supper and elected to drive back to my place to eat it in the warm.

On the way, I suddenly laughed out loud.
'What's the joke?' asked Jacqui.
'Oh, just the thought of what people will say when we tell them we're going to spend the next few weeks in a water tank!'
We all laughed at the thought. A touch of the *Monty Pythons*!
Back at my place with coffee and the fire on, Jacqui's day was completed by her finding that her Sweet and Sour was more like 'Sweet and Sweet'.
'The bloody sauce tastes like Raspberry jam!' she said, disgustedly.
The next day Rog phoned Terence Meaden to report the findings of the previous day. When he'd listened to the events in detail, Meaden told Rog what had been behind John Macnish's phone call to him the other evening.

'He phoned because he too had decided that Morgan's Hill would make the perfect site for a cropwatch,' said the professor. 'He wants to use the hill quite desperately and even offered to share when he discovered that we already had permission to use it. I told him that we were not interested in sharing the hill, so he will have to find somewhere else. However, today I received a call from David Morgenstern, Macnish's partner in the *Daytime Live* projects. He too tried to persuade me to share the hill. I'm afraid I gave him a bit of an ear-bashing – for one and a quarter hours!'

When Rog told me this later, over a pint at the *Bull* I was both delighted and filled with misgivings. Delighted because our early planning had worked out and filled with misgivings because we knew that Andrews and Delgado were working with Macnish and we wanted them kept well away from our site. I recalled that Andrew Woolley had said that he'd been approached by Andrews with a view to using Morgan's Hill as a site, only to be told that *CERES* had got there first. What we needed was to establish a presence on the hill as soon as possible. This had been arranged for the next day.

Tuesday 18th June 1991

We assembled at Terence Meaden's workshops at Bradford –on-Avon at 09.00. The caravan had been cleaned and was lettered with *CERES-Circles Effect Research* on the sides and end. Terence had already hitched it to his Peugeot estate. In the back of the estate was a load of scaffolding planks. These would make a 'roof' for the water tank and the radar scanner would be put on top. We set out for Morgan's Hill.

On arrival, we opened the gate and the small convoy passed through and on up the hill. There was another gate half way up the hill and this too, had to be opened and shut again.

Once through this second gate we drove up to the top of the hill before stopping and unhitching the caravan. Securing the HQ, we moved Terence's car back to the water tank. Soon, Terence, his son, Lionel and the Militaria shop owner from Bournemouth, Eddie Brown, were busy roofing the tank.

So far, so good. The caravan was behind the copse, out of sight from the road. Terence had been loaned four huge lorry batteries; these would be used to power the caravan electrics and the radar set. We had come to an arrangement with Andrew Woolley whereby we installed a battery-charger in an outbuilding in his farmyard. Two batteries would be in use with two on charge. A daily trip would eventually be required to swap batteries over. We could top up water bottles at the farm by means of an outside tap. Cooking and heat was supplied via Calor gas bottles.

All was ready. The radar was to arrive on Thursday morning. Pleased with our day's work, we locked up the caravan and went home.

Later that evening I had a call from Terence Meaden.
'Peter, I'm afraid we have to move the caravan,' he said.

What! Why?

'I've had a call from Farmer David Brown,' went on the Prof. 'He is very concerned that travellers might see our caravan and move onto the hill. He suggests we move to the back of the hill, near the Wansdyke.'

'But that's not much good!' I exclaimed. 'We can't put the radar monitor in the caravan there…it's too far away from the scanner…'

'Oh, well, he wants us to move the radar as well. He doesn't want us to use the water tank after all, for the same reasons.'

This was mighty suspicious. We'd already had all this out with the farmer. Eddie Brown was going to bring along his camouflage netting for both the caravan and the tank. We'd be next to invisible.

'Yes, yes, I know that,' agreed Terence. 'But he is insistent. Anyway, we'll still be able to walk to the edge of the hill and keep a lookout. And the radar will still scan the same area.' The radar was due to be delivered by Marconi the following day.

We had little choice, it seemed, but to accept the farmer's new conditions if we were to continue with '*Operation Blue Hill*'. But what a Bummer! It was understandable that no farmer wanted any truck with convoys of travellers, but Brown knew exactly what we intended to do and how little we planned to be visible. We'd also tried our hardest to keep our cropwatch a secret. That others now knew that, it seemed, down to the farmer himself; it appeared that he had told Macnish and Morgenstern of our presence on the hill. There was little doubt that word would now get around - so what did the farmer hope to achieve by 'outing' us? We would soon know.

The next day Terence Meaden towed the caravan to its new site adjacent to the

Wansdyke. We looked around and took stock of our new surroundings. We were now sited close up against a barbed-wire fence. Over the fence and a few hundred yards away were two tall towers used to carry aircraft directional beacons and transmitters for the Wiltshire Fire Brigade and Ambulance service. Gone was our forward lookout post at the tank. To look out across the fields we'd have to use the shelter of the copse; that wasn't too bad. We'd have to find a new site for the radar, though; it couldn't go on the caravan roof.

'That's no problem,' said the professor. 'I have a scaffolding tower that I can lay my hands on. We'll put that up and make a platform of planks on the top. The scanner can sit on there.'

And so it was. By the afternoon of the 19th June we had the scaffolding tower up and a platform on the top. Mid-afternoon a van with 'Marconi' on the side arrived and a pleasant chap got out and introduced himself as Graham Stocks. The radar set was a small marine one and it wasn't long before it was set up on the tower. The monitor was put in the caravan on the table and wires trailed between the scanner, the batteries and the monitor. Once connected up the scanner was set up and we were in business! The machine had a range of distances and we could, by changing the settings, 'see' as far as Alton Barnes. If a Plasma Vortex were to form within a radius of up to five miles around Morgan's Hill– we'd see it.

Operation Blue Hill was up and running.

This meant that someone had to spend the night in the caravan, as the cropwatch had to be manned at all times now we had the radar. I volunteered. Once the others had departed I wandered around the field a bit and up onto the Wansdyke. Then I wandered across to the front of the hill and looked down across to Bishops Cannings from the copse. Then back to the caravan again. It became obvious very quickly that however much one liked solitude and one's own company – cropwatching alone would speedily become boring. Especially if there was no means of making tea or coffee! I made a mental note to bring up an old kettle I possessed and tea, coffee and milk.

We now had a continuous weather log running in which the wind direction and force, cloud cover, visibility and temperature were to be recorded every hour. Weather recording equipment would soon be set up around the hill and an automatic weather station was to be delivered, on loan, on Friday. We also had a Duty Site Officer's log. Every event, every visitor was to be recorded. For the duration of the cropwatch a record would be kept of everything.

I kept the log during the night and, after an uneventful period of darkness, dawn came accompanied by thick mist. The good thing about the mist was that it meant conditions were not conducive for a vortex to form. I snatched some sleep. It stayed misty and had cleared little by 10.40 when I was relieved by one of Terence Meaden's friends, Monsieur Leichner. Jean-Francois Leichner was an engineer and a very likeable man. He had seen a possible interest in using a force similar to the plasma-vortex in an industrial capacity. I left him in charge and drove the 30 miles home

At four that afternoon I was back on site to relieve M. Leichner. Once he'd left the site,

I settled down to put the kettle on and brew some tea. A noise outside caused me to step out of the caravan. There were two youths wandering through the gate from the Wansdyke. I intercepted them and found out that they were looking for crop circles. I told them that we were part of a scientific survey on 'crop lodging' and they seemed to believe me. They said that they 'knew Colin Andrews and Pat Delgado'. I feigned ignorance. They left the way they came. I made my tea and sat down to watch the radar screen and eat a sandwich. The distant sound of heavy artillery announced that the army was holding a mock battle on nearby Salisbury Plain. This went on most of the evening. They had the weather for it; it was sunny with a slight breeze. Quite pleasant really.

At seven o' clock a Range-Rover drove slowly along the track and stopped by the caravan. Out jumped Farmer Brown. He wandered round to the caravan door where I met him.

'Evening,' he said, jovially. 'All going alright then, is it?'

I found this approach a little difficult to swallow as he had already gone out of his way to ensure that, from the start, things *weren't* going alright.

'Fine,' I replied.

'That's OK then. Bit lonely on your own? Never mind, you'll have some company soon. Colin Andrews and Pat Delgado arrive on Friday-they're setting up in the farmyard- and that BBC man-Macnish-will be arriving about then. He's going to put a camera or something on one of those masts. See you.'

He hopped back into his Range-Rover, turned and drove off again the way he'd come. I stood and watched him go, speechless with rage! Surely not! He'd not pushed us out in favour of the BBC and the dynamic duo? Whilst I pondered long and hard on this another car approached. It was Jean-Francois Leichner. I told him what Farmer Brown had said. I was so angry at the farmer's apparent deceit that J-F walked me round the hill to cool me down. I couldn't understand why the farmer had done this. We had an agreement! J-F was philosophical. He offered the suggestion that perhaps the farmer was joking or had a very good reason for moving us. By the time we reached the caravan again I had cooled down a lot and Jacqui had arrived.

We brewed a cuppa and she told me that Rog had gone with Terence to Heathrow to pick up the first batch of Japs who would form Professor Ohtsuki's team. We moved outside and changed the batteries over as the voltage had dropped considerably. Jacqui also said that there were unconfirmed reports of circles in grass at Market Lavington, a few miles to the east. Jacqui and I decided to take the batteries to the farm and put them on charge before going to look for these circles. This we did but, at Market Lavington, there was no sign of any circles, so we returned to site. Rog arrived shortly after we did and reported that the first batch of Japs was now safely installed in a hotel in Devizes.

The evening was now growing dark and the weather became much cooler. Rog's carphone rang. It was Terence Meaden. After a chat, Rog came back into the caravan where we'd all retired, as it was warmer.

'That was Terence,' he said. 'He tells me that he has had a call from Alan Rayner-there is a formation on Farmer Horton's land, behind his metal barn. And there's one at Newton St Loe.'

'What! You mean near Bath?'

'Yep. And one near Prestwick airport at Glasgow and one near Cirencester.'

God's Teeth! After a slow start to the season it looked like things were now moving! Rog elected to stay the night at the caravan. J-F Leichner left and Jacqui and I stayed a while longer, standing on the top of the hill and watching the artillery firing bright yellow flares to illuminate the manouevres. A heavy bombardment followed. We left Rog to his own devices at about 23.30 and headed home.

Friday 21st June 1991

I got up fairly early and after breakfast went out to do a few necessary chores after which I went to Newton St Loe. The circles were apparently by the main London-Bristol railway line. In order to get a good idea of the location, I drove along the A4 from Bath towards Bristol and turned off at the Globe pub roundabout. I had the idea in mind that by driving up the hill to Twerton, a suburb of Bath, I could look back down over the entire area in question, locate the circles and, returning to the A4, use one of two footpaths to get to the formation. However, from the top of the hill all I could see was fields of wheat. No circles.

I went back down the hill to the A4 and parked up in a gateway by a blue Ford Orion. Wondering briefly if this car belonged to Colin Andrews as he drove an Orion, I walked along the track to the railway. The railway here runs through the fields on a long embankment. I climbed this embankment to get a better view of the crops. No circles.

Walking back to the car I pondered over a map. There was another track a few hundred yards nearer to Bristol. I walked to this track and repeated the previous exercise. Once again I clambered up the railway embankment and surveyed the crop with my binoculars. Aha! There was a small patch of crop damage. It could be a circle. There was an object in the centre.... I scrambled down the bank and made my way carefully through the crop.

It was merely ordinary crop lodging. The object in the centre was an animal drinking trough.

So where were the circles? I had scanned the fields all around, both sides of the A4 and both sides of the railway embankment and had seen nothing. Deciding that this was probably a hoax report I went back to my Capri and drove off up the A4 towards Morgan's Hill. It took nearly an hour and when I drove up the hill, passing through the two gates, I found Rog alone.

He came out of the caravan looking tired and far away.

'Did you have a good night?' I enquired.

'No. First the army kept up a barrage for nearly an hour, then the wind got up and the caravan was buffeted by sudden shocks of wind for ages. Then it rained.' He sighed. 'I'm off home to bed.'

He wasted no time in getting into his car and driving off. I settled down for another day's cropwatching. It was another quiet day. At lunchtime a Philips Telecom van arrived to work at the masts behind us. At two-fifteen Terence arrived followed by an estate car. This turned out to be a chap named Paul Izzard from the company that was loaning us an automatic weather station. After introductions he and Terence got to work setting up this gadget a few yards away from the caravan.

The Philips van left at two-twenty five and as he departed so another car drew up. This was Professor Ohtsuki with one of his Japanese colleagues. Behind them another estate car was arriving. There were more introductions. Terence introduced me to the Japanese and then to the somewhat scruffy group of three or four people from the estate car. These latter (who it must be said, wouldn't have looked out of place amongst a group of some of the tidier New Age travellers) were a camera crew from a company called '*Juniper*' who were following Terence around that summer making a film on behalf of TV's *'Equinox'* series. They did some filming and were gone after about 15 minutes to meet and film Richard Andrews.

J-F Leichner now arrived. Ohtsuki told us that he had some 'pretty expensive' camera equipment coming over from Japan later that week. As a group of his students were also arriving then, the professor was hiring a mobile home to get around in. I took Ohtsuki and his colleague up onto the Wansdyke to show them the area where circles had formed below in previous years. M.Leichner then took the Japs to the other side of the hill and I took the opportunity to buttonhole Terence and ask him what he thought of Farmer Brown's comments regarding Macnish and co.

The professor frowned. 'I spoke with Macnish only last night,' he said. 'He claims he has nothing whatsoever to do with Andrews and his group.'

'But Farmer Brown claims that Andrews and Delgado will be setting up their equipment in Woolley's farmyard on Friday!' I countered.

'I don't believe it!' snapped the professor. 'No-one has any idea about their watch this year. It seems likely that they won't have one at all.'

Then he reached into his pocket, pulled out an envelope and handed it to me without a word.

It was a letter I'd written to the supposed landowner of the fields around Yarnbury circles asking for permission to enter his land. It had been returned to *CERES* by the Post Office. I'd put the wrong village address on it.

'Did you see the Newton St Loe circles?' asked the Prof.

'No,' I said. 'I tried all sorts of locations and even went up the hill towards Twerton, but couldn't see anything.'

Giving me a funny look, Terence strode off to the caravan and I followed, my tail between my legs.

At the caravan Terence took a sheet of paper and sketched a circle with a corridor and a smaller circle. He added a series of two or three boxes to one side of the formation. He handed it to me.

'Where's this?' I asked.

'Newton St Loe of course!' he retorted. 'My contact filmed it from the steps of an old signal on the railway embankment.'

I knew exactly where he meant. The signal was not an old signal. It was still very much in use but could do with a coat of paint. But the main point was that I'd been at that very location earlier and had not seen anything. This was bloody odd!

'Anyway, my son and his friend will visit this formation and measure and film it,' said the Prof. J-F Leichner came into the caravan. 'Terence, Professor Ohtsuki is ready to leave now.'

So was Paul Izzard. It seemed that the plan was for them all to visit the formation reported at Horton's barn and then for J-F to take the Japs to their hotel in Devizes whilst Terence went home for his dinner. J-F would then come back to relieve me so I could get some food. They went off in convoy and were shortly replaced by Jacqui, Andrew Woolley and one of his farmhands. Whilst Woolley and his workmate set to work with a tractor stacking silage bales, I filled Jacqui in on the day's events. After a while it seemed obvious that something had held J-F up, so Jacqui went off to find a shop and get me a snack. Meanwhile I changed the batteries.

Jacqui soon returned with a couple of sandwiches and some milk so I brewed tea. Whilst we ate, we wondered who would be coming along for the night stint. Nobody had heard from Paul Fuller (whose turn it was) but at nine-thirty he arrived in the company of Eddie Brown. I gave them both the run-down of the previous twenty-four hours events.

'Oh-oh. I don't like the sound of this,' muttered Paul, sipping his tea. 'If Macnish is moving in here with Condrews then I certainly won't be staying around to help!'

J-F Leichner arrived and, the site being well-staffed, Jacqui and I left for home just after midnight. Paul and Eddie settled down in front of the small gas fire to watch the radar as the weather cleared and the temperature dropped.

I finally got to bed at around 0200 on the morning of the 22nd June. At ten past seven the phone woke me up. It was Terence Meaden.

'There are circles formed at Lockeridge,' he said. 'It's important that someone goes to measure and film them. I can't go because I have to see professor Ohtsuki. You will have to go.'

Now, the worst thing that anyone can do is disturb my sleep. I wasn't quite with it after only five hours kip and thought Meaden had said '*Stockbridge*'- which was near Winchester, so there was no way under the sun that I was going to leap into action and speed off down to Winchester after only five hours in the pit! I declined to go and the Prof. got a bit stroppy and said he'd detail someone else. Fine. I didn't mind who went. Besides, I knew for a fact that there was a big travellers camp there, where a mass of hippies had gathered after being turned back from Stonehenge by the police. So any circles were sure to be hoaxes. Meaden rang off.

Later that morning I went to Morgan's Hill and relieved Paul and Eddie. They'd had a quiet night. I told them of Meaden's early phone call. 'He'll just have to go there himself,' grinned Paul. 'He can't expect us to run the cropwatch *and* do all his running around. I'll be back this afternoon,' he called as he and Eddie Brown left. Eddie had the longest journey: he lived in Bournemouth.

The morning and early afternoon was cold, overcast and rainy. I changed the batteries and put the old pair in my car ready for moving down to the farm for charging. The batteries were giving some concern; they should have lasted for up to 12 hours but were lasting less than eight even after a 19-hour charge. Something wasn't right. Perhaps we had a power leak down to earth. I looked over the wiring. All seemed ok.

A car arrived. The occupant introduced himself as a reporter from the *Observer*.

'Dr Meaden is supposed to be here soon. He's holding a press conference to release his new book,' explained the man. Press conference? That was the first I'd heard of that! Terence had said some days ago that he was going to tell the press about the book but hadn't told us he was going to hold a press conference at our 'secret' site. A few days before, Rog, Terence and I had been photographed at the site by the *Western Daily Press* and we'd gone to great pains to ensure that the camera angles hadn't shown the easily recognisable masts in the background and that the text hadn't mentioned Morgan's Hill. Now the national press was turning up. What next?

A photographer from the *Observer* was what was next. The two chatted together as a huge mobile home struggled into view and drove across the grass to the caravan. It was Professor Ohtsuki and a crowd of young Japanese lads-presumably his students. With Ohtsuki on site I went off to the farm and put the batteries on charge. On my return I found that a couple of photographers from the *Daily Telegraph* had joined the two men from the *Observer*. Then, another car arrived with one of Meaden's *TORRO* colleagues, Keith Mortimore and his wife in it. They'd come to set up a Stevenson's Screen (weather monitoring equipment).

Five minutes later, a convoy of six other vehicles wound its way across the grass to join the three other cars and a mobile home already there. With my car that made eleven vehicles parked on the field. So much for a 'secret site'! The only consolation was that this little lot couldn't be seen from the road - I only hoped nobody had seen them driving up the hill. Farmer Brown would be quite justified in throwing us all off the hill!

Then Paul Fuller and Rog arrived making thirteen vehicles in all.

The Japanese students were great fun. They spoke almost perfect English and were more interested in studying the *Racing Weekly* than crop circles – that is when Ohtsuki wasn't around! Apparently some of them were going to Ireland when their part of the cropwatch was over and they were going to the races there!

The weather turned cold and rainy now so Paul, Rog and I retired to the caravan whilst the press interviewed Terence Meaden and Yoshi-Hito Ohtsuki and photographers took their pictures at various locations around the site. We watched the press circus in silence. Paul was disgusted at the amount of press on site. ' This isn't good at all,' he muttered. 'It's getting more like *Blackbird* every minute!'

Eventually the press all left in one big convoy, Meaden and Ohtsuki with them. Some Japanese students were staying overnight so the three of us thankfully left at nine after giving them instructions on batteries and radar.

Overnight the students faithfully kept the log. At eleven-fifty they recorded what they first wrote in as 'Ball Lightning' but later amended it to what it really was – more army flares! The night was mainly cloudless and cold but as dawn approached so did cloud and by the time I arrived at the bottom of Morgan's Hill it was raining. I went straight to the farmyard to recover a set of batteries that had (again) been on charge for 19 hours or more and put them in the boot of my Capri.

At the hill I drove through the lower gate and closed it behind me. Half way up to the top gate I saw another car approaching me. It was a blue Ford Orion and as it passed I recognised the driver – Colin Andrews! I hurried on towards the caravan, heart in my mouth. Farmer Brown had been right!

At the caravan I found a dismal scene. The radar was at a standstill, the batteries having gone flat overnight. The rain was now pouring down and everything was waterlogged. The students headed for Ohtsuki's motorhome and warmth. There were Japanese everywhere now, forming a procession to and from the Wansdyke. I wandered over to see what the attraction was and found a large camera on a stand pointing down onto David Shepherd's fields. Presumably this was part of Ohtsuki's equipment. I went back to the caravan where I changed the batteries and loaded the dead pair into my car.

A quick trip to the farmyard to put these batteries on charge and I returned to the top of the hill to find more people milling around and a blue minibus parked on the grass. Terence Meaden's car was also there. I searched him out. Finding him by the Wansdyke, I took him to one side.

'Terence, this is becoming a bit of a shambles,' I said. 'What are all these people doing here? And what was Colin Andrews doing here earlier?'

Meaden looked sad. 'I-I really don't know...' he said at last.

'We cannot allow that to happen again!' I said. Meaden just shrugged.

The rain poured down.

'Come with me,' said the Prof. I followed him to where a short, stocky Japanese whom I'd not seen before was joining some cables together. Meaden introduced me to 'Mr. Ogawa of NTV'. It seemed that NTV, who were a Japanese TV company, had Colin Andrews under contract to them and had brought him onto our site to conduct an interview with him. But what was NTV doing there in the first place? Terence now excused himself and went off to his car where his wife was waiting. I walked to the caravan only to find it full of Japs! They were installing a video recorder and monitor for the Wansdyke camera. Why in our caravan? Just who were they? I was baffled by all this. Terence hadn't mentioned that all this was going to happen. A young white man whom Meaden had thought was an interpreter for the Japs came into the caravan and started to fix wires to the monitor. I asked him if he could convey our feelings to Ogawa (who spoke little English-apparently) that Colin Andrews should not be brought onto our site again. His reply shocked me.

'I'm the UK contact for NTV and I can answer your question,' he replied stiffly. 'We are contracted with Colin Andrews and we will bring him here as many times as we like.'

I was aghast! 'You can't do that! This is *CERES* site!' I exclaimed.

He stood up from his work and looked at me in an arrogant way before replying.

'I know there is friction between Terence Meaden and Colin Andrews but that's not my problem. I have a contract and I'll bring Colin here whenever I like.' He bent to his wiring again.

'Well, .you can keep him out of our caravan!' I retorted, angrily before leaving the caravan and going out into the rain. Meaden approached.

'My wife and I are going for lunch,' he said. 'Would you like to join us?'

I was, by now, soaked through and very angry. I politely declined his offer on the grounds that I'd look daft sitting in a restaurant in a pool of water. He nodded and left. I made for the caravan again only to find NTV still installing their equipment, a Japanese camera crew filming them doing it and several of Ohtsuki's students crammed in the only spaces left. You couldn't have swung a cat! There was nowhere to go except my car. I spent an hour or so sitting damply in the Capri whilst the ever-busy Japs installed a mobile generator. Then as the rain appeared to ease, I left the car and wandered to the top gate. A car came up the hill and I opened the gate for them. They were press. Once I'd closed the gate so another lot arrived. I spent the rest of the afternoon opening and closing gates for various press. I was very, very wet.

It was a puzzle to work out just what was going on. It seemed that Ohtsuki was working with NTV who were working with Andrews and Delgado. Terence didn't seem to have much say in what was going on. Why he had said nothing I didn't know. So much for a quiet summer's cropwatching at a secret location. The world would know where we were now. A blue minibus packed full of Japs approached the top gate. Ohtsuki's motorhome was behind it. I opened the gate and they passed through. Closing the gate I thankfully headed back to the caravan.

The *CERES* HQ looked as if it had recently returned from a pop festival. The inside was littered with paper, labels, empty drink cartons and tins. There was mud everywhere. Muttering angrily to myself and casting aspersions on the sex and ancestry of various people, I cleared the mess up and lit the gas fire to get some warmth into the damp caravan.

Eventually in late afternoon, Terence Meaden returned with his wife and J-F Leichner. They all came into the caravan and I put the kettle on. Whilst the kettle boiled, I told Meaden what the NTV Englishman had said concerning Colin Andrews. Meaden said nothing, just looked very sad.

Mrs. Meaden seemed shocked by my revelations. 'This is no good!' she cried. 'Terry, you must tell them to take their cameras away!'

Her husband said nothing.

Jean-Francois Leichner broke the uneasy silence by talking about a possible French plan to finance laboratory experiments with plasma-vortices and talk then turned to a planned conference on the subject to be provisionally held in 1992 in – Antwerp! Meaden also produced photos of the earlier Chilcomb formation. These were copies of pictures taken by the Americans who'd ventured into the circles. Terence passed them round. I studied the pictures closely. I still wasn't convinced: the circles were rough and ready. Jean-Francois ventured the opinion that it looked like the circles had been made '....by people trampling the crop....' I asked the Prof. what he thought now. '...I...don't really know....' was his reply.[1]

Soon, Terence said it was time for him to leave.

'Professor Ohtsuki and his students will man the site tonight,' he announced. 'So there is no need for you, Peter, or Roger to stay. I will call Roger on his mobile phone and tell him. The rain is likely to stay for a day or two anyway.'

After the Meadens and J-F had gone, I locked the caravan and walked to my car. I was still soaked to the skin and hadn't eaten since breakfast at 0700 that morning. It was now twelve hours later and I was starving. And still angry!

I drove home, had a hot bath and made myself some food. Then I wrote up the day's notes – just for the record!

Chapter Twelve
WARM WET CIRCLES

Rain-MoreRain-Circlevision move in-Circles appear under suspicious circumstances

That evening, Jacqui and then Rog arrived and we retired to the Bull for beer and a conference. I explained the day's proceedings to them. Jacqui put her glass of *'White Lightning'* down heavily on the table.

'So, it seems that we've gone to all the trouble to find and equip the caravan and are now being pushed out,' she snorted.

'That's about the long and the short of it,' I agreed. 'NTV have installed their equipment in the caravan and presumably will be using it there.'

'Did Terence ever mention that Ohtsuki was going to do this?' she continued.

I swigged at my 6X. 'Not that I've ever heard,' I said. 'I'm sure he would have told us.'

'So,' she went on, 'Colin Andrews can come and go on our site whenever he wants to?'

I sighed. 'Yep.'

'Well, this isn't good enough. We'll have to raise this with Terence!' she snapped.

Rog and I agreed. 'I'll come up with you tomorrow,' said Rog. 'We'll have a word with Terence if we see him.'

Monday 24th June 1991

Rog and I made our way to Morgan's Hill, arriving at around eleven. It was still pouring with rain. As we arrived at the site we noticed the radar scanner had stopped again....Examining the log, it seemed that the radar had stopped at 01.23 in the morning, the batteries having lasted only eight hours. NTV's generator had packed up as well. We took the batteries to the farm and brought back the spare set. The weather being still wet we didn't bother starting the radar. By lunchtime fog had set in. One of Meaden's friends called in. He was the man who'd lent the batteries. We told him that there seemed to be a problem with them.

'Shouldn't be,' he said. 'They're good batteries. Perhaps there's an earth leakage.'

I said we'd already looked for that but would try again. He said he'd call again the following day, and left. We switched the radar on. The batteries lasted a couple of hours. Ohtsuki now arrived with some students so Rog and I went to the *Waggon and Horses* for a late lunch. In the bar were Stanley Morcomb and Ralph Noyes so we sat with them. Ralph told us that the CCCS were '...on the verge of calling off their watch....' because of the miserable weather.

'Have you seen the Lockeridge formation yet?' asked Noyes. I replied in the negative.

'Why don't we all go up there and take a look?' he suggested.

Good idea. It would be nice to see something of the object of our watch at last!

After lunch we all drove up to the site of the circles, a mile or so from Alton Barnes. From the road nothing but the familiar 'shadow' could be seen and it was so wet that we didn't venture in. We didn't have permission anyway. Then another of Terence's friends arrived.

The Hon.George Bathurst was a retired gentleman who had a hobby in meteorology and frequently wrote articles for *J.Met.*

'Have you been in yet? He said, in clipped tones.

We said we hadn't.

'Right. I'll see if I can find the farmer!' he said and drove off.

Ten minutes later he was back, parking his old red Renault in a nearby gateway.

'Farmer's not in,' he said.

We left him gazing at the distant formation and went our separate ways: Ralph and Stanley back to the CCCS cropwatch and Rog and I to Avebury where we had a cream tea!

After Avebury we went back to the caravan and found it Jap-free! Rog left at six, as he had a riding lesson and I stayed on my own. There were no Japs around and the rain still poured. Time passed slowly and it was eight-thirty when I heard the sound of an engine and went outside to see who it was. A small motor-home pulled up. On its side were the words 'CLOUD 9'.

I stood and watched as the vehicle stood, engine ticking over as the driver gazed at the gate onto the Wansdyke. He noticed me and got out of the cab.

'Hi,' he said in a Scottish accent. 'Where can I park?'

'Not here, I'm afraid. This is private land. We're conducting a scientific survey. You'll have to go back down the hill.'

The driver seemed slightly bemused. 'No, no,' he said. 'I'm part of this set up.' He handed me a business card on which was written '*Skystalk Surveillance. Cloud 9 systems. M.Carrie – Director*'.

'That's me,' he said. 'Mike Carrie. I'm looking for somewhere to set up my surveillance equipment on behalf of John Macnish...'

WHAT! For a moment or two I was speechless. Eventually I managed to say '*Macnish...?*'

'Aye,' replied the Scot. 'He's running some sort of watch here along with David

Morgenstern, Colin Andrews and a bloke called Pat Delgado – This is Morgan's Hill, ain't it?'

'Y-yes, but you can't stop here-we've got permission to use this site!'

Carrie grew impatient. 'WE have the farmer's permission to be here!' he snapped.

Slowly, out of the mist, something was beginning to dawn on me and it involved Farmer Brown, Andrews, Ogawa, Macnish and a conspiracy...

Meanwhile, when Rog had left the site earlier, he went via the farmyard where, acting on a hunch, he checked the battery charger. His hunch was correct-the charging rate had been deliberately altered. That was why the batteries were going flat so soon. They weren't getting anywhere near a proper charge. He put the charging rate right and went on his way.

We never found out who changed the charging rate but, as the world and its granny knew where we were now, it could have been one of a dozen or more suspects. Someone who wanted the radar to be dormant while they carried out a hoax, perhaps? If so, they obviously didn't understand what radar did. Or perhaps they just didn't know exactly what equipment we were using and wanted it stopped anyway to avoid any chance of being seen.

Back on the hill, Carrie and his van had gone away at last – to where I didn't know. I couldn't believe this was happening. First the caravan was taken over by NTV and we were frequently pushed out, then Colin Andrews arrives and we're told he would come on to our site whenever NTV wanted him to, now Macnish and co were moving in.

What the hell was going on?

Even the weather was against us. Fog had been covering the hill now for over four hours. At nine-forty-five, with the fog showing no sign of lifting and no sign of anyone coming for the night shift, I packed up and left. When I arrived home, in spite of the fact that it was nearly eleven-thirty, I phoned Paul Fuller straight away. A sleepy voice answered the phone. 'Hullo?'

'Paul-it's Pete...'

'Oh, hi, Pete. What's up – has a vortex landed?'

'NO. Worse than that...'

I filled him in on the evening's events. Understandably he was horrified.

'How is this happening?' he asked, rhetorically. 'WE were supposed to have the hill to ourselves...how come Macnish and all these loonies are moving in?'

'God knows,' I said. 'It's all going wrong. I wonder what Terence will say?'

We'd find out on the following day.

Tuesday 25th June 1991

The day started badly. It was still raining. I was sitting in my car outside the post office in the village where I lived when my car was suddenly struck from behind by another vehicle driven by two young girls. To cut a long story short, I discovered that they had taken the car without permission of a relative and the driver had no licence. The Police were called and found out that she also had no insurance (when it came to court she was charged with 7 other offences as well). The Capri was still driveable although the back end was somewhat rearranged, so I was able to go to the hill that afternoon.

I arrived, in the rain, at 14.00 and was followed up the hill by Mike Carrie's Cloud 9 van. At the top of the hill, in the spot where we'd originally parked our caravan were two big cream-coloured motorhomes. People were roaming all around the front of the hill carrying equipment. The obviously recognisable equipment was sound detectors and cameras. I recognised David Morgenstern from the *Blackbird* TV coverage of 1990.

I got to the caravan and found J-F there. He said that Meaden's friend, Mike Rutty, the man who'd supplied the batteries, had been and was told by Rog that the charging rate had been changed. He had checked everything and was satisfied that the altered charging rate was the reason for the flat batteries. This of course, was the first I'd heard of it, so you can imagine that my already bad mood turned foul!

J-F left and I settled down to the routine of checking the weather station and recording the data. This was part of the duty site officer's task. Every hour he/she had to record the time/ wind direction/ wind strength/ cloud cover/ cloud type and range of visibility. If conditions were right for circles to form, then it was 'High Alert' and recordings were taken every fifteen minutes or more. This was reckoned to be an important task according to Terence Meaden. Of course, this could only be done if we could get in our caravan....

The rain still came down. Visibility was only a few dozen yards. Japs were everywhere. Rog arrived at six-thirty and looked sadly at the circus of which we were now a very small part. He said little and we sat and took data until Terence arrived at eight. His reaction to seeing the new arrival on the hill and in the very place which Farmer Brown had moved us away from?

He didn't seem in the least bit surprised.

Very odd behaviour, indeed.

Meaden wouldn't be drawn into talking about the new arrivals and I was in a hell of a mood so we avoided each other for the rest of that day.

The Duty Officer's Log records that Morgenstern and Carrie were about that afternoon and *CERES* had a visit from Paul Izzard of the Didcot Instrument Co. The weather settled down to a mixture of occasional rain and fog. I was at the caravan when we had a visit from David Morgenstern. He came into the caravan where I was clearing up after some NTV Japs.

'Hi,' he said and introduced himself. 'Look, we want to cooperate with *CERES*,' he said, aware of the icy atmosphere. I looked at him, coldly.

'My personal view is that as long as Andrews and Delgado are involved, then that won't be possible,' I replied. Any outfit with the CPR twosome involved would necessarily mean that they got all the publicity and Meaden's work would be sneered at, as it had been by them for the past couple of years.

Morgenstern said, 'They aren't involved.'

I laughed at him.

'Look, we know they are contracted to NTV and NTV have said they'll bring Andrews and Delgado here whenever they want. You are working with NTV so that means you are working with Colin and Pat.'

Morgenstern couldn't answer that. The rain started again and lashed at the window, drumming on the caravan's roof.

'And another thing,' I went on, 'As long as you and your programmes keep the "unknown intelligence" theory going, you'll all make money. If Terence Meaden was to pop up and prove that his vortex is responsible, solving the entire problem, then there'd be no more dosh in it-would there?'

Morgenstern's face lit up in a wide grin at this. He obviously had thought of that!
However, I had no authority to tell him to take a running jump off Morgan's Hill so I suggested he speak with Terence Meaden when he was free.
By now Macnish and his crew had equipment all over the place, including in the mast compound behind the caravan. As I left to go to the farmyard I could see the motorhomes on the front of the hill not only from the bottom of the hill but from the road and from the farmyard. It was now obvious that Farmer Brown had sold us out, moved us away from the front of the hill to make way for Macnish and his set up. When I arrived at the farmyard I discovered even more telling evidence of their presence. There, behind the barn and in full view of the road and the surrounding area, was a forty-odd foot mobile tower with cameras and other gear on it! It bore the legend 'Cloud 9'.
The farmer couldn't say that he was afraid of travellers noticing the *CERES* site-anyone who passed could see Macnish's setup. Although in reality it was now obvious that it was *us* who'd been set-up.
I returned home later that evening and phoned Paul Fuller. He was saddened to hear about the situation and vowed to try and collar Meaden for a meeting later that week.

'Eddie and I are of the firm opinion that *CERES* ought to pull out and go somewhere else,' he concluded.

Terence Meaden stayed on site all night to cover the 24th/25th shift. The morning of the 25th dawned with fine weather, spoiled by the odd shower. Rog turned up at 09.30 and shortly after was joined by various members of the press and radio. More Japs arrived. Terence was soon busy with interviews for newspapers and radio stations concerning his book '*The Goddess of the Stones*'. Even Rog managed to get in on the act, being interviewed by GWR radio about his part in the cropwatch. TVS had sent along a camera crew who took over the caravan to film various Japanese watching OUR radar and NTV's monitor.

And, at last, the sun came out. Which was just as well because as usual there was no room in the caravan and our team was out in the cold again.

Terence had moved into the caravan by now to be filmed by TVS. What happened next caused quite a stir.

At approx. 10.35, whilst demonstrating the ranges of the radar, the assembled audience had their attention drawn to an unidentified echo which appeared on the screen from the south-west and crossed the screen rapidly heading in a north-easterly direction. Meaden jokingly said that this was probably '....a UFO...' and all present rushed outside to see what it was. But it had gone.

What was it? Later on, Terence said that it was most likely to have been a meteorite. It certainly appeared to be travelling very fast indeed. From the distance of years and of experience, I personally would surmise that it was possibly a RAF or Navy jet fighter -- perhaps a Tornado or a Harrier – flying low across the terrain below the hills. It is not impossible that the radar signal travelled out from the hill and picked up the fighter. Certainly the area covered was in a MOD air corridor. If this was the case, then we were extremely lucky that the aircraft did not detect the radar signal and send back a 'jamming' transmission. This would have, in all probability, damaged the radar set and *CERES* would have had a lot of explaining to do to Marconi![1]

The weather now being warm, Rog was taken off by the TVS crew to be filmed in the Yatesbury circles. The wheat was still wet after all the recent rain and they all got soaked again.

Terence Meaden went home at about mid-day.

That afternoon, I had a phone call from Paul Fuller. He told me about the 'UFO' incident and that he'd been in touch with Meaden and they'd 'had words'.

'I wanted him to arrange a meeting with us all to discuss what was going wrong,' said the UFOlogist. 'I'm afraid that I ran down the entire operation, Pete,' he sighed. 'It's got too silly, what with all the Japs taking over our site, Macnish and Morgenstern muscling in and all the press – it's not good for *CERES* at all.'

'What did Meaden say?' I asked.

'Nothing much – he wouldn't listen and cut me short before saying he was busy and ringing off. He's going to get set up, Pete. Jenny (Randles), Eddie Brown and myself can see it coming. He's let all the loonies in and takes no notice of us. We're afraid that he's leaving himself wide open for someone to set him up like Pat and Colin were.'

This was true. Terence was now obviously enjoying the publicity. The entire *CERES* watch was ruined. Everyone knew where we were and the facilities that we'd worked so hard to put together were being used by everyone except us. All we were doing was opening and closing the gates for the visitors and guarding the caravan when NTV weren't there.

Which was what I said to Jacqui that evening at the *Bull*.

'Did you see that Terence was on the local TV news tonight-going on about some UFO he saw on the radar?' she said.

I groaned. 'No. I didn't see it-thank God! But Paul did. He phoned me up in horror. Terence of all people talking about seeing a UFO!'

Outside the rain had started again and it was now absolutely pissing down. The pub door opened and in walked a very wet – no – *soaked* Rog. He went straight to the bar without a glance to left or right and ordered a pint. He joined us and sat down soggily, a rather fed-up look on his face.

'Well?' I asked

'What's gone on today?' said Jacqui.

Rog glanced moodily at us.

'Nothing much,' he said and sipped his beer.

'What were Macnish and Morgenstern up to? I demanded.

He didn't answer straight away, then: 'Nothing. Haven't seen them,' he said tersely.

He wasn't in the mood for talking it seemed.

I was. 'Aren't they there?'

Rog looked at me. 'No.'

He wasn't going to open up. But I was fed up with the whole affair. Having my car smashed up hadn't helped, especially as the whole repair job was going to cost me money, as the other party wasn't insured.

'The whole cropwatch has gone stale!' I declared. 'The caravan we bought for *CERES* use is invaded by Japs. NTV are using the place as not only a monitoring room but as a base when Ogawa and his mini-bus are off on some trip. It's getting pretty stupid! They use our facilities while we run around in the rain! And above all, we aren't doing any real cropwatching- we're just guarding a bloody caravan! Paul, Jenny and Eddie are not at all happy with it either,' I added, drumming up moral support. '...In fact, they fear that Terence will leave himself wide open to a hoax along the lines of *Blackbird*!'

I paused for breath. Rog just shrugged and swigged his pint.

'Terence is just using us as 'tea-boys', put in Jacqui. 'He isn't interested in our contribution now that he's got all those Japanese around. That's because they are *real* scientists I suppose.....'

'NO!' snapped Rog. 'That's not the case.....'- But he didn't say what was...

'I just wish he would tell us just what the hell is going on! Everyone whom we've been led to believe is bad for *CERES* is turning up on site and being allowed to do so without his objections! He won't be drawn into talking about it. He seems happy for them to be there.' I was getting angrier by the minute.

Rog looked down at the table. 'Terence just isn't concerned about Macnish and co,' he said simply.

'Well,' I retorted, 'It makes us look pretty stupid then! He's in league with them if he won't push them out!'

Jacqui intervened and changed the conversation slightly.

'I'm going to town tomorrow,' she said. 'To buy a copy of the *Goddess of the Stones* as the free copy Terence promised us hasn't materialised.'

This was another bone of contention. Meaden had promised us all a free copy of the book we'd helped to promote by way of doing all the ground work for the cropwatch whilst he went off and did lectures, book-signings and TV appearances. So far, no freebie had appeared. [2]

Rog mellowed. He pulled a soggy leaflet out of his pocket.

'Some Yanks gave me this when I was at Yatesbury this afternoon,' he said.

Jacqui took it. The leaflet set out details of a three-day event to be held at Glastonbury during July. It was called the 'Corn Circle Experience' –or something like that. Speakers included Colin Andrews, Busty Taylor, Richard Andrews, John Michell, George Wingfield and the Earl of Haddington. Lectures were all priced separately, the cheapest being £10. Busty and Richard were also organising bus tours of circles sites.

Jacqui read all this with her eyes growing wider by the sentence. Eventually she spoke.

'We're on the wrong bloody side!' she cried.

I sighed. She was right. It was amazing; they had it all sown up. They were all on the money trail and having a lot of fun into the bargain, whilst all we were doing was guarding a bloody caravan in the rain!

We *were* on the wrong side!

Just to complete a perfect couple of days, Jacqui and I had a major 'domestic' on the way home and went our separate ways that evening. The relationship, increasingly rocky of late, was now effectively at an end.

The next day the site was manned, on occasions, by Japs. Nothing much happened and there's no record of where Terence and Ohtsuki were. I stayed at home, making my damaged car legal as some lights had stopped working after the collision. What Rog and Jacqui did I have no idea.

Thursday 27th June 1991

I spent the morning at work and later in the day set off for Morgan's Hill. It was raining as usual. I went via Beckhampton by way of a change of scenery and arrived at the bottom of the hill at around 19.30. I got out of the car long enough to change into my wellies and open the gate before venturing through rivers of water up the hill. I noted that the 'sky-stalk' wasn't visible for some reason but Macnish's two caravans were still pretty obvious to all and sundry. At the top gate I had to wait while a couple of wet horses with soggy riders passed. As I moved onward to our site, I noticed two red cars, one of which was Macnish's Stag, parked next to the motorhomes. There was no other sign of life.

At the caravan I found Rog, Terence and a newcomer. The latter was introduced as Robert Mackenzie, a balloonist who had researched some circles in Buckinghamshire on Terence's behalf. He showed us some pretty good photos of circles that he'd taken from a balloon. 'I hope to come along later when the weather is better,' he said, 'And bring along my "hedgehopper". It's a one-man balloon, which you wear on a harness similar to that of a parachutist. It would be perfect for looking at circles without going into the field on foot,' he explained.

He also had a selection of very interesting camera gear, which Meaden took a good look at, announcing that this could be of great help to *CERES*. Mackenzie left soon after, promising to keep in touch. To the best of my knowledge we didn't see him again.

Once the caravan was free of visitors, I challenged Terence about Macnish.

'Terence, are you involved with Macnish in any way?'

Outside there was a timely, if theatrical, clap of thunder in the distance.

Meaden thought briefly before replying, 'No.'

'Do you not think that Farmer Brown has let us down?' I asked.

Meaden's reply was swift. 'No – considering that he doesn't know that they are here!'

'But,' I went on, '...Brown was at Andrew Woolley's farmyard the other evening when that mast was there –he can't have missed it! And the motorhomes are clearly visible from the farmyard....'

From Terence's behaviour I could see that he wasn't interested in this line of conversation.

'All I can say is that Andrew Woolley told me that Brown didn't know about Macnish and also that it seems that NTV are jointly sponsoring both Ohtsuki and Macnish.'

This was difficult to swallow. I knew from my conversation with Morgenstern that NTV were working with him and Macnish, and now we knew that they were working with Ohtsuki as well.

'So, we now have the entire *Operation Blackbird* crew here, parked on the side of the hill where Brown said we couldn't stay because we'd attract travellers, and they are more

obvious to travellers that we would ever have been!' I was like a bulldog – I wasn't going to let go until I had the truth!
Meaden was growing more impatient to close the conversation.

'Anyway,' he said, shortly. 'Let's not waste time talking about such people.... Robert Mackenzie has much to offer us with his balloons...'

The conversation was now closed.

The sound of a car outside announced the arrival of another visitor. This turned out to be Jacqui. She came into the caravan and asked if she could borrow my waterproof trousers as she wanted to go and photograph some Hares she'd noticed in the next field. I threw her the car keys and she took the waterproofs from the boot of my car and went off to find the Hares.

'I'm thinking of organising a 'workshop' for Professor Ohtsuki to demonstrate his work,' announced Terence. 'This will be, possibly, on Thursday of next week...'

'I won't be able to be there,' I said, 'I have to work.'

'Me neither,' said Rog.

Terence was not disappointed. 'Maybe we can arrange it for Friday instead.'

'That would be OK for me,' I said, 'Although I don't feel that you have to arrange it round me – I haven't any useful contribution to make. Paul's contributions would be important.'

'It is important that everyone is present to *learn*,' said Terence. 'Professor Ohtsuki has some very interesting films to show.' He went on, a slight air of excitement in his voice, from which we gathered that Ohtsuki's films would be worth seeing. Jacqui returned, and as she did so, Ohtsuki's motorhome hove in sight. It was still raining, so we left Terence and his Japanese counterpart to it and went off for a pint.

Against my better feelings we went to the *Waggon and Horses*. There we found Alan Rayner and a couple of people we'd seen before, so we all got talking at the bar. The pub landlord joined in the conversation and during the evening I discovered that his father was a tenant farmer who farmed land near Bath. Asking whereabouts, I was told 'Newton St. Loe'.

Now, this was very interesting indeed, because Paul and I had been cultivating the theory that many hoaxed circles were 'association hoaxes', IE: the hoaxers were making a mystery for the researchers. For example, if a researcher said that he'd found circles in a place in Hampshire, then circles would frequently appear in similarly named places in other counties. If Busty said that it was strange that circles hadn't yet appeared in one place, then shortly afterwards-they would. In cases such as this, circles had appeared on land farmed by the father of the landlord who ran the pub most favoured (at that time) by circles researchers. This would be seen by many of the 'Unknown Intelligence' brigade as being the work of the 'Cosmic Joker' or evidence of the mischievous nature of the circlemakers. We (Paul and I) tended to think that it showed evidence of human intelligence......

Anyway, the evening drew to a close and we three left and went our separate ways under clearing skies, the rain having stopped at long last.

The caravan was manned by Japanese students that night. By 01.00 they recorded that the weather was '....*Dry, Fine...*'. By 02.00 it was '...*Cloudy, Fog...*' and the comment was added: '...*It's fine but I can't see clouds because the fog is deep....*'. By 04.00 it was '...*Fog, Fog, Fog!*' and the windspeed had dropped to almost nil. By 06.00 the fog was still present.

As was something else...

At 08.45 I was woken by the telephone. It was Rog.

'A circle has formed at the bottom of Morgan's Hill!' he cried, excitedly.

I was puzzled. 'Surely the conditions weren't right...'

'Terence says the conditions were perfect. It was a still night....'

I was still not sure. 'Where was the warm weather? It's too cold, surely?'

'Terence is happy. He's satisfied that the conditions were right.'

'What about Macnish and Co.?'

'It seems that they hadn't got their equipment set up at the time...'[3]

I arranged to see him up at the hill and rang off. Shortly afterwards, the phone rang again. This time it was Jacqui (we were still on speaking terms).

'What d'you think of it?' she enquired.

'The circles? Well, it's a bit doubtful on the face of it...'

'Precisely! It's odd that Macnish and Morgenstern have had all their gear set up until last night, when they aren't ready!'

I agreed. 'Yes. This is just what Paul and Jenny were afraid of. That someone would try to hoax Terence, catch him out and make him look a fool. That would give Andrews and Delgado the lead again.'

Jacqui snorted. 'Well, it stinks to me!'

'And me. But we have to allow for the possibility that the circles may be genuine. Trouble is, if that's the case then the 'Opposition' will make much of the fact that we don't seem to have been looking in the right direction when the circles formed. It's just the sort of 'Mystic Prankster' that Colin's always on about. I only hope Terence doesn't rush in front of cameras to declare it genuine.'

'Yes. That's just what Andrews and Delgado would love! I bet the BBC made it in the middle of the night!' she went on. 'Anyway, I'm going up to video it. Can I borrow your camera poles?'

I said I'd leave the poles in the kitchen whilst I went to work (Jacqui still had the key to my place) and she'd call by and collect them later.

The day was sunny (typically as I was at work) and Jacqui set off for Morgan's Hill via my place. She got to the hill to find it almost deserted except for a pissed-off looking Rog who'd arrived earlier and been unable to do anything as he'd been left guarding the caravan, having relieved an excited Terence Meaden at 18.00. Little had happened since then; George Bathurst had arrived and straight away gone off to see the new circles and a trio of walkers had passed through and stopped for a chat. It was recorded in the log that the latter were '...fully supportive of the Vortex theory....'. When Rog and Jacqui were eventually relieved by Eddie Brown at 21.00, they couldn't see the circles from the hill or from ground level due to fading light, so decided not to bother and went to the *Waggon* instead.

There they found the CCCS 'Supreme Soviet' (George Wingfield, Michael Green, Busty Taylor, Ralph Noyes) having a committee meeting in the small room. When it was over, Lusty Busty came into the bar, saw Jacqui and made a beeline for her.

'Here,' he said. 'There's a CCCS Barbecue on tonight. Fancy coming?'

'Yeah. OK,' said Jacqui.

'Right. It's on Farmer Horton's land, you'll have to follow me,' said Busty.

In Jacqui's car, they followed him out of the pub car park and along the A4 a short distance before seeing his Metro turn off onto a farm track. They followed him along the track and past 'Firs Farm' where Farmer Horton lived. Onward for a further quarter of a mile then Busty stopped and got out of his car. Jacqui stopped. Busty came back to her and whispered 'Turn your lights off now and follow me again.'

They followed him again for a few hundred yards then Jacqui pulled up.

'I don't like this at all,' she said to Rog. There was no sign of any barbecue or, indeed, anything at all. 'I don't like this at all,' she repeated. 'There's something odd going on. I'm going back.'

With that, she turned the car round and headed back to the Waggon, where Rog retrieved his car and they went back to the caravan where they met up with Paul Fuller who was covering the night shift. They stayed with Paul until after midnight before setting off for their respective homes.

Paul spent a busy night on the hill. The generator supplied by NTV to provide the power for their cameras and monitor was a troublesome beast; it kept conking out. That night Paul was bothered by a NTV man who appeared and started the generator at the same time as Rog and Jacqui left. The generator spluttered to a halt seven times between half-past midnight and two-forty. NTV gave up and left, returning for another attempt at 08.55, just before Ohtsuki arrived with his students.

Some of this I learned when I phoned Jacqui from work the next morning. She reported that Terence had been '....Delighted....' with the circles.

I wasn't around during the morning of the 30th June, for reasons which my diary doesn't record. However, I can say that Colin Andrews was brought onto the site by NTV and interviewed on camera in front of Carrie's 'Cloud 9' van. Rog and Jacqui at last went into the circles and managed to video them. Their opinion? '....Probably genuine...'[4]

Jacqui came round to my place that afternoon and showed me the video footage of the circles. On the screen they didn't look too bad. There was a large circle with a small corridor leading to a smaller circle. She had also videoed the first of the year's dumb-bells, the one at Avebury Trusloe which we'd all got so wet measuring. This formation had now apparently grown a couple of extra spurs!

We decided to go up to Lockeridge, which had now got a new formation, another small dumb-bell. Packing the camera-poles into Jacqui's car we set off and went straight to the new circle, knowing that if we went to the hill we would, in all probability, get 'stung' to guard the caravan for the rest of the evening!

At the Lockeridge circles we found a small group of New Age fans[5] admiring the circles so we quietly went about a survey. We found evidence to suggest that the top circle had been made first, then someone or something had moved down the hill a few yards to make the second circle, leaving a trail of flattened stems as they/it went. Having made the second circle, they/it moved back up to the top circle again, laying down a wider corridor of flattened crop over the narrow trail made earlier. This wider corridor flowed UP the hill. The underlying flattened crop lay DOWN hill and was about the width that a person would make as they trod it flat moving down to the place where they would make the second circle. From this evidence we deduced that this formation was undoubtedly a hoax.

Having taken many pictures to illustrate our findings, we headed back to the caravan.

It was deserted. The caravan was locked up, the radar stopped and NTV's generator quiet. Back to the top of the hill where I took a few pictures of Macnish's motorhomes- which were now partly covered with camouflage netting. They were deserted. We moved to the bottom of the hill where we could still see the motorhomes in spite of the camouflage. From there we called in at the farmyard and found Terence Meaden there, putting batteries on charge.

'I'm staying at the hill with Yoshi Hito Ohtsuki for the evening,' he explained. 'We've had a busy afternoon with lots of visitors. There's no need for you to bother to stay tonight as Yoshi will cover the night shift.'

I was grateful for this, as I was hungry now, having not eaten since lunch.

'There's a good Chinese restaurant in Devizes,' said Terence. I wasn't really into Chinese food so I said I'd probably go to the *Waggon*. Jacqui agreed so we parted company with the professor and made our way to Beckhampton.

At the old coaching Inn we found the bars full of people, including George Wingfield and several Germans. We managed to order food and eventually found somewhere to sit.

Unfortunately the table we chose was right next to Mike Carrie and one of Macnish's team, Roger someone-or-other. Both were well pissed and Carrie in particular was quite loud. He and his companion were making much loud talk about a 'Wallaby' – what it was about we had no idea but it seemed to amuse them no end. Then they recognised us and started to take the mickey out of our set-up. I refused to be drawn and countered by asking them about Macnish's company, 'Moonlight Productions'. Both denied all knowledge of it. Which was odd as that was the name Macnish had on the headed notepaper he'd used to write to Meaden earlier in the season. What we didn't know was that they'd changed the name to 'Circlevision'!

Carrie soon lost interest in this and decided to try to persuade Jacqui to go to bed with him. He was loud, very rude and very persuasive – but he was wasting his time. All the same it left a nasty taste in the mouth. Even more so when one remembered that these were the people who we'd been moved off our original site to accommodate. It was now 10.30 and enough was enough. We left Carrie and his companion eating giant 'knickerbocker glories' and went home.

We were now at the end of June. It had been a very wet month indeed, hardly conducive for circles to form or be researched when they did. Most of the *CERES* team had spent a day or so soaked to the skin on more than one occasion after finding that they couldn't use their own caravan because NTV were. It took a week to dry my trainers. The wet weather hardly seemed to match Meaden's theory of warm air moving over hills and meeting cooler air to form a vortex. Yet we had several formations. We also had several known hoaxes both in the Beckhampton area and in other parts of the country.

Generally, things were not going well for us.

Chapter Thirteen
THE SHORT STRAW
Alton Barnes again-The Sun appears-Jim Schnabel appears- The Son of God appears - Doubts appear

I was at work on the 1st of July and it was there that I came across a copy of the *West Wiltshire Advertiser* – a free advertising news-sheet similar to the *Bristol Journal*. To my amusement inside was an article in which George Wingfield and Terence Meaden slagged each other off. George was always one to speak his mind. But it wasn't his day, for on the same day I also found an article in the *Western Daily Press* where George was reported as having been barred from lecturing on Crop Circles at Bristol University due to the authorities there discovering that the contents of his talk would be about 'Aliens' and their apparent connection with circles – something which did not fit with the university's criteria for talks at that time.

Later, I had a call from Jim Crow. He informed me that Busty Taylor and Richard Andrews were to give a talk at the Bristol Watershed on July 3rd on the subject of the *'Mystical Side of Crop Circles'*. Jim promised to attend and surreptitiously tape the talk for *CERES*.

Tuesday 2nd July 1991

I arrived home from work that afternoon to find two messages on my answerphone. The first was from Terence Meaden, excitedly telling me that a new formation, a dumb-bell had appeared in East Field at Alton Barnes overnight and a giant complex had also appeared at Newton St Loe. The rest of the information was lost in static as Meaden's mobile phone lost its signal. The second message was from Rog telling me more or less the same. I made a quick call to Jacqui and swiftly changed out of my uniform. A quarter of an hour later I was on my way to Wiltshire.

Arriving at Alton Barnes some fifty minutes later, I found the road strewn with 'No Waiting' cones, which were being generally ignored by the handful of vehicles parked there. The huge crowds I had imagined would be there had not materialised and I was able to park with ease. I walked along the road to gain a vantage point over the crop and took a few photos of the formation. It was a three-in-line type of dumb-bell. I wandered up to Adam's Grave, the barrow on top of the hill, and took some more shots. On the way back down I passed a man taking photographs of flowers – seemingly oblivious to the crop circles in the field below!

Back at the edge of East Field I found Ralph Noyes, Stanley Morcomb and Mrs. Morcomb, standing looking out across the crop. I got talking with them and someone else joined in and produced a drawing of the new Newton St Loe formation. God's Teeth! It was massive! Apparently it covered most of the hillside on the south side of the A4 opposite the existing circles which I hadn't been able to find that time.

Two German girls stopped and joined in the conversation. They asked Mrs. Morcomb if she could take them into the field and explain about crop circles as they were new to the subject. Mrs. Morcomb said she was just about to leave and persuaded me to do it – not that I needed much persuading! I took the girls into the formation and gave them a brief explanation of the phenomenon without mentioning the different factions. Then I set to examining the circles myself.

I knelt down and without too much trouble soon found some intricate layering where the corridor met the circles. There was similar evidence of construction as that which

Jacqui and I had found in the formation at Lockeridge. I took a few photos and suddenly Rog was there at my side, mobile phone in hand. I showed him the layering. He agreed that it was suspicious.

A man appeared with a dog.

'Aha!' I said. 'If Colin Andrews is correct then this dog should be taken seriously ill and roll over!' [1]

The dog wandered happily in and out of all the circles without any ill effect at all.

A shout from the edge of the field and there was Jacqui, complete with video camera and my camera poles. She joined us and we took pictures and videoed the layering. George Wingfield now joined the gathering throng of researchers. Jacqui greeted him with a chaste peck on the cheek, which took the wind out of his sails!

'Well, ' he eventually said, 'This is a pretty good Plasma Vortex, I must say!'

'Yes, isn't it,' replied Rog, sardonically.

'I can't believe a vortex made this,' went on Wingfield.

'I expect it did,' I said, not wishing to tell him that we already thought it was a fake.

It was a lovely summer's evening, sunny and warm and we all felt light-hearted after all the rain during June. Even George didn't seem able to be his usual arrogant self.

A hang-glider flew low over the field.

Wingfield looked up at it as it passed over us.

'That's what I'll be doing tomorrow,' he said.

'Better be careful that you don't encounter a Plasma-Vortex, then!' I grinned.

We all laughed.

'Well, cheerio, George,' I said. 'Oh, before you leave here, have a look at the layering where the circle joins the corridor...'

Wingfield looked a little surprised but said that he'd probably see us in the pub later.

Rog, Jacqui and I went to Devizes to buy fish and chips and returned to Morgan's Hill to eat our supper. We were joined by Eddie Brown and his wife. Later Terence arrived with some Welshman. We all sat on the grass or on the one or two folding chairs and talked as darkness fell. Meaden was on the crest of a wave. He showed us a diagram of Newton St Loe as drawn by his son. It certainly deserved the appellation 'Complex'! Meaden had also been to Alton Barnes and was happy that it was '...Genuine...'

Just before ten, Ohtsuki and some students arrived and announced that they would be staying all night. I agreed with Rog that we'd cover Friday night and Eddie said he would be along again on Saturday. There was some talk about the 'workshop' possibly being held 'somewhere in Devizes' on the Saturday but nothing conclusive was arranged. Then we left for the pub, Terence electing not to join us.

We had a very good evening and were in the *Waggon* long after 'Last Orders' should have been called. Everyone was feeling pretty good – helped no doubt by the good quality 6X and the good quality weather. Even George Wingfield was in excellent spirits, a fact proved when he swayed happily past our table just before chucking out time.

Wednesday 3rd July 1991

I was busy at work today but had a morning phone call from George Bathurst to the effect that he could cover the Wednesday and Thursday daytime watches at Morgan's Hill but was not available Friday.

Rog and Jacqui decided to go to Alton again but on arrival found that the farmer was now charging £1 admission so they didn't stop. They went to the *Waggon* for lunch then to the hill. At the site they found the generator stopped (the usual state) and the NTV camera therefore not working. Three of Terence Meaden's friends, Harold Wingham, Max Woosnam and Bob Bass were the duty watchers for the afternoon, and they were in the caravan in the company of a young American lad who had not been seen around the site before. He was to spend a lot of time with the *CERES* team over the next few weeks as he was shortly introduced to us by Meaden as a student from Oxford university who was writing some thesis or other and was to be given every assistance. He was a nice lad but asked an awful lot of questions. His name was to become synonymous with hoaxing over the next couple of years and he was accused of being in league with the CIA and various governments and of being employed by them to mislead crop circles believers in an attempt to cover up the Awful Truth. His name?

Jim Schnabel.

Anyway, I digress. Jacqui and Rog had noticed that only one of the two motorhomes occupied by John Macnish and his crew was still there. They wandered to the front of the hill to see what was going on. The remaining motorhome was occupied by several Japanese people – presumably NTV. As the cab door was open, Jacqui and Rog moved closer to try to see what was inside. Perhaps, they thought, we can see what sort of equipment they are using. A Japanese woman appeared and swiftly curtailed these plans by closing the door and advising them to 'go elsewhere,'- Or words to that effect.

'Arrogant cow,' was Jacqui's description of the woman.

By 18.00 on that fine, sunny evening, Max and Bob had left. Jacqui and Rog followed soon after. Which was a pity because the next visitor to the caravan was one Reg. Presley. No, not one of Elvis's relatives, but from a similar background; this was THE Reg. Presley, of The Troggs – a 1960's pop group of some note. Reg. was very interested in crop circles and how they formed and he was wealthy. He could have been a useful contact – But. Reg. was a devout member of Colin Andrews' congregation and worshipped at the shrine of the Unknown Force. Jim Schnabel and Harold Wingham, still on site, signed him in, listened to his ideas and Reg went on his way. We didn't see him again.

Harold went on his way at 20.00, leaving Jim all alone until 23.20 when a few members of the NTV crew turned up to start the troublesome generator. It started eventually and they went away again, only to return at Midnight when the machine stopped. It was restarted and ran until just after two-thirty when it conked out again. Just before this last failure, Jim noted in the log:

'....*Frequent spots appearing on the left hand side of the screen for the first time...*'

Regrettably he didn't say which screen – the Radar or the NTV camera screen. It can pretty safely be assumed that it was the radar screen as this did record sudden spots from time to time. Often of short duration, we never found out what they were.

The fine, starlit night continued until 04.00 when mist and fog came down. The fog stayed put until after nine by which time the radar had shut down with flat batteries. A hazy sun broke through just in time to welcome Harold Wingham relieving a thankful Jim Schnabel who returned to Oxford and his bed.

Harold and Terence Meaden were the duty watchers for most of that day, a day that turned out to be fine, hot and sunny. Paul Fuller arrived at 21.40 and was shortly followed by Yoshi-Hito Ohtsuki and a couple of Jap students. However, any thoughts that Paul may have harboured about having company during his night-time vigil were dashed when the three Japs left an hour later. He perked up when a car approached at 23.30, but it was only some people from NTV who looked around and drove off again! Half an hour later they returned and started the generator, then vanished again.

Paul's night was frequently disturbed by strong winds buffeting the caravan but the morning dawned bright and clear and by the time he left the site at 08.15 to get some more water from the farm, the winds had died down and it was becoming quite hot. And about time too – it *was* July!

About this time I wrote to Dave Reynolds: '.....*Things are hotting up, here in the West, with hoaxes coming almost as thick and fast as the real things...The total number of events reported to date is 58, including 16 hoaxes. The latest complex was formed in the early hours of this morning (Friday), at about 05.30, and it's at Alton Priors. Terence has been in with the tape measure, and is convinced it is OK......According to the daily papers, Kikuchi has arrived, but I haven't seen him, and Terence has not said anything, so where he is, I know not. Terence is now talking in terms of the watching going on until harvest!!!!!!! At this rate, most of us will have to undergo rehabilitation when it's over, in order to settle down in our homes again...*'

It was true! New circles had appeared at Alton Barnes, in the same field as the previous 1991 lot. Terence had measured them, Keith Mortimore of TORRO had checked the weather readings and they matched Meaden's criteria, so both were happy. So happy in fact that owing to the late arrival of summer weather and crop circles, Terence was planning to keep the watch going until harvest. Home was rapidly becoming somewhere most of us visited only for the odd night's sleep!

There were the hoaxes to take into consideration as well. Whether we were becoming more careful as a group or whether the group's combined skills were combining to scrutinise circles with a more critical eye, we never had time to think about, but it was a fact that we were declaring more circles as being hoaxes than ever before. Some were obvious and there was no doubt that as the subject's popularity increased at a phenomenal rate, so the ratio of hoaxes and hoaxers rose in direct proportion. Nevertheless, in most cases the first thing that Rog, Jacqui, Paul and I looked for when we first entered a 'new' formation was evidence of hoaxing. Secretly, and as the reader can tell from the various conversations in this book, all of us (Meaden apart) by now working on the basis that the plasma vortex probably did not make any of the more complex formations; in fact, we tended to doubt that it was responsible for anything other than singles and ringed singles. Unlike the CCCS who tended to believe anything where their dowsing rods twitched as genuine, including a well-known fake at Southwell, Notts, which had been made by agricultural students. It was very quickly denounced as fake by locals, the students and *CERES*: the CCCS said it was genuine...

So, it was the 5th July and I had a lie-in, getting up at 09.30 to a phone call from Jacqui saying that George Wingfield's cancelled lecture at Bristol University had been reinstated.

We agreed to meet later on, probably at the caravan.

Once I was ready, I left home and travelled to the site, calling in at a very good chip-shop in Chippenham that I'd discovered. I took the chips with me to Morgan's Hill and arrived at the bottom gate at the same time as a small convoy of cars, descending the hill, arrived at the other side of the gate. I opened the gate to allow them to pass through. The fourth car stopped to close the gate but I called out that I would do it as I was going up the hill. I asked who they were.

'Circles researchers,' came the reply.

'Oh, for Andrews and Delgado, I suppose?'

'No. The sensible side – Dr Meaden...'

Blimey! This was a turnup for the book – someone on our side!

Two more cars approached one of those I recognised as belonging to Terence Meaden.

I waved him down. 'Hello, Terence – what's going on?'

'Lots,' replied the professor. 'There's a dumb-bell and five small circles at Alton Barnes, and these people are from the BBC who are making a mathematical film about crop circles and ellipses.'

The other car pulled up and in it were J-F Leichner and Paul Fuller. I went over to see them.

'I didn't know you were coming here today,' I said to Paul. 'I could have stayed home for another couple of hours.'

I was only jesting, but in the back of my mind was the feeling that they were all off with the BBC people and I would be stuck at the top of the hill guarding the caravan for the rest of the day and possibly even the night.

Paul shrugged. Terence came over to us. 'We're already late,' he said, 'We must get on and go to the farmyard. We have to be filmed in these circles here.'

During a short conversation with Paul, most of which I didn't catch, Terence mentioned someone called "Dodd". Paul reacted with horror.

'But he's the man who was responsible for a hoax, Terence!'

Meaden looked surprised.

'These circles are *absolutely genuine*,' he said.

'Are you sure?' asked Paul.

'Oh, yes,' replied Meaden. He went back to his car and drove off after the others.

Paul looked at me despairingly.

'Terence doesn't seem to know if he's coming or going,' I observed. 'I thought that I was coming here to relieve a Jap as George Bathurst couldn't make it today.'

Paul shrugged again. 'I'll speak to you later, Pete,' he said. 'We'd better catch up with the others.'

He drove off after Meaden whilst I drove up the hill to the site for another spell of monotonous boredom: The Short Straw.

Guarding the caravan had little to do with circles research, apart from keeping the weather log up to date. The entire original plans for mobile watchers had gone to pot. Rog, Jacqui and I all had CB radios in our cars but we were the only ones. There was a distinct lack of discipline amongst those present; people at the site tended to do their own thing rather than stick to any sort of cohesive plan. About the only fun one could have whilst stuck on the hill was to go to the top gate and watch out for new visitors getting an electric shock when they allowed the metal gate to swing open too far and come into contact with an electric fence. When the unsuspecting person reached out to grab the gate – Zap!

In his book. '*Crop Circle Apocalypse*' John Macnish describes the *Blue Hill* HQ as a '...*scruffy little caravan*...' and a '....*hole*....'. Yes, at times that was true, but not our doing. As it was being used as a general meeting-place for all sorts of people, many of whom we didn't even know and who trod mud and dirt throughout, it was hard for us to keep as clean and tidy as we would have wished. Most of the intruders didn't clear up behind them: that was left to us.

When I arrived at the caravan, there were a couple of Jap students there. One lounged around in the caravan whilst the other was racing a (presumably hired) Volvo saloon up and down the field. When a car approached and a Chinese-looking gent got out, I presumed he was from NTV and took no notice. He came up to me.

'Is Terence Meaden's car here?' he enquired.

'No. He's got it with him,' I said.

'Oh. He told me to go to his car and fetch his tape-measure,'

'Who are you?' (If he was NTV he could go and scratch!)

'I'm with the BBC team, filming with Dr Meaden.'

I relented. 'I have a measure in my car – you can borrow it.' I fetched the measure from my car.

'Thanks very much. I'll return it later.'

He departed and I was left with the wacky-racers for a while until, at 13.00, a mini-bus full of Japanese arrived. I had no idea who they were. They parked up a short distance away and stayed put. Shortly afterwards a four-man film crew appeared over the Wansdyke and came over to the caravan where they filmed one of the Jap students sitting by the radar scanner. NTV? No-one seemed to know and they left again.

By now I was getting bored. At 14.40 Max Woosnam arrived and so did one of Meaden's other contacts, an American chap named Rutter. We chatted for a while and I established that they would be there for the next couple of hours. I seized the opportunity to leave the site and go to Avebury as I was almost out of film. At Avebury I bought a film and an ice cream (the weather was still fine) and mingled with the tourists who'd come to see the stones. Many of these wore tee shirts emblazoned with crop circles logos. Post-cards of circles were available at the shop. More evidence that we were on the wrong side!

Returning to the hill, I stopped off at the farmyard. There was J-F picking up a set of batteries.

'Hi, Pete,' he called. 'I am going to the caravan to collect some of Ohtsuki's students and take them to Devizes. When I come back, we go for a drink?'

I agreed, said we'd arrange the venue at the hill and left him there. At the bottom gate, I met Paul Fuller. He'd just been interviewed for the BBC.

'But, Terence must promise to arrange a meeting when all this is over, so we can sort out what was good and what was bad about *Bluehill*,' he said.

'I agree. What's at Alton Barnes?'

'A dumb-bell and a few small circles. They will take a bit of explaining by Terence, especially as Ohtsuki found a footprint on the edge of a circle.'

'I'll say. I still don't understand how a fair-weather phenomenon can now occur in fog and drizzle,' I replied.

J-F had passed us and now returned with the two Jap students. 'I see you later in the *"Crown"* at Bishops Cannings,' he called as he went past. I waved my acknowledgment.

As Paul and I discussed the media circus which had overtaken the 'secret' cropwatch we'd 'carefully' planned, an all to obvious hydraulic platform with a camera crew in its basket was lifting skywards from a position at the side of the road. We watched as it reached the required height and swung out over the crop. Presumably they were filming the circles in that field. At least it was done for Meaden's benefit and not any of the others who'd invaded the site since we started the project.

Paul suddenly had a thought. 'Where did J-F say he'd meet you?'

'At the *"Crown"* in Bishops Cannings-why?'

'That's where we had lunch with Terence earlier. It'll be shut now.'

'Shit! I'd better get along then. Will I see you tomorrow evening?

'Tomorrow morning – it's the workshop.'

'What? Terence hasn't said a thing!'

'Oh, dear,' said Paul. 'It's in Devizes-do you know the town well?'

'A little, where is it being held?'

'Long Street. It may be in the museum rooms-I really don't know myself! Oh, God! I can see myself wandering around Devizes all day. And there probably isn't anywhere to park!' The UFOlogist wasn't very happy with the arrangements, I could see. He went on 'I don't want to leave Romsey very early as I'm expecting the latest batch of '*Cropwatchers*'. It's no good - Terence will have to get more organised. Next year the NTV lot will not come with him –he'll be industry or university sponsored he hopes.'

'*Hopefully* he will be sponsored. What we could do with is something like that 'Skystalk,' I mused.

Paul had to leave so I waved him goodbye and set off for the *"Crown"* which, as I now suspected, was closed. It was, and there was no sign of J-F Leichner.
Back to the caravan without a drink. I put the kettle on and wrote up my cropwatcher's diary. A mini-bus full of Japanese arrived. They sat around for ten minutes and left again. Just who were they?
J-F Leichner appeared.

'Sorry I missed you at the *"Crown"*,' he said. 'But the Japanese were hungry and I had to take them back to their hotel in Devizes.'

I gave him a cup of tea. When he'd drunk it we decided to take a walk around the perimeter of the hill. Up on the Wansdyke we looked down over Farmer Shepherd's land and could see Max Woosnam, Jim Schnabel and the American looking at some crop damage in the lee of an electric cable post. We wandered on round the hill and came to the front, looking down on the road from Blacklands to Bishops Cannings. The weather had been sunny but now a haze crept in and the wind became fresher. As we approached the top gate so we spotted a van from Philips Telecom (who worked at the masts) and Range-Rover. It was Farmer Brown. Spying us, he called out a greeting.

'Be careful, Pete....' Muttered J-F.

I promised I wouldn't start an argument as Brown walked over to us.

'Nice weather for a change,' said the Farmer. 'You can see a fair way from here...'

'I can certainly see why you moved us off the front of the hill....' I retorted, indicating Macnish's remaining motorhome.

The farmer looked embarrassed. 'They're well concealed' he said.

'And so would we have been, using the same type of camouflage,' I replied.

As luck would have it a small convoy of vehicles arrived at the gate. There were a couple of cars and a mini-bus. The convoy contained every Jap on the hill. They announced that they were all leaving the hill and would not be back until nine that night. Farmer Brown opened the gate for them and followed them down the hill. J-F and I continued our walk.

Back again at the caravan we spent a while chatting with Max, Jim and the other American before J-F and Jim had to leave. The three of us remaining talked on and I found out from Max that he and his friends felt exactly the same way as Paul Fuller and I did about the way things were going. It seemed that Max and Harold had been at the caravan a few days before and Terence turned up to do another of his press interviews. He'd put them out in the rain while he was interviewed. As Max, Harold and George Bathurst were all retired and none of them was under 65, they didn't think much of getting wet whilst Terence promoted his books.

We all agreed that something ought to be done to avoid any repetition of this on any future watches held by *CERES*.

By 20.00, Max and the American had left, Jim Schnabel had returned and Jacqui had arrived. Jim was staying the night so Jacqui and I departed to Alton Barnes to see the new arrivals. We pulled up at East Field and found the farmer was charging £1 a time to go in and there were still quite a few people there. The weather was growing hazier all the time and clouds were beginning to form, making the light too poor for photography. We left for the *Waggon*, in order to eat and where we found that Alan Rayner and Una Dawood (of the Beckhampton Group) were the only croppies we recognised. Rog arrived soon after (he hadn't been to the hill – how did he know we would be there? He'd actually arranged to meet Jacqui there but I wasn't supposed to know that!) and we sat in with

Rayner and chatted for an hour or so. Rayner showed me a letter, which revealed that CCCS member and small publisher Alick Bartholomew had persuaded the farmer at Newton St. Loe to open the field with the massive pictogram in it to the public. The CCCS had exclusive rights to put a small stall at the gate selling books, tee shirts and other circles 'memorabilia'. It crossed my mind that it was about time *CERES* started doing something similar in order to raise funds for future research.

Outside the weather had changed. Lightning flashes split the sky. As it was time to go, we made our way to the door where we were met by one of the most spectacular sheet-lightning storms I've ever seen. The sky was constantly lit by blue flashes giving an eerie, unreal feel to the landscape. We crossed the A4 to where the cars were parked and Jacqui tried to persuade Rog to go with her and climb Silbury Hill to watch the lightning. Rog prevaricated and shortly afterwards the decision was made for him as it started to lash down with rain. As he got into his car, Rog uttered a sigh. 'Some Bastard has nicked my CB aerial!' he said. So they had. That meant we were down to two radios.

Saturday 6th July 1991

It was a rough night on the hill for two Jap students and Jim Schnabel. Thunder and lightning along with heavy rain lashed the caravan, lasting until nearly three in the morning when the thunder and lightning died away, leaving just rain for the rest of the night. By dawn it was still cloudy but the rain had stopped.

Which was just as well as it was the day of the workshop. Following further information from Paul Fuller, I now knew that the workshop was being held at the museum rooms in Devizes. In spite of Paul's fears about lack of parking, I arrived in Devizes at 10.20 and parked right outside the building. The event was being held upstairs and I wandered up to the room where I found a lot of people milling around. I recognised Terence Meaden, Paul Fuller, J-F Leichner, George Bathurst, Jim Schnabel, Professor Ohtsuki and several Jap students. I was told by Paul that there was also a man who was to talk about Ball-Lightning, a J.Met reader called Peter Lewis and a couple of passing Americans.

Of course, the by-now-obligatory Japanese film-crew was present. I don't know who they were but I was assured by Paul that they were not NTV. Terence was fussing around, trying to plug in a large TV set, only to find that the Japs had used up all the electric sockets and he'd have to find an extension lead.

Chaos reigned for while, especially when Terence finally plugged in the TV only to find that he'd forgotten to bring the remote-control device and he couldn't start showing a video of Ohtsuki's. George Bathurst was deputed to return to Bradford-on-Avon to fetch the missing device. During his absence I think a talk was given after which George returned with the remote and we were off.

Professor Ohtsuki showed a very interesting video of how he'd discovered that he could reproduce the plasma-vortex under lab conditions. The vortex left small, circular marks in dust. Some had even got rings round them! The tape showed a tour of the Underground railway system where similar markings were discovered on tunnel walls, the theory being that mini-vortices were created by the sparks from passing electric trains combining with the hot air in the tunnels and the wind caused by passing trains.

This was brilliant stuff and, it has to be said, lifted the flagging spirits of the *CERES* team no end. It did cast further doubts on the complex formations, however and seemed to add more weight to Paul's and my feelings that all these were fakes. Which of course meant that very little of what we'd seen that year so far could be genuine. Paul and I agreed that probably up to eighty per cent of all circles we'd seen and inspected were known to be fakes. Another small percentage were admitted or witnessed fakes. Which left another percentage of circles which we suspected to be fake, but nobody had admitted making them, or been seen making them nor had they been inspected by us.

Only a handful could go on the database as 'probably genuine'. As circles reports were now coming in thick and fast as the weather had improved, it was clear that we would not be able to examine all the data until the season had finished. It wouldn't be right to make sweeping statements until all the data was in and information studied.

Ohtsuki's video over, it was time for a lunch-break and Paul and I headed for the '*Elm Tree*' nearby for lunch, accompanied by Peter Lewis. On the way I phoned Jacqui and told her where the venue was should she wish to come up to Devizes.

After a good lunch, the talks started again with Terence Meaden leading off with a talk about *CERES*. Jacqui arrived just as Paul Fuller followed Meaden with the UFO/Vortex correlation theory. He was talking about the way in which several crop circles researchers had claimed to have had a 'Close Encounter of the Fourth Kind –CE4' in some circles when J-F interrupted.

'…That could be explained by excess Nitrogen from the crop spraying process being imbibed in some way and causing hallucinations,' he said.

We all thought this was a likely explanation and one worth following up in the future.

Then the ball-lightning chap gave his talk after which the meeting dissolved into general chitchat about all sorts of things

At the close of the meeting, I told Terence that I would be at the caravan on the following day with Dave Reynolds. Dave was coming down from his Wolverhampton home by train and I was to pick him up from Bristol Parkway station and take him to the cropwatch. Paul and I helped clear up and whilst I was outside loading Terence's car, George Bathurst took me to one side and voiced his concerns about the way the watch was going. What he had to say echoed the feelings of Max Woosnam and Harold Wingham. Yet again, we agreed that 'something had to be done'.

That evening, Jacqui, Rog and I met up with Jim Crow for a beer and to hear the results of the Busty Taylor-Richard Andrews recent talk in Bristol. Jim had taped it but the quality of the recording was poor. From what we could glean from the tape, the talk gave the usual impression that all circles were the results of some mystical but as yet unknown force. Dowsing was discussed as a way of telling beyond doubt whether a circle was genuine or not. In short, nothing new.

Sunday 7th July 1991

Professor Ohtsuki and his students manned the site all day until the arrival of Terence Meaden at 10.45. An hour later, Meaden left to return again at 14.30. Paul Fuller arrived at 18.55 as Meaden was leaving.

I went to the station to pick up Dave Reynolds but on arrival there his train was booked as 40-50 minutes late so I had time to go and pick up Rog first. Returning to the station we were just in time to see the train in the platform and Dave walk out of the entrance.

On the way up to Morgan's Hill we related the past few weeks events to him.

When we got there, at around 19.20, Paul Fuller was waiting. We all trooped into the caravan and Dave made himself comfortable as this would be his home for the remainder of the weekend. Terence Meaden arrived and, after greeting Dave, an attempt was made to discuss the coming week's staffing arrangements, but we were interrupted by the arrival of a camera crew from National Geographic. The team consisted of two men (one of whom was an American) and a female sound recordist. They'd come to interview Terence and Paul.

Then another film crew, this time the Japs who'd filmed the workshop, arrived and wanted to interview Dave Reynolds about an article he'd written for J.Met about a chap called Plott who'd drawn what could be sketches of the wind causing crop circles in the Middle Ages. Rog and myself, surplus to requirements, mooched about outside: not entirely a good thing as the weather was taking a turn for the worst again and the sky was clouding over.

The Japs finished with Dave, packed their gear into a van and drove off. Dave came over to Rog and me, now joined by Paul with a grin on his face.

'They've left us all prezzies!' he announced, handing out small square boxes. Each box contained a small wooden affair with a bell hanging from it.

'It looks like you hang them in the wind and the bell rings,' said Rog.

'More like a fishy-fly-paper type device!' muttered Dave, looking at his which indeed resembled a fish, with the paper wind-catcher on the bottom of his bell resembling a fly-paper. Paul looked at his and pulled a face as he tried to assemble it. Later he hung it in the caravan and left it there. We took ours home. I've still got mine although I still don't know who exactly it was who gave it to me!

It was dark by now with squally showers. National Geographic required their camera gear set up in the caravan for another shot. Those of us not involved had to stand outside. I got chatted up by the sound recordist, whose name was Di. We shared a cup of tea and shivered together in the cold, dark night. She was older than me by a couple of years, but not bad looking. We never met again after that evening!

Meanwhile, NTV had arrived nearby and set up a barbecue dangerously close to the petrol tank on their minibus! The night became lit up with garish lights from the flaming barbecue and the arc-lights used by National Geographic.

We learnt a lot about filming during this project. Phrases such as '....*11-take One*...' and the oft-repeated calls for '....*Atmos!*...'[2] became part of everyday language whilst filming was taking place. Interviews were punctuated by the sound of the clapperboard.

Rog and I left at 23.30 and were shadowed by a police car as far as Calne. We later discovered that there had been a 'Rave' party on nearby Roundway Down that night.

After work the next day, I was at the caravan by 1900 with fish and chips for Dave Reynolds and myself. I saw from the log that he'd been alone (apart from NTV nearby) from 01.00 until 0600. NTV left then, to return at 09.25. Yoshi-Hito Ohtsuki arrived with his students at 09.50. NTV left the site at 10.15 and took their generator, camera and video-recorder (the latter had been installed in our caravan...) so it looked as if they were finished. Ohtsuki had departed at just after mid-day. Terence had put in several brief appearances. Dave was alone when I arrived. Having no transport of his own, he hadn't been able to get out for food so was grateful for the food I brought with me.

The Japs had left the caravan in a mess, so Dave and I cleared up, filling rubbish bags from not just the caravan but outside as well. We swept out the caravan and wiped over the tables and work surfaces. We were reclaiming our caravan after just over two weeks of Japanese occupation. Now the heat had died down and the 'visitors' were gone, perhaps the *CERES* cropwatch could continue!

Rog arrived at 20.20 shortly followed by Terence Meaden in the company of George Bathurst. I decided that I'd like to see the Alton Barnes circles. Dave said he'd like to come along, as he'd not seen any 1991 circles yet. Rog declined. Terence stayed behind to talk to a couple of visiting Germans who arrived about then.

Dave and I arrived at Alton Barnes late evening. It was still light but the drizzle had set in again. We found the field empty except for a couple of figures in one of the circles. There was nobody at the gate to take any money so we set off across the field to the circles. As we approached the circle with the figures in it, so we noticed one of them was acting very strangely. The two were a male and a female. The male was the odd one; he was walking round and round the circle, staring unseeingly into the middle distance. His female companion seemed to be meditating. As we examined the by now well-trodden circle, so the man, who was wearing a blue track-suit (as was his companion) walked to the end of the smaller circle and just stood, staring at the horizon. His hands were folded over his navel and, from the back view it looked for all the world as if he was having a wee! He wasn't. He was communing with something much higher. He was The Son of God.

David Icke, ex-professional footballer, ex-TV sports commentator had taken time out to indulge in a spot of Earth-saving.[3]

Later that evening, Dave Reynolds made an entry in the site log:

'…..*P.Rendall and D.Reynolds return from Alton Barnes having met the Son of God and transcended to a new understanding, being at one with the vibrations….*'

As the late Frankie Howerd might have said, '…Titter ye not!'

Chapter Fourteen
WONDERFUL CIRCLES
More hoaxes-The Vortex makes an appearance-Baldrick-Dundry

On the 10th July, Jacqui and I went to Cannington, near Bridgwater, Somerset, to follow up a report of a single circle there. Looking at the map, we had doubts when we saw that the circle was dangerously close to an Agricultural College. A phone call to the farmer had revealed that he had already '....had a team from *TORRO* look at the circle...' –which was news to all of us as nobody we knew had been there. Arriving at the field in question, we swiftly found the circle. It was a single circle and was on a slight slope. In all ways it fitted Terence's theory. It had obviously been made at least a week or so prior to our arrival as the flattened stems had continued to grow towards the light, lifting off the floor of the circle. We measured the circle and drew a diagram for Meaden before leaving.

Students at the college later admitted making the circle.

Whilst we were in Somerset, Rog had completed the night shift with nothing to report except that it was '....a perfect night....'. He left for home and bed at 08.15 and the next person to arrive was Terence Meaden at 10. Terence left at mid-day and returned at 1500, as did Paul Fuller and some friends from the UFO world. Jim Schnabel arrived that evening and stayed overnight.

On the following day, I returned from work to find a message from Terence on my answerphone. There was a new formation near Marlborough, just outside the town on the Swindon road. Apparently it was another 3-in-line like Alton Barnes. I tried to contact the Prof. on his vodaphone but all calls were diverted to an answering service. I gave Rog a call and it was arranged for him to pick me up later and we'd head off for the circles.

By the time Rog arrived I'd spoken to Terence at last. He was on his way back to the caravan after spending a wet morning and afternoon in the field measuring the new formation. It had rained constantly and he was soaked. He told me that all except the northernmost circle and its corridor had been measured. Could Rog and I finish off the job? No problem. We set out for Marlborough and arrived in the famous High Street about an hour later. Turning left at the bottom end of the street we found the circles about a mile and a half along the Swindon road. It was a good one; 3 circles joined by a corridor angled across the slight slope of the field. But! To the left of the circles was a smaller formation which cast doubts upon the whole shebang...it was a circle with two smaller circles in it and two short spurs at 6 o' clock and nine o'clock. It looked for all the world like a frying pan with two eggs in it! Somehow we felt that there was no way a Plasma Vortex could make that.

And, of course, if it was a fake then there was immediate doubt about the main formation.

We parked up in a disused field gateway and got our measuring and camera gear ready. A woman approached.

'Isn't it wonderful?' she breathed.

'Not bad as formations go,' replied Rog.

'Yes, but isn't it wonderful that WE'VE got it in Marlborough,' she went on. 'It must prove something...'

'It proves that it isn't Little Green Men,' I said.

She looked disappointed. 'Are you sure?'

'Oh, yes.'

A few other stray people approached. Rog and I set off across the field. We measured the end circle and corridor and took a few photos as the light was going. Making our way back across the field we could see some more people had gathered at the gateway. Just as we got back to the car, local medium Isabelle Kingston and a car load of CCCP arrived to join the gathering throng which, by the sound of it, included several French.

On the way out of Marlborough I used Rog's mobile to phone Terence at the caravan and advised him that our mission had been successful.

It took us about twenty minutes or so to arrive at the top of Morgan's Hill. We found a slightly bedraggled professor of physics trying to get warm in front of the tiny gas fire. We joined him and I gave him the details of that day's work and also the measurements of the Cannington circle which Jacqui and I had been to. He was puzzled when I told him that the farmer had said that a *TORRO* representative had already been there. None of us could think who that might have been. It became a mystery like the Germans at Charlton and the Canadians at Upham.

The sound of a car outside brought two Frenchmen to the caravan. Terence seemed to know them and introduced them as Yves Chosson and Robert Fischer, two members of VECA, the French version of BUFORA. They would be staying in the area that night so Terence offered them the use of the caravan for the night. Little did we know what a two-edged sword that would become; the caravan was rapidly becoming a guest house for any stray people who happened to have a passing interest in crop circles, no matter what they thought made them.

Eddy Brown and his lady arrived at 21.30 and said they were staying until the early hours. We all had tea and Terence, Rog and I left at 23.00.

Robert and Yves didn't get a good night's sleep though. The radar shut off with low power at 03.55 and they had to go out in the cold and change the batteries over. One item of interest from their stay was that they recorded a small plot appearing on the screen about a mile away. The trace lasted for 10 minutes. Nobody ever found out what it was.

This was the sort of thing that we'd planned on having mobile teams for. If there had been a couple of people there, one of whom was linked by radio to the caravan, then that person could have driven off to investigate. Yves and Robert certainly weren't going to leave their relative comfort to go and see what the cause was.

Neither Rog nor Jacqui, nor I went to the caravan on the 11th or 12th. Yves and Robert took advantage of their free accommodation and stayed all morning on the 12th. About the only thing of interest to happen was that a Hercules transport aircraft (based at RAF Lyneham, near Chippenham, not far to the south) flew over the site and did not register on the radar. A different Hercules, flying a few kilometres away, did. This was probably because the nautical radar we were using was 'sideways facing' and not able to scan vertically.

Yves and Robert left after nine and nobody else turned up until Paul Fuller arrived twelve hours later. Terence arrived to spend a couple of hours with him. After midnight in what would become a regular night-time visit, Yves and Robert returned to spend the night in the caravan, on this occasion, with Paul.

I had a phone call from Meaden when I returned from work on the afternoon of the 13th. A new formation had been reported at Broad Hinton, on the road between Avebury and Swindon. The night had been misty and drizzling – similar conditions to the night when the circles had appeared below Morgan's Hill; I'd questioned then how those circles could fit in with the vortex theory – I had immediate doubts about this new formation. Terence had other evidence however.

Recently, there had arrived in Wiltshire a person well-known to followers of Earth-mysteries and to psychics. A person once described by none other than Arthur C.Clarke as the greatest materialisation medium of modern times: she was Rita Goold. Rita, a pleasant, plump woman in her late forties or early fifties, had paid a couple of visits to our caravan but I'd not had the chance to talk to her. She and a friend, Arthur Mills, were following the circles mysteries with interest and spending time with CCCS teams out watching. Now, Rita had been in touch with Meaden.

'Rita has reported seeing what could have been a plasma vortex last night,' said the Prof. 'She was with some CCCS at Alton Barnes when she saw a tube of light come down over Golden Ball hill [1]. It split into two and vanished.'

This was interesting. Conditions were not really right for a vortex to form according to the original theory but Terence had 'updated' the theory a bit after the Morgan's Hill circles. Now we had circles forming when it was wet, cold and misty instead of warm and breezy, and a tube of light to add weight to the theory. Did Terence want us to go to Golden Ball to look for traces of this 'vortex'?

'Hmmm. No. I think perhaps you'd better go to Broad Hinton first, ' said the Prof. 'Once news gets around, it'll get trampled and taking the measurements will be a waste of time.'

Rog and I set out for Broad Hinton. There was a little confusion as to where Weir Farm –the place where the circles were said to be – actually was, as it wasn't marked on the OS map. We drove into the village from the A4361 hoping that the farm was obvious. However, we began to have more doubts about the formation when we noticed that not only was the village holding its annual fete that coming weekend, but there was a barn dance being held as well: at Weir Farm! The fortuitous arrival of a crop circles formation at such a time would mean good publicity for the weekend's events.

Bearing all that in mind we found ourselves back on the A4361 again. I suggested that we go to the place marked on the map as 'The Weir'. We did and, after asking a couple of locals for directions, found the farm. A call at the farmhouse brought the news that the farmer was up at the circles formation. This was said to be just below the escarpment of the Marlborough Downs, to the east of the farmhouse.

We drove up the track and found the farmer setting up a mouldy caravan, presumably for someone to sit in and charge the usual entrance fee and, if the CCCS were quick enough, to sell books, postcards and tee-shirts of the latest formations.

The farmer was a genial type and allowed us to measure and photo the formation (another three-in-line dumb-bell, this time with arcs at each end). When we'd finished measuring – a task that took time as people were now arriving at the circles and asking lots of questions – the farmer told us an interesting tale. It seems that he'd been up at the bottom of the escarpment a day or so earlier, mending a fence. It was a murky morning with poor visibility. His attention had been drawn to a 'grey, pear-shaped' object which seemed to sit on the fence for a few moments before following the fence line and rising up over the hill.

'You'll think I'm daft,' he said. We didn't. We asked him if he'd be willing to write it all down for Terence Meaden. He agreed and I promised that the Prof. would be in touch. The work done, we headed back to the caravan.

On arriving at the caravan, we found Terence and Jacqui. We handed over the measurements of the Broad Hinton circles and told the Prof. about the object seen by the Farmer. Meaden was well pleased, especially when we told him that the farmer would write down exactly what he remembered seeing. We made some tea and chatted about the possibility that the circles we'd just seen may have been made as part of a publicity stunt to promote the village fete and barn dance. It couldn't be ruled out.

The sound of a car outside took our attention. A man in his 30's got out followed by a plump woman of about the same age. They came over to the caravan. Terence, who'd tensed at the thought of another interview, relaxed.

'It's OK,' he said. 'I know him'

The couple entered the caravan and Terence introduced the man as '...Malcolm Garnett [2]. He is on our side and has frequently come into our showrooms in Bradford on Avon to buy my books on the subject.'

Garnett nodded to us.

'These are my team,' said Terence, introducing Rog, Jacqui and me in turn. He turned again to Garnett. 'And who is this young lady?'

'Oh, this is Glenda [3] – she's a friend,' replied Garnett.

They stayed for an hour or so. The talk was all about circles and causes of circles. Garnett was obviously very interested but on a more basic level of interest to the rest of us. 'Glenda', as far as I recall, said little or nothing; shades of Busty Taylor's companion at Silbury three years earlier. During the course of the conversation, the subject came up that circles were not necessarily being found under hills and escarpments as indicated in Terence's theory of the eddy vortex.

Jacqui argued that circles found thus ought to be treated as suspicious where they were of such distance from the hill that a natural vortex would have been unlikely to be the cause. 'But,' she added, 'I am surprised that circles haven't been found near Dundry Hill.'

Dundry Hill is a ridge to the south of Bristol. Jacqui and her parents lived a couple of miles from the location. Immediately to the north of the hill, housing began, but there were fields on the top and southern slopes. No circles had been found anywhere near Dundry. Ever.

Terence claimed that vortices were really quite a rare phenomenon, only being so 'common' in Wiltshire and Hampshire because the huge cereal crop fields provided a perfect canvas for traces to be found. That was possibly the reason why circles had never been found at Dundry.

The evening wore on and soon everyone except Rog and I left for home. The weather, cloudy for most of the day, remained so until around one in the morning when the wind dropped. A low mist formed around the bottoms of the valleys. We were on High Alert conditions. We remained on alert for most of the night but by four in the morning the mist had got so thick that the top of Morgans Hill stood out like an island in a silvery grey sea. We couldn't have seen a plasma vortex if one had occurred more than a few yards away. At five, with dawn imminent, we packed up and left the site to patrol the surrounding area in the hope that something might have happened in the corn fields that night.

It hadn't.

We went home.

But! Something *had* apparently happened. At Bratton. From what we learned later, it seemed that Malcolm Garnett had dropped his lady friend off and gone to spend the night on top of the white horse. There, just after two, he had noted a white/yellow light to the south of the area. Slowly descending for approx. 25 seconds against a slight westerly breeze the light was, in Garnett's opinion, not a flare. He'd apparently been in the army or something like that and reckoned he knew the difference. Daylight came and he searched for traces of what he thought had been a vortex, but to his disappointment, found that it must have come down on uncultivated land.

Oblivious to this, Rog and I met up again later that day and spent a relaxing afternoon at an air display at Badminton. We had planned to go to Golden Ball hill that evening to look for traces of Rita Goold's 'vortex', but I had to work a night shift and Rog's elderly mother was burgled. My phone was out of order so I couldn't let Terence know. In the end, nobody went. [4]

Terence covered the Monday shift and spent a sunny day on the hill. I called him that evening to arrange the week's duty cover. He was to do a book promotion for the *Goddess of the Stones* at Waterstones bookshop in Bath on the Tuesday and everyone else was busy so it looked as if we'd be shut during the daytime on that day.

As it turned out, *Operation Blue Hill* wasn't closed on Tuesday. A certain little Frenchman named Yves Chosson or, as he was now known to us, 'Baldrick' –after the character in TV's *Blackadder* – stayed at the caravan during the morning and Eddie Brown took over later that afternoon. Baldrick was becoming a bit of a pain. At that time he was sneaking back to the caravan every evening and using it as a doss-house. Paul, Rog and myself thought initially that he was there with Meaden's blessing, because of the French connection. Meaden didn't realise this and certainly hadn't given his blessing, but, it has to be said that Terence naively allowed anyone who showed some interest in the subject to fill gaps in the shift roster. It allowed him to have the site manned whilst he got on with book promoting and the like. The trouble was that the *CERES* people (Rog,

Paul, Jacqui, Terence and me) were sharing the costs of the gas for the cooker and heater, the tea, milk and sugar. People like Baldrick and Jim Schnabel who were there for their own reasons, were not contributing. The problem would have to be addressed.

Tuesday 16th July 1991

The events of this day cast things in a different light. At lunchtime I had a call from Terence Meaden. He told me that there was a new circles formation. It was near Bristol. It was at – Dundry! *Dundry*! That was bloody odd!

HTV were after an interview with *CERES*. I was off to work, Rog was at work and Terence was off to his book promotion. Could Jacqui do it?

'No chance,' I said. 'If a TV camera was pointed at her she'd go to ground faster than a rabbit!'

'Could she go and look at the formation?'

'Possibly. She lives near there now.'

Terence gave me the farmer's details and I promised to try and get hold of Rog myself. At work, I phoned Jacqui.and told her of the formation.

'...There's a circles formation on *Dundry Hill*...?' she repeated, in a strange voice. 'I don't believe it! What did I say only the Saturday night just gone? That I was surprised that circles haven't been found near Dundry Hill.....'

'Terence wants to know if you'll go and have a look at the circles, ' I said. 'But he wants you to contact the farmer first.' I gave her the farmer's number.

Later that afternoon she called me back. 'Can't get hold of the farmer, ' she said, '-but I've got hold of Rog and he's coming with me to see the circles.'

(Funny how she always managed to get hold of Rog when Terence or I couldn't...)

Anyway, Jacqui and Rog set out that afternoon for Dundry. On arrival at the farm they found two youths who said that the farmer was out. They went up to the field but couldn't get near the formation as a large trailer was in the gateway and there was a notice there saying 'No Entrance – Keep Out!' Also there was a radio car from BBC Radio Bristol who couldn't get in either. When they found out who Rog and Jacqui represented, Rog was persuaded to give an interview in which he said that UFO's had no part to play in crop circles research.

Jacqui rang me at work again that evening to report where the formation was.

'It's on the west side,'she told me. 'It's a dumb-bell with a cross-bar and I can see it from the top of my road....'

Now this was really odd. I knew what Alan Rayner would say if he knew about the Saturday evening conversation. '..*That would be the Cosmic Joker at work.*.' And Busty Taylor would no doubt, have a similar answer.

But surely it couldn't be! Was there after all some superior being at work playing tricks on us? Or was it a prankster of a more human nature? It was not the first odd coincidence to happen during the cropwatches and it would not be the last. So many people were allowed to mingle freely with *Blue Hill* staff, and there were so many hoaxers at work that it was inevitable that somebody would find out where we lived and play a trick on us. It had already happened to Cloud 9's Mike Carrie whilst he was in Wiltshire. Hoaxers had noted the address of his HQ and gone off to Leicestershire where they made some good circles right next to his office!

Jacqui had videoed the Dundry circles from the morning local TV news so after work I went straight to her place. The video showed a pretty rough dumb-bell with two lines of standing crop in one circle-much like the early season dumb-bell at Prestwick, near Glasgow. Over a cuppa we spoke at length about the 'coincidence'. Neither of us was convinced that it was anything other than a hoax. But who had put it there?

'The way I see it,' Jacqui said, 'it's too much of a coincidence. I mention circles at Dundry on Saturday night and on Monday night-a formation appears. Somebody must have been listening!'

'But who?' I argued. 'There was only Terence, you, me, Garnett and Glenda there, Rog had nipped out for some grub. Terence wouldn't have done it, I didn't do it, I'm sure you didn't, Rog didn't...so...'

'So that leaves Garnett or Glenda!'

'Unless somebody has bugged the caravan!' I suggested, jokingly. Jacqui looked serious.

'There are a few people around with the technical know-how to do just that,' she warned.

It was true. With the collection of film and TV people, strangers and electrical engineers who'd flitted in and out of the caravan over the past few weeks, the expertise needed to plant a small bug or taping device had been there. We vowed to examine the caravan at the first possible opportunity.

The next morning I went to the caravan. The day was bright but cloudy and I took advantage of the lack of rain to clean out the caravan, remove Baldrick's sleeping bag and hunt for the 'Bug'. I gave that caravan a good search, inside, outside and underneath. The only odd thing there was an audio amplifier. Nobody knew how it had come to be in our caravan. Most of us had assumed that it was part of the NTV setup, but when the Japs left, the amplifier stayed behind. Taking no chances, I removed it from the caravan and put it in the boot of my car, later transferring it to my garage. In the remote event of a bug or tape device being in the amp-it would not be of use to any hoaxers now. [5]

The work being done, I brewed tea and sat outside in the sun, reading a book on Freemasonry. Later still, I walked to the front of the hill and looked around the area where Macnish and co. had been (they'd pulled out during the early part of the month). Little signs remained other than some flattened grass. Returning to the caravan I found that nobody else had turned up. As I was on duty at three that afternoon, I would have to leave soon. Just after twelve I locked the caravan and left, meeting Jim Schnabel at the top gate. I told him about the Marlborough and Broad Hinton circles (he'd apparently been back in Oxford for the past day or so) and arranged to meet him on Thursday as I had a day off then.

When I got home, there was a message from Terence Meaden on my answerphone. A circles formation had been reported at Barbury Castle, an ancient camp just east of Swindon. It had been reported to Terence by aerial photographer Richard Wintle.

'....It's the most complex formation ever seen....'

Oh, Hell!

'This important formation MUST be measured!' said Terence. 'And it's down to you. I cannot do it as I'm meeting representatives of *Juniper TV* at Westbury station and taking them to lunch. This will take all afternoon and some of the evening.'

Blimey! That must be some lunch!

'Sorry, Terence. I can't do it - I'm shortly off to work. You'll have to phone Rog.'

Shortly after, Meaden called again. 'I've phoned Roger-he isn't in.'

I said leave it with me and I'll try later. I managed to get Rog on the phone just before I left for work. I explained that we were all otherwise engaged and that the measuring was all down to Jacqui and him. He seemed a little reluctant but agreed to go. At work that afternoon, I rang Jacqui and explained to her what Terence said needed doing.

'I've left the tape and notepad in the kitchen for you and Rog to pick up,' I told her.

'I'll want the camera-pole as well,' she said.

'Sorry. From what Terence says the formation is so big you'll have no time to take pictures. There's so much measuring to be done and it will get dark by nine.'

From the sigh at the other end of the line, I deduced that she didn't think much of this. Then she dropped the bombshell:

'I've just spoken to Rog – he can't leave home until after seven o' clock.'

Hopeless! By the time they got to Barbury it would be nearly dark...

Chapter Fifteen
TRICKERY
Barbury and the straws-The Great American Confession-Upton Scudamore-A Chorost of disapproval-Hoaxers

I spent an uneasy afternoon at work that day. The weather as usual for that summer had turned nasty and by the time came for me to leave work at eleven it had been dull and drizzling for several hours. The unease was due to the feeling I had that the 'alliance' of people who were looking after *'Operation Blue Hill'* was falling apart. Terence Meaden was spending less time at the hill and more time promoting his book or measuring circles. Those of us who had planned the operation with him were spending most of our time there still doing little other than guarding a caravan. Any old Tom, Dick or Harry who passed through was being roped in without the slightest check on their real reasons for being there. I was also getting the impression that Rog and Jacqui were becoming less and less interested in helping out and more interested in spending the time together elsewhere.

And me? It was true to say that I was also becoming disillusioned about the whole affair. Terence was accepting far more circles as being genuine than Paul Fuller or I would. Still, in spite of the odd disagreement, there was that old thing called discipline. We'd planned it, set it up and we'd see it through and sort out the wheat from the chaff during the winter.

When I got home that night there was a phone call from Rog at eleven thirty.

'....It's a fake!' he announced. 'It's complex and bloody huge – but it's a hoax.'

'What's it like, then?' I asked, mind boggling.

'It's a sort of huge triangle with a circle with a cross in it at the top. Then there's a circle with a part bar across it at the bottom left and another circle with a cross at the bottom right. Underneath the triangle is a multi-ringed single. But it's massive,' he repeated.

'What makes you think it's a hoax?'

'A vortex couldn't make this!' said Rog. 'Not only that but Terence got here before we did and even he says it's fake. George Wingfield arrived and told the farmer *"..... You could get £10,000 for this. It's your next holiday or a new Range-Rover...."* [1]

'He said WHAT?'- I couldn't believe George would be so daft. Rog repeated what he'd just said. 'Not only that,' he went on, 'But Jacqui found a clump of damaged stems which looked as if they'd been flattened with ropes or planks or something. She showed these to the farmer, George and Terence. The farmer took the stems away!'

'Good Lord!' This was incredible!

That night I settled down with a glass or two of wine, safe in the knowledge that I didn't have to travel to Barbury Castle at first light to finish the measuring.

Of course, we all know now what Barbury really looked like. It was even more complex than I imagined from Rog's description and in fact it roughly resembled the CCCS' logo. I won't go into the controversy that surrounded the circle's provenance nor the various theories about who or what made it: that's all been done before. Suffice it to say that certain parties were convinced that Barbury Castle's new arrival pointed to a whole new dimension in circles research, others were equally as convinced that it was made by Government Spies, whilst others still were sure that it was a very clever fake.

It was our first real taste of Land Art.

The day following Barbury Castle's discovery, Terence phoned me and told me that the *Daily Star* was sending a reporter down to have a look at the Dundry formation in response to his claiming it as fake when they asked him about it. Could I liase with the reporter? No problem. I phoned the *Star* and arranged to meet reporter Virginia Hill at the *Black Lion* pub in Whitchurch at lunchtime. I also phoned Jacqui and asked if she wanted to be there.

Lunchtime came and off I went to the *Black Lion*. I met Jacqui there and shortly after Virginia Hill arrived with an agency photographer in tow. A quick drink and a few questions and we set off up to the circles. Parking in Dundry Lane we walked into the farmyard and found a sign saying 'To the Circles. £1'. We paid a quid each and walked up through the wheat to the crest of the hill where the formation was. It having been wet the night before, the wheat retained the water and we all got wet again. On arriving I the formation, Virginia asked me how I could tell it was a fake.

Easy. There was no flow of crop. The outer edges had been flattened by something that I deduced was probably a piece of wood. Then everything inside was just flattened any old how. There were masses of broken stems. It was even bad by current hoaxing standards! Then, as we progressed around the tatty formation, so I discovered some broken pieces of batten thrown in the crop just outside the formation. These pieces, if joined, matched the width of the 'pathway' made to form the outline of the formation. I also found a few pieces of paper including a 'Pay and Display' parking ticket from a Bristol car park. This latter might be a pointer towards the hoaxers as the lads taking the money said hardly anyone had visited the circles so far because of the weather.

Virginia was happy with all this. The photographer was happy with the photographs he took, I was happy that I'd been able to prove the formation to be fake. Jacqui, however, was far from happy. A picture I took of her at Dundry that day shows her with a long, miserable face. Perhaps it was the wet.

We took our leave of the *Daily Star* reporter, leaving her to go and confront the farmer with the fact that he had a fake on his land, and with Jacqui, I set off to see the Barbury Castle formation. An hour and a bit later we arrived at Barbury Castle via a network of lanes and tracks. There were several cars already there, one of which we recognised as belonging to Busty Taylor. The hill on which the 'castle' was sited rose high above the field in which the circles lay so we scrambled up the slope to get a grandstand view. From the hill we could see the whole impressive layout of the artwork which was Barbury Castle's crop circles formation. It was certainly an impressive sight and must have taken a few hours to make [2]. Looking across the formation we could see Busty at work with his long camera-pole, accompanied by what looked like Richard Andrews and Ron Jones. It was a pity, I thought as I took a few pictures myself, it was a pity that parts of the crop had 'lodged' (fallen over, weighted down by rain and blown by wind) overnight. It spoiled the perfection of the formation.

We left shortly and drove to Broad Hinton to get some more pictures of the dumb-bell there at Weir Farm. I was not too surprised to see that this formation had now sprouted an additional circle at one end; this had happened to the first of the season's formations, that at Avebury Trusloe and there were a few other reported similar incidents. Somebody was trying to replicate the 'additional ring' fuss of 1988 [3] and get all the researchers going. WE weren't going to be taken in and, let's be frank, these 'add-on' circles were so rough that anyone who thought them the work of anything else but hoaxers deserved stuffing with the rough end of a pineapple!

From Weir farm we went to Marlborough via a road across the downs. Along this road we spotted a 'Linear Complex' at a place called Preshute Down. We stopped and parked up on the verge to take some pictures. The complex was a sort of 'Alton Barnes #1' but with only the one dumb-bell. It was also so neatly laid out, so precise-looking that we instantly labelled it 'Hoax' on the grounds that Nature, should she be involved with the circles, couldn't make something *that* neat. Our short stay here was cut short by the arrival of two members of the Wiltshire Constabulary in a police car. One wound down his window.

'You aren't permitted to park on the verge. Move along,' he said.

Sounded daft to me, there were no notices to that effect. However, we moved on and headed back to Morgan's Hill.

We arrived at the hill at around 18.55. We were the only ones there. A look at the log revealed that, as usual, Baldrick had spent the night there. Jim Schnabel had arrived at five to ten and left at three after making a note in the log: -

'......I stumbled across a dumb-bell formation in the grass, about 50 metres SE of trailer. Tried to duplicate it nearby with feet, to see if it is a hoax. Not sure……has such a small dumb-bell ever been found…?'

Now, there was a story to this. After Jacqui and I had been to Alton Barnes (the day we met George Wingfield) the subject of discussion on more than one occasion had been the layering of the crop where the corridors joined the circles. My argument was that it had been the corridor that had been laid down first, then the circles, and then the corridor widened on top of it. One day, we'd trampled down a small area of rough grass near the caravan in order to prove a point. We managed to replicate the layering in miniature. Having succeeded, we forgot all about the 'trial'. It was this that Jim had come across. I left a note in the log with a brief explanation.

This evening, however, Jacqui and I had been at the caravan for half-an-hour when Jim returned. Rog was not far behind him. The weather was cold and raining so we all stayed in the caravan huddled round the tiny gas fire and drinking coffee. Jim Schnabel was very talkative and asked lots of searching questions about how we viewed the whole affair and what we thought of circles in general. I remember saying that there were so many fakes around and so many circles being reported that we were just trying to collect all the information possible with a view to spending the winter months putting it all together. We were, I said, trying to be as objective as possible. However, between ourselves, I could say that Paul and I were convinced that about 80 percent of everything we'd actually seen was a definite hoax. Jim asked so many questions that at one stage I asked him why he wanted to know so much. His reply was that he needed to ask the questions as he was preparing a thesis on the physiological background to the circles affair.

At that stage, we believed him.

Later on, hunger called so Jacqui, Rog and I went to the '*Waggon*' to eat, Jim declined to accompany us. He left soon after we did. The log for that evening shows that Terence Meaden arrived at the site at nine. He left at eleven, probably because Baldrick had turned up.

The following day was Friday and I was on early shift. That afternoon and evening I stayed home alone to catch up on a few jobs around the house and have an early night. I've no idea what Jacqui and Rog did. Up at Morgan's Hill, Baldrick was at the caravan until nine. Terence arrived at nine-thirty and left at ten. The site was unmanned until 14.00 when Jim Schnabel arrived. Fifty minutes later he left again (that day a group of circles had appeared at Alton Priors-near to Alton Barnes). Meaden came back at 17.20. He'd spent a long day at Alton Priors, measuring the circles, and had been 'Elsewhere on the Downs' (log entry). He was at the caravan for only a few minutes. Jim Schnabel came back, presumably from Alton Priors as well, at about the same time. He stayed a little longer, but was gone by 18.30. Baldrick was another one flitting in and out that day; he arrived at 19.00 and left fifteen minutes later. Jim returned again at 22.30 and left at 23.45, whilst Baldrick finally came back well after midnight to spend the night at the caravan. He'd been at Alton Priors as well. What on earth he was doing there until nearly midnight was anyone's guess. However, a large American (who seemed to think he was a Viking) called Jon-Erik Beckjord, who ran some sort of museum in the States, had arrived in the area. Erik the Viking believed that aliens were responsible for the circles in the corn. Baldrick had been seen spending quite a lot of time with Beckjord, so perhaps they were plotting something together.

Saturday 20th July 1991

At six on Saturday morning, Baldrick left the caravan to go back to Alton Priors. Jim Schnabel spent most of the day coming and going at the caravan and at 15.00 was joined by Rita Goold. Paul Fuller in turn arrived at 16.20. This time it was Paul's turn to be quizzed by Schnabel. Jim left later, just after Rita. Paul had a relatively quiet time after Jim's departure. A couple of walkers turned up on their way to nearby Cherhill and chatted to him about crop circles for a while. After they'd gone it was back to the quiet of a summer's afternoon on a lone hilltop in Wiltshire until 18.00 when Terence arrived.

Driving up through Chippenham, I tried my CB radio to see if any of the others were around. I eventually made contact with Jacqui Griffiths just after Chippenham: she was travelling up from Bath on the A4. Rog meanwhile, was heading towards Chippenham via Castle Combe and the three of us linked up near Calne. We remained in radio contact until we reached the bottom of Morgan's Hill at roughly the same time.

Paul and Terence seemed pleased to see us. I broached the subject of Baldrick with Terence on the grounds that if he was one of Meaden's friends, then could he please keep the place a little tidier? I was surprised to find out that he was not a friend of Terence, merely an acquaintance who happened to be French. We decided that Baldrick would have to go!

At 20.45 Terence announced that he was going home. Paul was staying the night, as were Rog and I. We all decided to follow Terence to the bottom of the hill and go to the pub for grub. At the *Waggon and Horses* we found the place full of a collection of weirdoes and nutters. Sorry, but that was the only was I could describe the people in the pub that night. There were traveller types with tatty old clothes and sweatbands(!) and a few who were just weird. There was a strange atmosphere in the bar. Erik the Viking was in there chatting with Baldrick, Richard Andrews talking with Rita Goold, Jim Schnabel talking to most people. However, we were hungry so food and drink was ordered.

Whilst at the bar I noticed that there were several copies of the *Crop Circle Enigma* – the CCCP book – on sale behind the bar. I talked the pub landlord into agreeing to sell a few copies of Terence's book as well as it turned out that the landlord had no idea that different factions were involved in trying to solve the mystery of the circles: he thought that we were all CCCS!

After chucking-out time, Jacqui went home, leaving Paul, Rog, Jim and me to go back to Morgan's Hill. As we approached the hill we noticed the lights of a car moving up the track leading to the top of the hill. We couldn't think who we knew who would be arriving at that time of the night, except of course, Baldrick.

It wasn't Baldrick, but a group of four youths, somewhat the worse for drink. By the time we'd parked up at the caravan and wandered back to where they'd parked (on the spot where Macnish and his group had been) they were trying to pitch a tent. Not easy in the dark and even more difficult when you're pissed. We asked one of them if they had the farmer's permission to be there. They claimed they had. We couldn't argue, as we had no information either way, so we left them to it. They were gone by dawn.

It was whilst we talked at the caravan that Jim Schnabel revealed that he was planning on writing an article about the circles affair. This was a surprise as we all thought he was student writing a thesis.

'If I were you, ' I said, 'I'd speak to Terence first, after all, you've been taken into his and our confidence. There's a lot we'd rather not have in the public domain yet. At least, not until we've had the chance to evaluate all the evidence from this year and 1990.'

Jim refused. 'If I was to check it out with Meaden I'd set myself up for the accusation that he was censoring my article.'

'All the same, it's only polite to mention it, Jim. You've been a guest here. We've let you know a lot that we wouldn't have told a stranger, because you told Terence that you were a graduate writing a thesis.'

Schnabel grinned. 'I am writing a thesis-but I might go public with it!'

There was no reasoning with that so we left it to him to tell Meaden. We, of course, would let the professor know about the article whenever one of us saw him first. The 'article' turned out to be a book '*Round in Circles*' and an article in a Sunday supplement in collaboration with another player in the circles story who, at this point, hadn't been cast. He was Robert Irving, of whom more later, in Book Two.

Whilst we were all talking with Jim Schnabel, a plan had been hatched. Jim was keen to see what was going on at Bratton (I can't remember why, but I think he wanted to know how to get to the top of the hill and wanted us to show him). Paul was none too keen on driving over to Westbury at that time of night as he'd had a couple of pints. Eventually it was agreed that Jim and I would go to Bratton and keep watch whilst Rog went to Alton Barnes. Paul would stay at the caravan.

Jim and I arrived (in separate cars) at the top of Bratton camp at around one-thirty. I established radio contact with Rog, who then left Morgan's Hill and drove to Alton Barnes. From the top of the hill, near the site of the 1990 Blackbird watch, we could see the smoke issuing from the chimney of the cement works. This was a good landmark and could be seen for miles. On this occasion the smoke was almost horizontal, which gave us a good indication of wind strength and direction. At this time the wind was too strong for a plasma vortex to form. There was eight-eighths cloud cover.

Just after two, the wind dropped and we were on alert. A car drove up, saw us there and hastily drove off again. Rog reported that the wind had dropped almost to nothing at Alton Barnes. By two-thirty all was very still. The skies began to clear. Twenty minutes later Jim and I saw a small ball of light low in the sky in the direction of north-northeast. We estimated it to be about eight to ten miles away. It vanished quite quickly. A flare? Doubtful as the Army firing ranges were behind us. It remained a mystery.

Just before three, Jim Schnabel left for his lodgings. Ten minutes later Rog called up.

'There's some car headlights up at the car park near Adam's Grave,' he said, quietly.

Five minutes later he came through again. 'There's a series of blue flashes from the car park area-looks like the light from a flashgun.'

By three-thirty the wind had picked up again and the cloud was coming back. There was no sign of anything happening, either on the human or meteorological fronts. We called off the watch and went home

After being out for most of the night, I spent most of Sunday morning asleep. Except that I was awakened at eight-thirty by a phone call from, of all people, Baldrick.

''Allo? Pierre? Il est Yves. I 'ave left the caravan but I 'ave to leave it unlock. Zere is no key!'

Whenever we had to leave the caravan unmanned, the door key was hidden in the battery box on the front of the caravan. This was only supposed to be known to a handful of people. Baldrick wasn't one of them, but he had found out. Now, after spending the night in the caravan as usual, the little Frenchman had come to leave and discovered that the key was missing. He'd found my number on a *CERES* fact sheet in the caravan and called me from a phone box.

Paul Fuller had been the last to have the key-he must have taken it home with him. I advised Baldrick to shut the door and hope for the best. I'd be there as soon as I could. Then I went back to sleep for an hour or two more.

I arrived at the caravan that afternoon at around 15.00 to find Rita Gould waiting in her car. I invited her in and put the kettle on. We got chatting and I asked her about her work as a medium. She laughed. 'I'm not a medium,' she smiled. 'You must be thinking about somebody else.'

I wasn't. This was undoubtedly the same Rita Goold who had conducted seances for years and was well known to psychic researchers like Andy Collins. I didn't know why she wanted to deny her 'past' but, as it wasn't really relevant to the circles game, I decided to leave the subject for another occasion. Whilst we drank tea, Rita, who was a great chatterbox and gossip, mentioned that Andy Collins and a group of fourteen friends from Essex had arrived at Alton Barnes the previous evening.

'...They came and sat in the circles,' she chuckled, '...Then after a while suddenly said, *"These are the wrong circles"* – and left to go to Marlborough! What d'you make of that?'

What indeed! She continued:

'....Then, after dark, I was sitting in a folding chair by the side of the field with a farmhand, watching the fields, when we saw lights in the latest set of circles. Well, we had to investigate, so we quietly crept across the field and found a group of youths in one of the circles. And they were smoking! Well! The farmhand asked them what the hell they were doing and do you know what they said?'

I hadn't a clue.

'...They said that they had permission to be there! The farmhand said that they did not and they said that they had the farmer's permission and that they were CCCS. He said "I *AM* the farmer – GET OUT!" The kids then said "Look out-we have a Wolf-Dog!" – and a poodle ran out of the corn!'

Rita laughed at the memory.

'Then,' she continued, '....The youths asked us if we were Meaden's group. We said of course not. It was suspicious though; they were all wearing combat gear and dark scarves to hide their faces. IF they were CCCS then they broke all the rules by being there without permission, smoking and taking a dog into the crop.'

At that point a small convoy of vehicles arrived outside. Terence Meaden, his wife and an attractive French girl got out of one car. Terence introduced the girl as his niece, Caroline. Then two Frenchmen from the UFO sceptic group VECA came across, followed by a National Geographic camera crew who wanted to film Terence. Two lads from another car were introduced as two academic students who 'may be able to help in the future'.

National Geographic were keen to get on and wanted to film Rita telling the story about some events she'd witnessed during Condrews and Fandango's 1989 cropwatch in Hampshire. They all trooped off to the far side of the hill, whilst Mrs. Meaden and Caroline chatted to the two Frenchmen. The weather being cloudy but quite warm, I seized the opportunity to lay out my waterproofs and wellies on the grass and wash them down. Whilst I was doing this, Jacqui arrived and VECA and the students departed. It was time for coffee.

Terence and Rita joined us later. Rita was, of course, the star of the show. She loved the cameras and the attention – but then, didn't we all? This was our 15 minutes of fame! Terence was having more than fifteen minutes of fame, though.

'We have to leave now,' he said, 'National Geographic want to film me at Bratton this evening.'

National Geographic and Rita Goold departed, followed within half an hour by the Meadens. To complete the musical chairs feeling, Rog now arrived! The three of us who were left drank coffee and sat around in the warmth of a Wiltshire summer evening, waiting for the next lot of circles to crop up. We didn't have to wait long: at 19.40, just as we were considering what to do about eating that evening, Rog's mobile phone rang.

'Roger, it's Terence. I'm at Upton Scudamore. There's an exciting new formation just been found. I'll need help to measure it. Can you attend?'

'Oh, I expect we can. Where exactly are you?'

'Near the railway line. It's the same field that the ringed singles appeared in last year.'

We knew it. A couple of miles on the Westbury side of Warminster.

'OK, Terence, we'll be there as soon as we can.'

As we made ready to leave, so a problem loomed large.

'How do we lock the caravan?' muttered Jacqui.

I thought for a moment.

'Rog, could you ring Paul and ask him if he's got the keys?' I asked. 'And Jacqui – do you have any stiff wire in your car?'

While Rog dialled the UFOlogist's number, Jacqui rooted around in the back of her car and came back with a coat hanger. 'Any good?' she asked.

Perfect! I went into the caravan, closed the door and locked it from the inside. Then I climbed out through a window and locked the window behind me by means of poking the straightened coat hanger through the window-rubber. Rog meanwhile had got connected to Paul Fuller.

'Oh, Hi, Roger. I know why you're calling; Yes, I've got the keys. Sorry. I'll bring the keys back when I come up to the caravan on Monday evening.'

Our goal was just over twenty miles away and it took us roughly forty minutes to arrive at Upton Scudamore. We turned off the A36 just past the turning for Chapmanslade and drove as far as we could down a track. No sign of Meaden. We retraced our route and followed the A36 towards the roundabout on the outskirts of Warminster where we turned off towards Westbury. From the bridge where the bypass crossed the railway line we could see the tiny figure of the professor in the middle of a HUGE barley field. Back we went to the track we'd originally gone down and we parked up.

After crossing two fields we were still nowhere near the Prof. Then we came into the enormous barley field but still couldn't see anyone. Surely he hadn't gone home? Then, Jacqui called 'I can see him,' – and there he was, with someone else we didn't recognise, about half a mile away! Rog and I strode on along the tractor-lanes. It looked as if we would have to go right round the entire field to get to Terence.

'That's it!' announced Jacqui, sitting down. 'I've had enough!'

We left her to recover and moved on. Luck! Within a few yards we came across a footpath which ran across the field and would lead us to where Terence was standing. We called back to Jacqui and walked on with renewed vigour. Rog's mobile rang.

'Hello, Roger. It's Terence. Where are you?'

'About 100 yards away!'

Terence introduced his companion as a local doctor who'd come across the formation and phoned the Professor. The formation was astonishing. There were two circles joined by a corridor. A further corridor led out of the second circle to end a few yards on in a sort of 'trident' shape. Either side of the first corridor, not joined to it, was a series of three 'boxes', joined at the top by a 'crossbar'. These looked not unlike a set of cricket stumps with bails on. But the really stunning thing about this formation was that the barley in the circles and boxes had not been completely flattened, but was 'knitted' into an intricate woven pattern. It looked for all the world as if the crop had been flattened by rushing water. To stand on it was to break it. How on earth could this have been hoaxed? [3] Hoax it surely had to be though, because to try to fit it into any part of the Meaden vortex theory was impossible.

Nearby was a scroll and a few small singles. We set about some rapid measuring because it was now gone 21.00 and dusk was falling. Treading in the main formation resulted in broken stems galore. It was such a pity to damage the circles. We estimated that the nearby singles had been there for about a week as birds had eaten all the seeds. The work done we went our separate ways: Terence and the doctor to the nearby services where they'd left their cars; the rest of us back across the fields to our cars. By consensus, we three returned to the services for food as it was now past 22.00 and we didn't know if the chippers in Warminster and Westbury would be open on a Sunday. It was also too late to get pub grub. The fish and chips in the services was half-cold and horribly expensive, but it was better than nothing.

Monday 22nd July 1991

I went to Jacqui's house this morning and we went to Upton Scudamore again. This time we had Jacqui's video camera and were going with the express intention of taking video footage of the formation we'd seen the night before. This was to enable us to spend time carefully studying it after the season had finished, as we still couldn't work out how on earth it had been made. At the field we'd just finished filming the circles when Jacqui spied a small figure approaching.

'Oh, God! It's Baldrick!' she cried.

Sure enough, the diminutive Frenchman was making his way across the crop towards us. Of course, he recognised us straight away. Word had got round about the formation and Baldrick was just one of many 'croppies' who were heading towards Upton Scudamore. As the Frenchman began to set his camera up, we bade him farewell and left.

That afternoon I went to Morgan's Hill by myself, arriving at 15.30. The caravan was empty and locked. I opened the side window with the bent coathanger, clambered in and cooked myself a small meal with some food I'd brought with me. The weather was cloudy and breezy. After I'd eaten I went for a walk around the hill and at the top gate met Andrew Woolley with his two dogs. He called out to me and came across to where I stood at the top gate. He had a frown on his face. I soon found out why.

'I need a word with your lot,' he said. 'This grass..' –he indicated the top of the hill with a sweep of his hand- '…This grass is a crop. We are intending to cut it again soon. You must stop driving over it. Stick to the road. Mr. Brown is very angry that cars are not using the road. If things don't change pretty soon, he'll have you all off the hill.'

Now, I knew that it was not any *CERES* personnel doing this. However NTV and their associates had not bothered where they drove, nor did Professor Ohtsuki who frequently drove his motorhome across the grass. His students weren't particular about using the road either. But the main culprit was none other than Baldrick! Yves would drive through the top gate, use the road to a point just beyond the copse then take a straight line across the grass to the caravan. He'd been warned about it before. I promised Andrew Woolley that we would ensure that nobody drove across the grass again and later that afternoon I wrote a note to this effect on every remaining page of the Daily Log and Weather logbooks.

While I was talking to Andrew Woolley, I saw Terence Meaden's car climbing slowly up the hill. I opened the gate and waved him through, noting that he had another man in the car with him. Once they were through I shut the gate, left Andrew Woolley to continue his walk with his dogs and headed off to the caravan to see who our latest visitor was.

When I reached the caravan, Meaden and the newcomer were still sitting in the professor's car, deep in conversation. When he saw me. Terence opened the car door.

'Peter, this is Mike Chorost. He's an American science writer. He's over here to study the crop circles.'

I shook hands with the yank. He was a small man with rapid-fire speech. He and Terence lapsed into conversation again so I went into the caravan to wait until they'd finished. It wasn't long before they came into the caravan and sat down. From the tone of conversation I could see that there was some difference of opinion taking place. I listened, interested. To my surprise it was obvious that Chorost's point of view seemed to be lodged firmly with those of CCCS-which was odd for a 'science writer'. But then, he *was* American.

'It's no good, Dr Meaden, you cannot carry on expecting people to accept your views,' said Chorost. 'You must prove your point.'

'What!' exclaimed Meaden. '*I* must prove my point? I've been in this game longer than anyone else- why should I have to prove anything?'

Chorost was getting worked up now. 'Look, you're like that astronomer who thought that the sun stood still whilst the earth revolved around it. You are barking up the wrong tree. You keep changing your theory to make it fit the evidence.....'

At this Meaden exploded. 'I haven't changed my theory one iota! It's always been the same! Some of the points have been changed in the light of new evidence-but that's science!'

Chorost was getting pretty angry now. He accused Terence of being a 'straight-line scientist'. I chipped in.

'Look, it's not only conventional scientists who are involved-and if you knew Terence Meaden you'd know that he is about as far from being a straight-line scientist as you can get.'

'And what about you?' demanded the Yank.

'I'm an engineer by trade,' I replied, '..And I have had a great interest in 'Earth Mysteries' for many years, But from an investigative standpoint. I don't accept all I see and read. I have looked at many crop circles over the last few years and seen many hoaxes, but I think that Dr Meaden has a theory which is worth investigating-otherwise I wouldn't be here and neither would my colleagues. We've all given up a lot of our spare time to help Dr Meaden. At least *CERES* has a cross-section of people in it. Other organisations seem only to consist of those who want to believe that crop circles are there to be worshipped-just the sort of people whom Terence has written about in the *Goddess of the Stones*.'

Chorost wasn't impressed. He took the view that Meaden's theory should embrace 'other' likely causes of the circles. I argued that that was partly the reason people like Paul Fuller and I were there-to give the subject the benefit of the paranormal researcher as well. *CERES* was comprised of a cross-section of individuals with all sorts of beliefs. And we had all come to the conclusion, after several years, that there was no evidence of paranormal or extra-terrestrial involvement whatsoever.

By this stage Chorost was getting really angry, presumably because we had a counter argument to each argument he put up.

'Look,' he gasped. 'I'm getting kinda worked up about all this. I need to walk around a bit.'

He left the caravan and vanished into the darkness, muttering to himself.
Oh, hell. Had I said too much? I glanced at Terence Meaden who was grinning broadly. He gave me the thumbs up.

'He is difficult,' he grinned. 'I wouldn't normally bring someone like him here, but, surprisingly, he has influence with American Science magazines – even though he supports the 'other side'.'

After nearly ten minutes, Chorost returned. He had calmed down a lot and accepted a cup of coffee. Happily, he had taken the time out to contemplate all that had been said (and it was a lot more than I have written above) and we returned to the subject of crop circles. Chorost now accepted that Terence Meaden and *CERES* were entitled to have their theory and reasons for coming to the conclusions we had regards the circles. He was now happy that Terence's vortex theory had a basis in science. He himself still believed that there was also some other force at work but he was entitled to his opinion and Terence and I would not hold that against him. Eventually, it was time for Mike Chorost to leave and we all parted on friendly terms. Terence left with him and as they set off down the hill so a set of headlights could be seen approaching the bottom gate.

Shortly after, as I prepared to settle down for a night's watching, Baldrick's car appeared round the copse and sped straight across the grass to park next to the caravan! The little Frenchman was surprised to see me and even more surprised to get a mild bollocking for driving across the grass and being told that he had to sleep in his car. I had put a message on his sleeping bag (which he left at the caravan) suggesting that he sleep elsewhere as he wasn't even keeping up the log whenever he stayed the night. I also wrote that after the following Thursday he would have to stay somewhere else, as we would be using the caravan every night. We weren't but he wasn't to know that.

The night stayed fine but a strong breeze meant that there were no 'alert' situations. However, at 04.06 I recorded two quick 'blips' on the radar approx. 1.8 miles due north of us. This would be in the area of the bowl below the Cherhill White Horse – a place where circles had appeared in the past. On this occasion though, nothing was found when the area was inspected later that day. These 'blips' occurred frequently in different places throughout the watch. They would appear on the screen as a spot, which would quickly fade. As well as the Cherhill blips there were occurrences in the region of Alton Barnes and Stanton St. Bernard. One could speculate that these blips were electrically-charged atmospheric vortices registering on the radar, but without expert interpretation we were unable to claim that as factual evidence for Terence's theory.

I left shortly after dawn and Baldrick must have sneaked into the caravan after my departure because he made a couple of entries in the weather log. The morning passed without anything out of the ordinary being reported. The weather did its usual and turned to rain with a thunderstorm being recorded during the afternoon. Terence, who took over the watch from 10.00 along with Prof. Kikuchi, was visited at 17.00 by three Germans from Tempo magazine. They were later joined by George Bathurst. I returned for the evening shift but didn't stay the night. Neither did anyone else.

During the afternoon I'd received a phone call from Rog. He'd been contacted by Dave Barratt of GWR Radio, the local independent radio station for the South West. They wanted to make a documentary about crop circles and somehow had got Rog's number. Rog was invited to take part in this documentary.

'Fine,' I said, wishing him luck. 'But OK it with Terence first so that you know what he is happy for you to say regards the '*Goddess*' stuff.'

This was not censorship. Terence Meaden had, during the 1990/91-winter season, shown us a vast amount of the information he had gathered towards his theory that ancient peoples had seen and worshipped those mysterious circular ground markings left by whirlwinds/vortexes. Only some of that information had been published in the *Goddess of the Stones* and two more books were planned. It was helpful to know what could be mentioned if one was asked about future plans or theories in this direction. That was why I urged Rog to speak to Terence before taking part in the documentary. However, much to my surprise, Rog dismissed my suggestion. 'I don't see the need for that,' he said.

Later still, Terence Meaden phoned. 'Didn't we give him a pasting last night,' he chuckled, referring to the Chorost visit. 'Still,' he added, 'It was necessary. Busty has been in touch,' he went on, 'For the first time in four or five weeks. He's been flying and reports ringed circles near Salisbury and at Sixpenny Handley on the Blandford road. Could you visit these? I have to go and meet Professor Kikuchi.'

I said that no, I couldn't, because nobody would be at the caravan otherwise. However, Eddie Brown had been in touch and was coming up from Bournemouth to cover a night duty at the caravan soon. I'd ask him to look in at Sixpenny Handley. Meaden agreed. I told him that Rog had been invited to take part in the GWR documentary. 'I sincerely hope you've been asked to take part as well,' said the Prof. I replied that I hadn't, and he was quite surprised. I changed the subject. 'Baldrick needs to be spoken to again. He's still using the caravan as a doss-house whenever he can and still persists in driving across the grass. Andrew Woolley was doing his nut about it the other day. Could you have a word with him-in French? He might understand it better in his own language.'

Meaden agreed to this.

The following day's duty at Morgan's Hill was covered by Terence in the morning and myself for the evening. It rained all day. Eddie Brown phoned my answer machine to say that he'd been to Sixpenny Handley, found the fields partly harvested but failed to find any trace of the formation reported there. He got soaked into the bargain.

Chapter Sixteen
HARVEST HOME

Hoaxes and more hoaxes-Harvest-Jim's theory-Blue Hill finishes after 60 days on the hill

Nobody logged in at the '*Blue Hill*' site until 19.00 on the 26th when Jim Schnabel arrived, failed to let go of the top gate in time and received an electric shock from the cow fence. He was followed on site by Paul Fuller, a visitor called Paul Ferguson, Terence Meaden, Roger Davis and Jacqui Griffiths and a trio of interested Dutch visitors. Most of these had gone by 22.00, leaving the Dutchmen, Paul, and Terence. I arrived at half past midnight. Terence gave me some press cuttings for the files and announced that he now agreed with the rest of the team's doubts over the earlier Newton St. Loe complex.

'The way I see it,' he mused, 'Several major cities have had a complex formation made close to them. Swindon had Barbury Castle, Bristol had Dundry and Bath has Newton St. Loe. As we are certain that Barbury and Dundry are both fakes it follows that Bath has to be fake also, as there are doubts about its authenticity. I feel we must label both the Newton St. Loe formations as 'Doubtful' in the database.'

This was good news. Both Paul Fuller and I had been pushing Terence to be more careful about authenticating circles straight away and at last it seemed that the message was getting home.

By a quarter to one, just Paul and I were left to cover the night turn. We were on alert most of the night as the winds dropped. Nothing much happened except that a couple of flare-like objects were seen in the sky in the direction of Urchfont at 02.00. They probably were flares: with so much of the area surrounding us being in use by the Army (who held regular exercises) flares were quite common; that didn't stop people reporting them as UFO's or Plasma Vortices.

At dawn, I departed leaving Paul to cover the day watch. He had an uneventful morning until just after mid-day when the Range-Rover of Farmer Brown arrived. The farmer was not at all happy.

'I'm sick and tired of you people driving across the grass!' he complained. 'Andrew Woolley has spoken to you about it but it still goes on!'

Paul tried to explain that it wasn't actually one of our group who was the culprit and that we had warned people to keep off the grass. The farmer wasn't listening.

'That grass is a crop,' he stormed. 'I'm going to padlock the top gate! You'll all have to leave your cars at the bottom of the hill!'

That would be very awkward indeed. Paul smoothed things down by saying that we were probably only going to be there for another week or so and that he would ensure that a notice was written and placed on both sides of the top gate to warn people to stay on the road. The farmer seemed to take this in good faith and relented. 'OK, I won't lock the gate,' he said. 'But any more tyre tracks through my silage grass and you're all off the hill!'

Paul agreed that this was fair and when the farmer had gone, he set about making the notices. Of course, as I later mentioned to Paul, if Farmer Brown hadn't poohed on us and let NTV/Circlevision muscle in on our agreed site, we'd have kept ourselves to ourselves and all these extra visitors would have been unaware of our presence.

Yet again this damaging of the crop was the fault of Baldrick. He'd now been warned several times to keep to the road. He'd been told three times that week to stay out of the caravan unless invited in. The trouble was that he knew where we hid the keys; we had to secrete the keys about the van because there were so many different people who were officially using it on *CERES* business and we couldn't get copies made for all of them. It was getting to the stage where he'd have to be told to Sod Off. If being polite wasn't working then perhaps rudeness would.

Jim Schnabel arrived that afternoon, as did Keith Mortimore from the Tornado and Storm Research Organisation. Keith had come to change the recording sheets in the weather stations, which had been set up around the site. Rita Goold dropped by and said she had a story to tell Paul. Jim Schnabel soon departed to go to Alton Barnes (yet again! Whatever did he do there?). When the others had left, Rita took Paul to one side and told him the following tale.

It seemed that Rita had met up with a couple of young men during one of her nocturnal watches at Alton Barnes. These lads had been sitting in their car at West Overton (not far from West Kennett) when they'd heard voices in the night. They had ventured into the field where the noises came from and had observed a group of around six people all dressed in black flattening a rough shape into the crop with the aid of planks of wood. Frightened of the consequences of being spotted, the lads had left the field and gone to where they knew someone else was crop watching and there they told their story to Rita.

Rita being no fool had even got the names and addresses of the lads. She gave this information to Paul Fuller who duly recorded it in the duty log. He also advised Terence Meaden, who turned up after 18.00. Meaden in turn told of some circles reported at East Kennett, which were thought to be hoaxes.

And so it turned out. Paul, Terence and Rita went off to East Kennett only to find a poor copy of the Alton Barnes 1990 formation. Terence was driving, of all things, an E-Type Jaguar! His Peugeot being in for repairs to the starter motor, the Prof. had borrowed one of the classic cars which was for sale in his showroom. Unfortunately, both Terence and Paul parked in a field adjacent to the Kennett formation. They hadn't noticed that a horse was sharing the field. This horse fancied a snack and decided that the E-Type's bonnet looked tasty. Having found that it wasn't to his liking, the equine vandal tried to sample a touch of Metro bonnet for afters. This too, wasn't much of a meal so the nag returned to the greener grass, leaving a Jaguar and a Metro in need of a little attention from a spraygun.

Terence, Paul and Rita also called in at the Lurkley Hill (West Overton) fake, which was one of the worst they'd seen. To their amusement, they found the CCCP's Michael Green in the circle with a film crew. He was declaring the circle to be '….genuine….'!

By now, the reports of circles coming in were far too many for us to make any sort of assessment as to their connection with any possible plasma-vortex. As mentioned earlier, we were merely recording the information and leaving the evaluation until the winter months. However, we could say which ones we knew or thought were hoaxes. The total of fakes by the 28th July stood at 33 positive hoaxes, 6 'doubtful' and 2 'uncertain'. And these were mostly the circles that had actually been visited by one or more *CERES* personnel. There were many more we'd had reported to us but hadn't been able to visit. The 'insects' which were appearing, we gave no credence to at all.

When I got home from work late on the evening of the 27th July, there were messages on the answerphone. Jacqui had called to say that she had received a call from Rog who in turn had heard from Terence, that a new formation had appeared at West Kennett. Terence had also called to say that we'd apparently missed some circles at Upton Scudamore when we'd been there the previous week. He was there measuring these circles when he phoned. He also mentioned the West Kennett circles, adding that he had reports of more circles at East Kennett and at Ogbourne, near Marlborough.

Sunday 28th July 1991

Terence Meaden had been forced to stay at the caravan overnight, as the E-Type wouldn't start. The night had been mostly foggy and therefore uneventful but the following day turned out fine and sunny. This brought people out in droves. Not only did walkers appear on footpaths but also the farmers took advantage of the fine weather to start harvesting. Combine harvesters began to appear in the cornfields: the crop watching season would soon be over.

Jim Schnabel was the first to arrive and, soon after, Morgan's Hill was blessed with quite a congregation on that Sunday afternoon. Terence Meaden's wife and son turned up to rescue him; I arrived and shortly afterwards, so did Paul Fuller with Richard Wintle, an aerial photographer who'd been the first to discover the Barbury Castle formation. Wintle had more photos to show us all including some weird shapes which we thought 'fake' just from the pictures, including nine 'Olympic' rings in a field at Ogbourne. The Meadens and Jim were going to have lunch in a restaurant in Tisbury-which wasn't exactly local. 'It's cheap, though,' grinned Terence. Paul and I didn't fancy this idea so we later went off to the *Crown* at Bishops Cannings to try to get some food after leaving a note for Jacqui Griffiths who was travelling up separately. We were successful, Paul enjoying a curry whilst I had cottage pie. This pub was closer than the *Waggon and Horses* and had the advantage that it wasn't full of crop circles enthusiasts, most of whom didn't believe in the Meaden theory and seemed to openly dislike us. This was possibly due to the antics of people like George Wingfield, who was openly critical of anyone who didn't believe in the 'unknown energies' or UFO involvement in the circles. He thought that we were part of a Great Government Cover-Up and were inventing the vortex to conceal the Real Truth. Whatever that was supposed to be! This made time spent at the Beckhampton pub increasingly uncomfortable for us, so we started using the *Crown* instead.

We all met up at the caravan later that afternoon. Jacqui Griffiths had arrived and some time was spent trying to get Meaden's errant car started. After a while spent at fruitless endeavour, we gave up. The E-Type would not go. The Meadens departed for home to arrange rescue for the Jag, Terence promising to return at about 17.30 with another car. Jacqui, Paul, Jim and I all went to see the fake at East Kennett. We set off in separate cars, arranging to meet at Silbury Hill car park. It was full of cars. Paul decided to go on to Lurkley Hill. Jacqui drove slowly past as I found a space. 'I can't find anywhere to park!' she yelled. 'I'm going to follow Paul.' God knows where Jim Schnabel had gone. I locked my car and walked up the track to West Kennett barrow. Halfway there a clutch of tourists passed me on their way back from the barrow. Bringing up the rear of this group was.... Jim!

'You can't get in to the formation,' he called, '...But you can see it from the barrow. See you.'

He wandered off down the track and I went on to the Long Barrow. Jim was right. Standing on top of the barrow one had a good view of the circles. I took a few shots with a long lens on the camera and went off to meet the others at Lurkely Hill. At Lurkely Hill I parked up and found Paul and Jacqui at the roadside. 'It's a horrible mess!' declared Jacqui.

Paul made to get into his car. 'I'm going back to the Blue Hill site to fetch Terence-if he's there,' he called. 'I'll be back as soon as I can.'

Jacqui returned with me to the circle. They were right. It was horrible. No 'flow' – just trampled and battered down crop. We sat in the circle and took some pictures and just watched people come and go for a while. Then Paul and Terence turned up, Meaden driving his son's Volvo this time.

'*National Geographic* have arrived,' announced the Prof. '...They wish to interview me again.'

OK. We'll watch. I might even meet Di, the sound recordist again! As we waited for the Nat.Geog. team to arrive, a black Fiat Panda shot up the road and parked at an odd angle on the verge. Jim Schnabel was driving and appeared to be looking for something as he was ducking down to floor level in his car. The camera crew and interviewer arrived, but, to my disappointment, with a different sound recordist. They set up their gear at the roadside and started to film Terence. Jim Schnabel got out of his car and walked purposefully towards them. In his hand was a small tape recorder, which he thrust at the interviewer.

'*Jim Schnabel – Washington Post!*' he announced, much to everyone's surprise. '....*Can you confirm or deny that you paid students from Southampton University to hoax circles?*'

The National Geographic interviewer looked mildly shocked by this sudden interruption.

'Hoax? What hoax?' said someone.

'That one for a start!' cried Jim, pointing at the circular mess in the field.

'No. Not us,' retorted the interviewer, '....And while you're at it, Buddy, shouldn't you be asking our permission to record us?'

Schnabel shrugged. 'So you're not guilty, then?'

'No. We *did* get some people from Southampton University to make a circle for us all right. It's way over there behind that hill....' -He indicated a vaguely Alton Barnes direction – '....But it was done as an experiment – alright?'

Schnabel looked sheepish. 'OK,' he said and switched off his tape.

'Remember, you ought to ask before taping people's voices!' said the interviewer, sternly.

Jim nodded, head down like a naughty schoolboy being told off for running in the corridor.
The camera team now made to move off up the hill a little way. Jacqui and I started to follow, only to have our way blocked by a cameraman.

'I'd kinda like you to stay away,' he drawled, '....He gets kinda shy if there's people around...'

'Who gets shy?' I asked.

'Dr Meaden....'

'What? Terence – shy? Cobblers!'

The cameraman smirked. 'We-e-l-l – the camera gets shy!'

I was angry by now. 'Look, this is England! It's a free country, sunshine!'

The Yank gave a particularly horrible leer and walked off behind his colleagues.
Jim Schnabel got into his car and drove off. Jacqui and I followed the camera crew to where they were about to film Terence, sitting in a field. Three other youngsters arrived and were welcomed by the Nat.Geog. lot. These latest arrivals were two boys and a girl and turned out to be the witnesses to the Lurkely circle's creation, as mentioned by Rita Goold. They were filmed giving their version of events. We could hear some of the interview:

'*.....Yeah. We saw them. It really pissed me off, 'coz, -like-I'm really into circles, and to catch hoaxers at it-well...*'

Terence wandered over and we walked into a nearby dumb-bell formation, a hoax made some time ago. It had had add-on circles and spurs, which had been made recently. Terence told me that the 'students' mentioned by Jim were our old adversaries, The Wessex Skeptics. They were 'experimenting' with the faking of circles.

'God knows why,' muttered the Prof. 'They could have taken up the invitation to follow *CERES* for the summer-they would have seen plenty of fakes then.' He was becoming a little disillusioned with all the hoaxes we were finding. We vowed to keep tabs on the Horrible Skeptics from now on. We'd also keep an eye on Sonny Jim – *Washington Post*? Who was he kidding!

Meanwhile, Rog arrived at the caravan at 18.30 and found it empty. He watched alone until 20.00. Nobody else turned up so he went home again. Terence returned to the caravan after midnight and stayed until morning – an E-Type Jaguar was far too valuable to leave unattended on top of a hill all night! Jacqui and I made our separate ways home.

The next day Terence managed to get the E-Type recovered and he went home for the morning, only to return with Agronomist John Graham. I didn't see them as they had moved on by the time I arrived in the evening. The harvest was now going ahead rapidly as the current spell of dry weather continued. As I drove up the hill towards the top gate I could see the combine harvester busily cutting its way through the circles which had appeared under our noses only the previous month – although it seemed like years ago, now.

The caravan was deserted and as it was such a pleasant evening I tidied up and then sat out in the evening sun, writing up my notes.

The Sun sank slowly into the west.

A hiker passed by and stopped to have a chat about circles. He was fully supportive of the scientific theory and had little good to say about those who believed that Little Green Men were creating crop circles. Regrettably, he was in a minority. The weekend just gone had seen a three-day 'conference' at Glastonbury. Entitled 'Investigating Crop Circles', it promised:

'......*Lectures, an open Debate, an exhibition, Dowsing walkabouts, Tours, celebration and an opportunity to meet people investigating Crop Circles...*' there would also be a 'Circle dance'.

Speakers included Isobel Kingston (the large medium we'd met at Beckhampton in 1990), George Wingfield, Colin Andrews, Richard Andrews, Busty Taylor. Oddly enough, even though it was billed as an opportunity to meet people investigating the circles, nobody associated with *CERES* was invited to take part. This was a portent of things to come. The great publicity machines were rolling and anyone who'd as much as waved a pair of bent coat-hangers in the general direction of a crop circle was now able to class themselves as an 'Expert'. There was no attempt to provide an open forum with speakers from different disciplines. The CCCS have to shoulder a lot of the responsibility for this: from their inception they made it clear that they 'knew' what was causing the crop circles and it wasn't a Plasma Vortex but something far more sinister. A scientist like Meaden was just part of the Government Cover Up. These people had far more astute business minds than Terence Meaden, however. They recognised the potential for marketing Tee shirts, Key rings, posters, photos and now conferences. Tickets for the 1991 Glastonbury Conference cost £80 each. That was more than you'd pay for a ticket to a top-class rock band in London in 2002.

And - If you wanted to go on an optional tour of Crop Circles sites – you paid extra.

It could be argued that Terence Meaden was naïve and, without detriment to the professor, this was probably true to a certain extent. Meaden operated within the bounds of his own discipline at first. He had an excellent pedigree in that he was a Professor of Physics and the founder of the Tornado and Storm Research Organisation (TORRO). He was also an amateur archaeologist. By 1991 he'd spent nearly ten years researching the circles and their weather/historical connections, only to be usurped by Colin Andrews in 1989/1990. Andrews, whether consciously or by accident, knew how to manipulate the Press. He seemed to have the knack of appearing as 'Mr. Ordinary Guy' and got the press and public on his side. Even when he made mistakes he retained his popularity because that seemed to prove his 'ordinariness'. Meaden, unfortunately, because he wore a suit and tie and had 'connections' and letters after his name, was lumped in with the 'Establishment'. This was a shame because those of us who got to know Terence Meaden found completely the opposite.

We had now arrived at a situation where the original researchers (Terence and Paul Fuller) were being largely ignored, and a whole host of newcomers to the subject were commanding huge fees and getting all the publicity. We began to get the feeling that the subject of crop circles was being pulled away from us, along with our credibility. How true this was would become obvious later that same year.

Back at *Blue Hill* and Eddie Browne arrived to take over from me on the evening of the 29th July. He spent a quiet night, roaming around the hill, watching through night-vision binoculars. Not that there was now much to watch for as the fields were being rapidly stripped of crop by the whirling blades of the combines. Nearby, as Eddie kept watch and kept up the weather-log, slept Baldrick, curled up in his sleeping bag in the back of his car.

I was working during the daytime on the 30th July so could not attend *Blue Hill*. Terence Meaden made several visits with Prof. Kikuchi and finally departed the site at 19.00, after which the caravan was unmanned until Baldrick arrived at midnight. He purloined the keys and spent the night in the caravan. The weather, which had been overcast for much of the day, now turned to rain, as noted in the log at midnight by Baldrick. He made no more entries until he signed out of the site at 10.30 on the morning of the 30th.

Meanwhile, the 30th being Jacqui's birthday, she and I went out for a drink. Before I left home, I had a phone call from Rog. He told me that GWR's Dave Barratt was coming to his (Rog's) house the following night to shoot some more footage for the video. Could he come round to my place before Barratt arrived to take a copy of the *CERES* database? No problem. I did suggest that perhaps Dave Reynolds ought to be asked to take part in the video as he was studying for a Ph.D., was looking for a future job in meteorology and was the future of *CERES*. Apart from Terence the rest of us were just enthusiastic amateurs.

Rog didn't respond to that.

He came round early evening the next day and took a copy of the database. This time I suggested that it might be a good thing to avoid commenting on unknown or dubious hoaxes as we were still collating the information. Rog didn't reply.

After he left to keep his appointment with GWR, I left for Morgan's Hill. I arrived there at 19.30 and found the site deserted. Noting the fields to the north of our site to have been harvested, I put the kettle on. Just over an hour passed before Terence Meaden arrived again. He came into the caravan with a look of surprise on his face.

'Hello, Peter – what are you doing here? I thought you would have been being filmed by GWR.'

'I wasn't asked,' I replied, equally as surprised. 'Anyway, I could really only duplicate what Rog would be saying. I did recommend that Rog ask Dave Barratt to interview Dave Reynolds as he was really the future of circles research as far as *CERES* was concerned.'

Terence nodded slowly.

'I have been flying with Busty Taylor,' he said. 'And it has left me so depressed. We saw hoax after hoax after hoax. There are fakes at Lockeridge, Milk Hill, West Kennett, Silbury Hill...there's an 'Insect' at Normanton, a 'Curly-whirly' shape at Amesbury and another nearer to Salisbury...Sixpenny Handley is a 'curly-whirly' and there's a phallus complete with testicles near Westbury!'

He sighed. 'We flew over a circle near Westbury which Busty said had been there a week and already it's had spurs added to it...'

'Cheer up, ' I said. 'At least we are identifying the fakes, which hopefully will be one in the eye for those trying to catch us out.'

Terence smiled, wanly. 'TVS came to film me the other day,' he said. 'Half-way through the interview they mentioned the Wessex Skeptics. I'm afraid I let fly. Said it was a shame that people of their intelligence should waste everybody's time trying to catch others out rather than spending time with us seeing what we do when a circle is first reported.'

I agreed. We drank more tea then called it a day at 21.30, as we were both quite tired.

Meanwhile, Rog spent most of the evening being filmed and interviewed, then went round to Jacqui's place.

That night the caravan played host to Baldrick. Again he kept no log between midnight and 07.00.

Tuesday 1st August 1991

I was working a twelve-hour shift that day, so didn't get to the caravan. Terence Meaden and Jim Schnabel covered the shifts there during a bright but cloudy day during which another two fakes were discovered, at Beckhampton and Kennett Avenue. I was visited at 20.45 by Jacqui who took me to the *Bull* for a drink. There we met Rog. Sitting in the garden of the pub, there was a definite tension in the air between the three of us, for varying reasons. At first, little was said, but eventually Rog said a few words about the filming. Apparently the finished video was to go on sale. Barratt had given Rog a couple of free photos of crop circles, which he'd also chatted about on film. Rog passed them round.

'They're quite recent,' he said, '...And look pretty genuine to me....'

I was aghast! The photos were of the recent Lockeridge formation (which Terence and I had christened 'Fishograms' because of their shape) and the Amesbury 'Curly-whirly'! Both hoaxes! I was about to say something about these but decided against it. Rog thought they were OK and I thought they were crap. Arguing wouldn't help. We parted without falling out over it and Rog arranged to pick me up the next evening for a visit to the caravan.

Wednesday 2nd August 1991

Rog and I journeyed to Morgan's Hill that evening in relative silence, arriving at 20.25 to find the place yet again deserted. With the crop fields being rapidly harvested, visitors and helpers were becoming less frequent as there was little to do. Even the field in which our caravan stood had been harvested for a second crop of silage. We noticed that the automatic weather station had gone-recovered by the company who loaned it to us. Inside the caravan it looked as if nobody had been there since Baldrick left earlier that morning.

And it looked as if we'd seen the back of the little Frenchman. He'd left a note saying that he was '...*leaving England on the 3rd August....*'. –So we wouldn't have to worry about him driving over the grass any more. We'd also found out what he'd been up to. It seemed that he had teamed up with Erik the Viking and another disaffected member of VECA. Between them they'd decided that whatever was making the circles needed encouragement to carry on communicating. Erik had worked out that the circles he'd seen in person and in books were actually a long-lost language that he called 'Tifinag' – or something like that. Erik, Baldrick and the other one had persuaded the farmer at Weir Farm to let them carve a message into the crop, in exchange for money.

So, armed with petrol strimmers, they'd cut the phrase '*Talk To Us*' in the wheat [1].

Paul Fuller now arrived at the caravan and we were in the middle of a coffee when Rog's mobile rang. It was Jim Schnabel. It seemed that he was calling from Bishops Cannings, was excited about something and was now coming up to the hill to tell us.

Sure enough, he was there within 15 minutes and came in to the caravan full of excitement. He sat down with us.

'Listen here, you guys! I was talking with the farmer at Lockeridge earlier. Y'know that new fake formation there....' – I glanced at Rog, he was stony-faced- '...Well, the farmer heard people drive away just before the circle was found. Then,' went on the American, '...There's that new formation at Beckhampton. Another hoax.'

So, where was this leading?

Jim pulled a copy of the OS map 'Swindon and Devizes' from his pocket. He spread it over the caravan's table.

'Look here, if you join Lockeridge and Beckhampton with a line – whaddaya got?'

A straight line?

'No! They form the bottom line of a triangle!' cried Jim, triumphantly.

Oh, yeah. Why didn't we think of that...?

Jim took his pen and extended the sides of the triangle to an apex.

'There! If you draw lines from Lockeridge and Beckhampton towards Barbury Castle, you get the point of the triangle somewhere on Avebury Down!'

He glanced round at three surprised faces.

After a few moments, I spoke up. 'I had been privately working on the assumption that the hoaxers were working along a ley-line,' I said. 'And if I'm right then it follows that the next hoax will be somewhere in the vicinity of Firs farm-near the fields where the 'Scrolls' appeared last year, followed possibly by one at Cherhill.'

Jim wasn't put out by this. 'That's as maybe,' he said. 'But d'y'all reckon my theory is OK?'

'We-e-l-l – I suppose so....' muttered Paul Fuller.

'Seems Ok to me,' said Rog. I nodded.

Jim was pleased. 'OK. Tonight we all go to the point of the triangle and watch all night for the hoaxers. I reckon they'll strike again tonight.' He looked at his watch. 'We all meet in the car park at Silbury Hill at...say...23.15?'

It was agreed and Jim left to go to his Bed and Breakfast accommodation to 'tidy up'.

We had a couple of hours to kill. Paul didn't want to go to the *Waggon* as it was '..Full of Loonies..' so we decided on an alternative. There was a pub called the *Bell* further along the A4 towards Marlborough, we'd go there. But first I wanted to call in at the *Waggon and Horses*. I wanted to see Alan Rayner and thank him for the cooperation he and his group had given us throughout the season and also to offer our congratulations as we'd heard he was shortly getting married. Paul would go on ahead to the *Bell*.

Rog and I carried out the 'Public Relations' exercise successfully and Rayner was pleased to see us. With the season now drawing to a close we possibly wouldn't meet him again that year. Paul Fuller had been right not to come with us, though: the place *was* full of loonies.

We went on to the *Bell*. No sooner had we bought a pint than in walked Jim Schnabel. I was stunned. We hadn't mentioned we were going there – how did he know? Jim seemed equally surprised when I asked him how he knew. He didn't answer but was anxious that we get moving.

'Do you know what I'd do if I were the hoaxers?' I said as we drank our beer. 'I'd send all the researchers off on a wild goose chase then make a fake circle right where they'd just been earlier...'

Jim's head jerked up sharply. 'You are just too damned clever...' he snapped. I never found out whether he was being sarcastic or not.

Anyhow, we wouldn't leave until we'd drained our glasses, then we set off in convoy to the car park at Avebury village. Here we left our cars. Rog now put a spanner in the works by saying that he couldn't stay all night. As I had driven up with him, that meant I couldn't stay either. He was also cold as he had no jacket or jumper...Paul Fuller rescued the situation by loaning him a sleeping bag from his car, which Rog draped across his shoulders.

Jim was now champing at the bit so we set off along the road which led out of Avebury to the Ridgeway, Paul and Rog falling behind as we climbed up towards the Downs. Eventually we arrived on the ancient Ridgeway and walked along it for about a mile or so until Jim stopped.

'I'm not quite sure where we are,' he muttered. 'We should be North of a small copse, but I can't see in the dark.'

We wandered on for a further hundred yards or so. Jim stopped again.

'Wait here,' he ordered. 'I'm going to climb over this barbed wire fence to have a scout around.' So saying he vanished into the darkness.

Half an hour passed.

Suddenly a white ball of light streaked across the sky, descending from left to right before vanishing. Paul saw it as well as me, but Rog was looking the other way. 'It could have been a flare,' suggested Paul, but I thought not: if it had been it would have stayed around longer. Was it a shooting star? Perhaps, but it was unlike any shooting star I'd ever seen or have seen since. Possibly it was a piece of space debris burning up as it fell to earth. Or it could have been Jim! [2]

Shortly afterwards, Jim reappeared, scrambling through the fence. 'I found the field I was looking for,' he announced. 'But it's way down the hill and can't be seen from the Ridgeway.'

This cast doubt on Jim's triangle theory. If the hoaxers were to make a circle at the point of a triangle, then arguably it would have to be easily seen to make their efforts worthwhile. We were not convinced by the theory any more than we had been back at the caravan and decided that we'd given Jim the benefit of the doubt so now it wasn't worth going on. Rog wanted to go home and I, of course, had to go with him. Paul also elected to leave. Jim decided to stay-or so he told us.

Paul retired to the caravan for some sleep and Rog and I went home, arriving back in the Bristol area around three in the morning.

The next morning there was a large peanut shaped hoax in the 'scroll' field at Beckhampton...

Paul stayed at the caravan all day. He was disturbed only by a few walkers out enjoying some more reasonable weather. Rita Goold paid a visit during the afternoon, staying for an hour and a half. She listened to the tale of the night before and laughed.

'That boy did something similar the other night at Alton Barnes,' she said. 'He was watching the fields with me when he suddenly vanished. Within five or ten minutes of him disappearing a group of blokes in combat jackets and dark clothes appeared and started asking me silly questions and making silly comments. After they left, Jim reappeared.'

Jim Schnabel himself was not seen until just after 17.00 that afternoon. Jim didn't stay long. He left just in time to meet up with Farmer Brown. Paul, who had gone to the top gate to let Jim out, saw what happened next. The farmer was once again, angry. He'd driven by the hill and noticed not just the lower gate open but the top one as well. He'd come up to deliver a bollocking to the culprits. The culprit was now sheepishly apologising. Jim had been in such a hurry that he'd forgotten to close the gates.

I was at home that afternoon when the phone rang at 16.00. It was Terence Meaden.

'I'm just letting you know that I won't be at the hill today. I have to read through the proofs for the follow-up to the *Goddess of the Stones*. Oh, by the way – there's a new formation appeared. It's a hoax...'

'Hoax?' I echoed. 'Not at Barbury Castle...' I was thinking that perhaps Jim had been right...

'No. It's at Beckhampton-the field the scrolls were in last year...'

You could have knocked me down with a wheat stalk! I had been right! So did that mean that Jim Schnabel was in league with the hoaxers? I told Terence of my theory and of Jim's theory. He was sceptical about Jim's involvement but agreed that we would have to 'keep an eye on Jim' in the future.

Rog picked me up again that evening and when we arrived at Morgan's Hill I had to hold the gates open for a large BMW to leave the hill. When we got to the caravan, Paul Fuller and Eddie Brown were there. Paul explained that the visitors were '...Three Germans-it's OK, they're on our side!'

We settled down to a 'conference' about Jim Schnabel. I ventured my opinion that he may have been employed to lure us away from the area to give the hoaxers a chance to make another formation without the danger of being seen. This was plausible, I said, especially as the CCCP's watch – a caravan on land not too far from where the new formation had appeared – had been withdrawn some weeks previously.

Rog, strangely, wouldn't hear of Jim having anything to do with hoaxers. Eddie and Paul thought it very likely that he was involved and cited the incidents that happened when Jim was at Alton Barnes with Rita. Paul was still of the opinion that the white light he and I had seen could have been a flare of some kind set off by Jim. We came to a majority conclusion that Jim Schnabel was in future, not to be trusted until proven otherwise.

This was now almost the end of the cropwatch. There were to be no more night watches at the caravan as there was nothing to watch from the hill. All the fields around us were now harvested. There were only a few left uncut in the district and they wouldn't last long. At 2100 we decided to adjourn for a pint. Paul was still anti-the *Waggon* so we went to another fairly local real ale pub, the *Ivy* at Heddington, near Calne. This was deemed to be sufficiently out of the way to be free of 'Loonies', and this proved to be the case.

With a pint or two in front of us we sat at a table and talked about *Operation Blue Hill* and the lessons to be learned. There were many. Not the least was the need to keep any future cropwatch site a firm secret! Next year, we vowed, would be different. Little did we know then just how different 1992 was to be. Next we had to decide what to do about hoaxes. Should we publish all we knew about hoaxes to let everyone know that we hadn't been fooled by them? The counter argument was that if we did publish all our information then that would just give the hoaxers the information needed to carry on making bigger and better hoaxes and avoid been caught by *CERES* in particular. By the time Paul Fuller left at 2300, we hadn't made any decision and couldn't therefore recommend anything to Terence. Eddie, Rog and I stayed at the *Ivy* for another 30 minutes or so, not talking about crop circles but watching some local girls playing darts!

I took the caravan keys home with me that night. Terence had the only other spare set. Nobody could now access the caravan unless Terence or I were present.

That was effectively the end of round the clock cropwatching for 1991. Terence Meaden paid short visits to the caravan on the 4th and 5th August. I was back on site on the 7th as the man from Marconi was coming to remove the radar set and scanner. Terence joined me for a while and when the work was done, we went to see the Firs Farm Fake. It was very, very rough. We were joined in the formation by a group of middle aged women, all of whom believed the formation to be a genuine phenomenon. We didn't express our views! Friday 9th August saw Terence and I at the caravan once more where we put all the batteries into Terence's car and went to Andrew Woolley's farmyard where we recovered the battery charger and worked out how much we owed him for use of his electricity. 17th August saw another visit from Terence when he recovered the barograph. On Sunday 18th August 1991 the Stephenson's Screens were taken down and in the evening Terence and I removed the caravan to Bradford-on-Avon.

Operation Blue Hill was over after 60 days!

Chapter Seventeen
TROUBLE IN THE STUBBLE
The Tomlinsons-The Skeptics again-Clench Common-Doug and Dave

Although the cropwatch was over, the work wasn't. There were still reports coming in of circles all over the country. These had to be collated and entered into the *CERES* database. Most got the label 'Hoax' against them if there was sufficient evidence to suggest that. If the evidence was circumstantial then the circle was labelled 'possible hoax'. Other labels were 'Possibly genuine' and 'Genuine'. There were very few of the latter. It was looking like a very sad year indeed, although only for *CERES*. Other groups, the CCCS for example, were collectively enjoying their first real summer in the cornfields so everything was new to them. They saw very few hoaxes.

There were still highlights to enjoy; whilst in the 'Fishogram' at Firs Farm one day, I was talking to a person who showed me that all the stems from a small circle there had vanished.

'....They've been taken away for analysis by Aliens...' she breathlessly told me. I agreed with her. Indeed they had. There was not one stem left in the circle. They had indeed been taken away by Aliens, or, at least, *AN* Alien. What I didn't tell her, because it would spoil her day – and she wouldn't have believed me anyway – was that the stems had been cut with a pair of secateurs and taken away by an 'Alien' who was none other than....Baldrick! The Frenchman had obtained the permission of the farmer to cut the stems and take them back to France where he intended to have them 'analysed' in some laboratory or other.

One day, not long after *Blue Hill* had finished, I was talking with Terence Meaden over lunch in a pub. He showed me a copy of a map of an area near Guildford and announced that he had a very good report of an eyewitness account of circles forming.

'This is such a good sighting that it is imperative that it remain secret,' he said. 'There is likely to be an article in the newspapers very soon.'

He filled me in on the basic story. It seemed that a couple living in a village called Hambledon had been out walking through a wheatfield one day in May 1991when they were caught up in a strong 'Whirlwind' which had proceeded to rush around them violently and made their hair stand on end. When the wind subsided, there were a series of crop circles laid down around them. They had been so stunned by this event that they had contacted Terence Meaden. The professor had been out to speak with the couple, the Tomlinsons, and was happy that they were as genuine as their account seemed to be.

This was amazing. After the disappointments of the summer, it seemed that *CERES* was going to come up smelling of roses after all. Terence promised to let me know when the article was due. It came out in the Mail on Sunday on the 25th August 1991. There was the account of the whirlwind making its circles, complete with a series of diagrams explaining how a Plasma Vortex was responsible for the event and how it worked. The article filled most of a page and was accompanied by a picture of Terence Meaden and the Tomlinsons standing in a field of ripe wheat with the Marlborough complex (by now looking very rough) in the background.

With the publication of that article, we were back on top. A seemingly solid eyewitness account to add to the collection of eyewitness accounts held by *CERES* and painstakingly researched by Paul Fuller. And it was published in a prominent newspaper- surely this was evidence that Terence had been right all along. This was one for the CCCS to beat! Even the CPR couldn't top this! Whilst we rejoiced, Paul Fuller set out to carry out his usual meticulous scrutiny of the evidence.....

Paul carried out a survey by means of putting adverts in local shops asking for other witnesses to come forward. Nobody did. He found that no one had seen these circles other than the Tomlinsons. Which was a bit strange. The path the couple had taken on their walk was well used by other people. It was also odd that the farmer hadn't noticed anything when he combined the field at harvest. And the first anyone had heard of the circles was when the Tomlinsons had written a letter to a national newspaper, entering their sighting in a competition the paper was running to find out what caused crop circles. There was a substantial prize for the winner.

There was another who had doubts about this case. Jim Schnabel had been advised by Terence Meaden to go and speak to the Tomlinsons so that the American could hear a good report of a circles formation being made (Terence was still labouring under the misapprehension that Jim was a student working on a thesis). Schnabel found that although the Tomlinsons had been amazed at the sight of a series of circles being laid down around them and had rushed off home to write down what they'd seen, they hadn't bothered to take any photographs of the circles. Not only that but nobody else had taken any photos either – which was odd as most of the country had become 'circles conscious' thanks to all the press and TV publicity. Jim began to have doubts. Over the next few weeks he travelled to Hambledon, visited the site of the circles, and went to speak with locals and the farmer. He found that there was absolutely no evidence whatsoever for the Tomlinsons circles. [1]

Terence Meaden remained convinced that the Tomlinsons were genuine – they seemed so sincere. By the time Paul Fuller presented the results of his investigation - which showed that considerable doubt had to be cast on the veracity of the Tomlinson's case and deflated the whole affair- sadly it no longer mattered. And anyway, a far more interesting formation had appeared near Cambridge-a Mandelbrot set. This is a shape randomly generated on a computer by a 'chaos theory'-something that would only be known to students of physics and computers. *We* thought it to be a very clever hoax-but of course everyone else thought it proof of a higher intelligence at work.

The harvest was now almost finished, but as long as there were fields of corn still uncut then there were people still flocking to Wiltshire to see signs of any circles and to worship at places where they'd been. Those of us who had other lives to lead now tried to get on with them. A brief respite was necessary to catch up with all the household jobs that would need attention before the winter set in and spare time would be taken up with the analysis of all the data we'd collected during the summer. One morning I was just finishing some repairs to my garden fence when the phone rang.

It was Terence.

'I'm going up to have lunch at the *Waggon and Horses*,' he said. 'I am to meet some people from the USA who are interested in making a film about the circles. I'd like you to come along to meet them. *Juniper* TV will be there as well-they want to film us examining some circles.'

It was a fine day so I decided to take a ride up to Beckhampton on the Honda 90 motorcycle I used for work. It took over an hour to reach the *Waggon* and when I walked into the bar, the place was, as usual, packed with a mixture of circles fans, tourists and jockeys from the nearby stables. Terence was sitting at a table with a couple of men. He introduced me but I can't now remember who they were. One was something to do with Warner Bros. I think. Over lunch several aerial photos of circles were passed around. One in particular showed a couple of circles in a field. These circles, I commented, were fake. One wasn't even round, resembling a fifty pence piece in shape rather than a circle. They were apparently somewhere along the road between Marlborough and Pewsey. We decided that, from the evidence of the photos, the circles weren't even worth a visit.

Jim Schnabel passed by and waved a greeting.

I asked Terence what we were doing with *Juniper* that afternoon.

'As you know, *Juniper* have been following me around all summer,' he replied. 'They are making a documentary about our work with the circles. They have a few circles, which have appeared, on David Sheppard's land at Baltic Farm. They want us to be filmed whilst we examine these circles.'

I'd seen the *Juniper* crew enough not to entirely trust them. This was possibly because they were all dressed in the same manner as most of the followers of the 'Unknown Intelligence' theory. OK, I realise that this is being prejudiced. I have nothing against 'New Age' people, being an avid follower myself, but experience had shown that most (not all) 'New Age' people did not believe Meaden's theory. The production company was almost all comprised of people whose manner of dress would not be out of place in a travellers' camp. The one exception seemed to be the production company's researcher who looked like a young farmer.

Anyway, after lunch we made our way to Baltic Farm, Terence in his Peugeot and me following on my Honda. We passed the farm and turned off along a track, stopping where a small knot of vehicles was parked. I parked my bike and joined Terence who was talking to Jill, the *Juniper* 'person-in-charge'. I was surprised to see Jim Schnabel there and horrified to recognise Robin Allen, Martin Hempstead and a couple of other members of the Wessex Skeptics. I smelt trouble.

Initially all went well. The idea was that Terence and I were to examine the circles and testify as to their authenticity on camera. We were, of course, on our guard with the Skeptics present. The first circle was easy. It bore few of the characteristics of the circles we'd been looking at for years. It was accurate but too accurate. We found obvious footprints, broken stalks and traces of human construction. Worryingly, some of these signs were similar to those we'd found at 'genuine' circles in the past and had assumed that they'd been made by visitors who'd got there before us. We moved on to be filmed in the second circle, having declared the first one a fake.

The dreaded Martin Hempstead was brought into the circle. Hempstead was renowned for his abrupt and rude manner. Once he got into his stride it was always difficult to get a word in edgeways. However, Terence was well prepared. He recalled the evidence we had that the Skeptics had been making circles for *National Geographic*, amongst others, and got in first. He accused Hempstead and the Skeptics of hoaxing circles. This took the wind out of the Skeptic's sails. He blustered and stammered for a second or two. Meaden continued, 'We know you've been making circles....and we suspect that you are the hoaxers!' he argued.

It didn't take much to get Hempstead angry. He now became very, very angry indeed as Terence laid into him. A loud and unpleasant argument ensued. Hempstead admitted that the Skeptics had made circles but argued that everyone knew where they were.... at Lockeridge. He admitted that they were now '...*learning how to hoax them better*....' – at which point I suggested that that was an irresponsible thing for people in their position to do (the Skeptics were all academics). The argument got more and more heated and insults started to fly. All the while Jim Schnabel was standing nearby, pocket tape recorder in hand.

Eventually I decided that I, like Mike Chorost that time at *Blue Hill*, needed to cool down. Arguing with the Skeptics was a bit –no, *a lot*-like banging your head against a brick wall whilst standing in the fast lane of the M4: dangerous, futile and it hurt! I left the circle where Meaden and Hempstead were still arguing loudly and went to stand a short distance away. I was joined by one of the Skeptics who was dressed in a blue overall jacket and trousers and looked more like a soft drinks delivery driver than a university academic. I didn't know his name and he didn't introduce himself.

We watched the heated argument for a while without speaking, then the Skeptic started making barbed comments about Meaden and his theory. He suggested that Meaden's vortex was a lot like the 'Emperor's new clothes' syndrome and that the professor was altering his theory as more complex formations appeared. Then the Skeptic questioned not just Meaden's theory, but also the scientist's background! He questioned where Meaden actually qualified in meteorology and why there was '....no evidence of Meaden publishing anything at all before 1976.....' [2] I'd had enough of this. If these people could debate the subject in a calm and collected manner then I was prepared to listen. There was no doubt in my mind that a lot of what they were saying made some sense. After all, Paul and myself had been arguing that there were many more fake circles than we'd previously thought and had little doubt that when we came to analyse that summer's data during the coming winter months, we'd find more hoaxes. If only the Skeptics would stop trying to antagonise people and try a more polite approach, then, in retrospect, I am sure we could have worked together. They had different ideas. Their argument was that Terence Meaden had a good theory up until the point when he'd managed to explain away Alton Barnes 1990 as the results of a plasma vortex. From that moment onwards they had, they said, tried to convince him to examine his findings with more care. As academics themselves, they could not see how science and the Meaden vortex could explain away anything more developed than a single circle or a ringed circle.

Perhaps, if they'd left Martin Hempstead and Robin Allen in the laboratory, they might have convinced us of their argument.

Anyway, I found this Skeptic just as unappealing as Hempstead and Allen and his version of the 'needle game' with me was successful.

'Bloody Skeptics!' I exploded. 'Why can't you just listen to what people have to say instead of turning every debate into an argument? Why do you all have to be so bloody rude and insulting? Do you honestly think you'll win us over like this?'

The Skeptic merely smirked. He'd done what he set out to do-wind me up. Realising that any further conversation would be a waste of time, I turned on my heel and stormed off to my motorcycle to wait for Meaden.

Some weeks after this event, Terence Meaden received a rather rude letter from this particular Skeptic, who turned out to be one Dr David Fisher. He included a dog muzzle for Meaden to present to me to keep me quiet should we ever meet with Fisher again in future. For some months after, I also received a lot of odd 'junk mail' through the post; the sort of junk mail that could only have derived from somebody filling out forms or questionnaires in my name. I am not suggesting that the Skeptics or Dr Fisher in particular were responsible but it seemed a bit of a coincidence after the affair of the dog muzzle.

Towards the end of August, Terence once again phoned and suggested we meet for lunch at the *Waggon*. It seemed that *Juniper* wanted more footage. Having been assured that the Wessex Skeptics would not be there, I agreed. This time I drove up. There were not too many people at the pub this time and I once more made the acquaintance of Stanley Morcomb and his wife who were sitting with Terence.
Soon we were joined by the *Juniper* producer and her researcher.

'We have some exciting circles for you to see,' said Jill, the producer. 'We'd like to film your reaction to them and give us the benefit of your knowledge.'

Stanley Morcomb and his wife were permitted to come along as well on the proviso that they and I kept out of the circles and kept quiet while filming was in progress. We were to follow the Juniper team to the farmer's house where we would pick up the farmer and move to the circles. And so we set off, all in separate cars. Juniper leading, followed by Terence's Peugeot 406, Stanley Morcomb and with me bringing up the rear. We took the A4 to Marlborough, then turned off on the Pewsey road. A few miles along this road and we stopped. Terence came back to my car.

'Jill wants me to follow her to the farm,' he said. 'Could you and Stanley wait here for us?'

No problem. I parked up on the verge and switched off the car engine. I got out and wandered ahead to where the Morcombs had parked. Terence and the Juniper car sped off and a short distance ahead, turned off down a track. Neither the Morcombs or I could fathom out why we had to stay there, but we accepted it. Perhaps the farmer didn't want stock frightened by too many vehicles? We hadn't a clue. We chatted for perhaps ten minutes or more. Suddenly, a car shot out of the track down which the others had driven. It was followed by the *Juniper* car and Terence's Peugeot, all going at a fair old rate of knots.
With surprised looks on our faces we watched this convoy speed by before recognition set in. Stanley Morcomb started his car engine whilst I sprinted along the road to my car.
Shit! A stream of slow-moving traffic was coming from Marlborough and we needed to turn round and follow the others back the way we'd come! Vehicle after vehicle trundled

by. Stanley managed to turn and shot off down the road in pursuit. It was a few more moments before I could do likewise. I shot off back towards Marlborough, but was now at least two or three minutes behind Terence. Soon I was back on the outskirts of Marlborough without a sign of Terence or *Juniper*. I passed the Morcombs coming back the other way again! Turning again at the first available opportunity, I once more sped off towards Pewsey.

It was futile. I was soon back at the farm entrance again without sight or sound of Terence and co. I seemed to have lost the Morcombs as well. I pulled up in a gateway and cursed loudly. I had no idea which circles the Juniper team was taking Terence to or where they could be. They could be anywhere in Wiltshire or even Hampshire for all I knew. Just because the farmer lived nearby did not mean that the land on which the circles were was also nearby. With extensive farming, the land could be miles away. In the back of my mind was a nasty feeling that this was a set up; *Juniper* had *wanted* to lose the Morcombs and myself. Realising that I could search all day without finding them, I headed back to the Avebury area.

I didn't see Terence or the Morcombs again that day. The professor phoned me that evening to find out where I'd been. After I explained, he told me that *Juniper* had taken him to see some circles at a place called Clench Common. He gave me the map reference.

'It is a pity you weren't able to find us,' he sighed. 'They were beautiful circles, Peter. Just plain singles with a lovely swirled pattern. Just like they used to be.'

It was after he'd rung off that I got out the map of the area and plotted the circles sites from the references.

I couldn't be sure, but from the map and Terence's description, the location looked very similar to the place where the '50p' circles we'd seen in the photo the week before had been......

And now, at the end of August, came the first of several body blows, which would change the entire shape of crop circles research. One evening I had a phone call from Terence Meaden. He was clearly upset about something. He had, he told me, been set up by *Juniper*. The circles at Clench Common which he'd been asked to inspect on camera and which the Morcombs and I had missed out on, were fakes after all. *Juniper* had asked to film a final interview with Terence, at his home, where they had informed him, again on camera, that the circles he'd waxed so enthusiastically about had been made by......the Wessex Skeptics! My heart sank.

'I was taken in completely,' muttered the professor. 'After all those hoaxes I was so pleased to see plain, simple circles...and the farmer's explanation of the night the circles formed.....it all fitted. So I answered all their questions just as they wanted me to.'

Oh my God. He'd been led right up the garden path....no wonder they wanted to lose the Morcombs and me.....If I'd been there I felt sure I would have been able to warn him that this was the '50p' circle which both he and I had already declared fake.

'Busty Taylor was also there,' went on Terence, 'He was duped as well.'

I felt so sorry for Terence. Whilst it was true that we'd had one hell of a job that summer convincing him that many circles were hoaxes, he had been at last coming round to accepting the fact. He'd even recently told a reporter that, during 1991, he had seen more hoaxes than in all the other years put together. It was now also obvious that our suspicions about some people were correct. The whole entire range of press coverage of the circles over the past four years had been biased towards the 'Unknown Intelligence' brigade. We'd had to put up with the TV people and the Skeptics trying to catch us out all year and they'd at last succeeded. The only consolation was that one of their own kind had been caught out as well-no offence, Busty.

However, when the programme, as *Equinox* was shown that October, it was Terence Meaden's humiliation that was shown in full: Busty's was restricted to a few, nicely edited lines.

Before that the news was leaked to the dailies. Several articles were published (even in the *Daily Sport*) which showed how Terence had been caught out by Farmer Pitt and the Skeptics. Just to show how the Press believed in fairness and equality, there was no sign or hint that Busty had been caught as well. The press was happy that they'd caught the professor out. They had achieved what they'd set out to do.

Gloom settled over the *CERES* camp. Or at least, what was left of it. By now Rog and Jacqui were hardly ever with us. They spent most of the time horse riding together. Dave Reynolds was busy studying for his Ph.D. Terence and his wife went on holiday to their house in Normandy for several weeks, leaving Paul Fuller and myself to sit in nervous anticipation of what would happen next.

But, while *CERES* feared the worst, the rest of the circles supporters were having a ball. The Grand Old Man of Earth Mysteries, John Michell, had got involved in circles and had organised a 'Cornference' to be held over the weekend of 7th-8th September at, where else, Glastonbury. Tickets were priced at £30. There were lectures by Colin Andrews and Pat Delgado, Richard Andrews and Busty Taylor, Michael Green, George Wingfield et al. The place was packed. Enthralled folk listened in awe to Colin Andrews telling them that the earth was in '....severe trouble....Mother is *crying*...' he choked.[3]

Colin had a lecture tour arranged for 1992; Taylor and Richard Andrews had a lecture tour arranged for that winter where they would lecture in nine cities in the USA. Crop Circles were certainly paying for some people.

CERES personnel weren't invited to speak at the 'Cornference' and none of us coughed up the Thirty quid to attend.

On the Sunday, whilst all the principal speakers and other rising stars were being entertained to drinks at George Wingfield's Somerset house, I was wending my way into Bristol to work a Sunday night shift. It was just after midnight when I had a telephone call from Paul Fuller.

'Pete, something terrible has happened,' he gasped. 'Some people from Southampton have confessed to making crop circles for years. There's going to be an article in *Today* paper in the morning.'

It seemed that Independent Radio News had picked up on the story and were running it.

We agreed not to bother Terence in France as there was every chance that it could be a fake item. At 00.30 Paul rang again. It was all true.....Fuller had given a short radio interview and had been played tapes of Pat Delgado admitting that he'd been had. It seemed that the game was, at last, up. Paul agreed that we should tell Meaden and he would call the Prof.

I can't remember the rest of that night. I left work at seven in the morning, heard some of the confessions of two retired artists on the radio and went home to bed. The telephone started ringing at around nine and carried on throughout the day. Newspapers- the *London Evening Standard, Bristol Evening Post*; TV-ITN- rang twice; BBC Radio's *World Service*; Overseas radio, *Time* magazine, all rang me that morning. The calls continued through the day and into the evening. Terence Meaden, at his French hideaway, had got wind of the breaking revelations and fended off all enquiries to Paul Fuller and myself. I hadn't even seen the newspapers and it wasn't until I switched the TV on for the *One o' Clock News* that I really got wind of the full story and heard the confessions of Doug Bower and Dave Chorley.

There can't be many, if any, people who have an interest in crop circles and who have not heard all the tales surrounding Doug and Dave. The full story is to be found in Jim Schnabel's *Round in Circles* and John Macnish's *Cropcircle Apocalypse*. Briefly, two artists from Southampton claimed to have started the entire affair back in the early 1980's. They'd made circles at first with an iron bar, then with planks and rope. They had become incredulous at the growing band of 'believers' and created wilder and wackier formations, convinced that people would soon cotton on to the hoax. People didn't so Doug and Dave made more and more circles, infiltrating circles groups, particularly CPR, and then going out to make circles 'to order'. Then they got angry that people were making money out of the circles when it had all started as a joke and decided to retire.

They tried to interest a couple of papers in the story but it was *Today* which cottoned on to the fact that if these two were telling the truth, then there was one hell of a story here. And so it was that an 'Insectogram' was manufactured and Pat Delgado led in to 'authenticate' it. Which he did; Then the press revealed that it had been made by Doug and Dave. From that moment on, one could imagine that the entire subject would take on water so fast that it would soon sink without trace.

Not a bit of it.

Pat Delgado was man enough to realise that Doug and Dave were telling the truth and he fell on his sword. Colin Andrews, as usual, blustered and bluffed his way out of it. But he was also finished – at least in the UK. It would not be long before he was resident in the one place where he could be assured of some kind of future on the lecture circuits – the USA. George Wingfield merely shrugged it all off by claiming that it was all part of a major Government Conspiracy and carried on as normal, although increasingly dedicating more and more time to ferreting out the hoaxers. Busty and Richard Andrews carried on as normal. The CCCS carried on as normal, nodding wisely and wagging a remonstrative finger towards those *naughty* boys from Southampton who had tried to spoil their summer games.

In France, Terence Meaden answered very few phone calls but there was little doubt that a cold front and deep depression had settled firmly over the meteorologist.

I was as shocked as everyone else was, but in a way, I wasn't surprised. There were so many fakes that someone, somewhere had to be responsible for making them – other than the Wessex Skeptics, that is. I was also very relieved that apart from the Clench Common affair, we hadn't been caught out by hoaxers! Apart from the early circles, we at *CERES* had cast all the later circles revealed to have been made by D & D as hoaxes; All the ludicrous 'Insectograms' and the like of 1991 had been dismissed. Luckily.

And so, 1991 went downhill from there. The CCCS, Colin Andrews and a lot of upper middle-class people who wanted to worship crop circles continued with their money-spinning lectures and talks. Books were published and photos sold. Key-rings and T-shirts were still on sale. The *Cerealogist* and *The Circular* magazines continued to be published with no loss in sales. *The Cropwatcher* also continued to be published, with more emphasis on Doug and Dave.

And in the wheat fields the ploughs dug deep into the chalky soil.

End of Book One

FOOTNOTES

Chapter 1
1...He wasn't alone in thinking that an 'aerial component' was involved. Lots of circles looked just as if something had descended into the crop, leaving the circular depressions. The appearance of circles underneath overhead power lines tended to dispel that theory.
2...BBCTV One o' clock News, 26 July 1990
3...Julie Blay talking to Terence Meaden
4...It's still not clear who was in these aircraft

Chapter 2
1...He was referring to Dr Meaden
2...I'd tried to photograph stones in the south circle but each time I tried, the camera refused to function, indicating flat battery. When I left the circles-the camera would work; when I went back-it wouldn't. A replacement battery solved the problem. Was there residual energy in those stones which drained an already low battery? On another occasion, driving past the same stones, a friend's mobile phone lost its signal whilst we were inside the circles, but regained the signal when we left the stones.

Chapter 3
1...A failure of the escape mechanism caused the canopy to be blasted off the aircraft as if the pilot was ejecting. With the canopy gone, the unfortunate pilot was sucked out of the plane by depressurisation.
2...Name changed
3...Years after, in 1996, I was driving through a place called 'Crackstone' in Gloucestershire, when the air vents in the Peugeot 306 I was driving suddenly started pumping smoke into the car. I stopped rapidly, grabbed a fire extinguisher and opened the bonnet. There was no sign of any problem other than a smell of burnt wiring. When the car was later examined by a Peugeot mechanic, no signs of any problem could be found. Not far away from where the problem occurred stands the 'Long Stone' and not far away is an area once fabled for standing stones, the 'Devil's Churchyard'. Strange but true.

Chapter 4
1...Name changed
2...Most people who were there that evening thought the same-I don't know why.
3...A BUFORA publication 1986
4...If you go to any remote spot in Wiltshire or Hampshire, you are frequently not far away from a military establishment, owing to the large military presence in these counties.
5...*The Black Alchemist* by Andrew Collins. ABC books, 1988
6...As eventually told in *The Seventh Sword* by Andrew Collins. Century, 1991
7...Co-authors of *The Green Stone* and *The Eye of Fire*, Grafton Books 1984/1987, 1988.

Chapter 5
1...Name changed
2...This was at Telegraph Hill, just off the A272
3...This was *Operation White Crow* organised by Colin Andrews and Pat Delgado
4...The sound was later discovered to be a bird – the *Grasshopper Warbler*
5...This was the circle Rog, Jacqui and I had seen the previous summer. Later, its creation was claimed by Doug Bower who'd made the circle when the CPR watchers weren't there.

Chapter 6
1...Interview with *Today* newspaper, July 1990
2...The Class 59 locomotives, built by General Motors for quarry firm Foster-Yeoman
3...I honestly believe Dr Meaden thought that they were just interested in circles and he hadn't caught on that they were actually finding circles as 'Messages from the Gods'.
4...Names changed

Chapter 7
1... He didn't manage to find anything
2... Another version of the process is that when laid down by whatever means, the stem of the wheat is exposed to degrees of light and temperature that it wouldn't normally get when standing straight. See *'Truthseeker's Review'* issue 5 1995. *'Interview with The Spiderman'*
3... EMF = ElectroMotiveForce

Chapter 8
1... Try it for yourself and see.....

Chapter 9
1... They didn't
2... I still have the video evidence...

Chapter 10
1... Doug Bower and Dave Chorley made this one, hence the 'DD' signature

Chapter 11
1... Doug and Dave made this, an early 'Insectogram'

Chapter 12
1... The radar we used was a 'sideways facing' marine radar. In other words it sent out horizontal beams. A low-flying fighter crossing the landscape to the west of Blue Hill would have been flying lower than the radar and would have been likely to be picked up. RAF and Navy jets used this route almost daily. This was almost certainly the UFO Meaden saw on the screen.
2... It never did. Nor did we get a copy of his second book, *The Stonehenge Soloution*.
3... We later learnt that some of Carrie's detectors were faulty and had been switched off.
4... This circles formation has been credited to the UBI (United Believers in Intelligence), later known in 1992 as the 'Squirts' (see Book 2)
5... We took pictures of these youths. They were later identified as three of the UBI.

Chapter 13
1... This was an oft-quoted tale: that dogs would fall ill whenever they approached a crop circle. Pants. I saw lots of people take their dogs into circles with never an ill effect.
2... *Atmos!* The call for an atmospheric recording-background noise in other words.
3... This was during the period when Icke had decided that he was the Son of God and had a mission to save the planet. He added a female companion to his family group. This was the woman he was with at Alton Barnes in 1991. The following year, Icke admitted that he had 'been a little mad' in 1991. He is still pursuing some mission or other and still sells books.

Chapter 14
1... Circles researchers first attributed the name 'Golden Ball hill' to the possibility that it may have been associated with the phenomenon in the past. Research showed it was named after the prolific gorse which grew there.
2... Name changed
3... Name changed
4... Later in the season, someone, possibly Jim Schnabel, ventured the opinion that Rita had actually seen approaching car headlights reflected off the low mist.
5... I later dismantled the amplifier but found nothing obvious inside. We never found out whose it was or how it got into our caravan. It went to the tip.

Chapter 15
1... George was probably referring to the entrance money the farmer could get.
2... From what I later learned about hoaxing (see Book 2) I would estimate Barbury was probably created by 6 people in approximately 3 hours.
3... This was the ringed circle which, after being measured by all the investigators at the time, 'grew' an extra ring overnight. (Some say it was always there but not noticed at the

time). This caused Colin Andrews to challenge Dr Meaden's theory at the 1990 Oxford conference.
3...Doug Bower and Dave Chorley later claimed this as one of theirs.
Chapter 16
1...After working out that the 'Aliens' were leaving all these messages in the form of different types of crop circles, Erik and co. left a message for them in *English*! What was wrong with the 'Aliens' own language of 'Tifinag'?
2...In retrospect, no, it couldn't have been Jim. The light was just like the light I'd seen at Stanton St. Bernard in 1990 (see Chapter 6).
Chapter 17
1...No reports of these circles have ever been uncovered.
2...Terence Meaden had been living in Canada before 1976, where he had been Associate Professor of Physics at Dalhousie University. He had published extensively before 1976 including a 1966 book on the Electrical Resistance of Metals.
3...It was fashionable at that time to link crop circles with the Hopi Indians, some of whose graphics resembled some of the formations. The Indians referred to the planet as 'Mother'.

Bibliography

The John Turner programme, February 1988 - BBC Radio Bristol
Crop Circles, Harbingers of World Change (Ed. Alick Bartholomew) (Gateway Books 1991)
The Black Alchemist – Andrew Collins (ABC Books 1988)
The Seventh Sword – Andrew Collins (Century 1991)
The Circlemakers – Andrew Collins (ABC Books 1992)
Alien Energy (Review copy only) – Andrew Collins (ABC Books 1994)
Circular Evidence – Pat Delgado and Colin Andrews (Bloomsbury 1989)
The Latest Evidence – Pat Delgado and Colin Andrews (Bloomsbury 1990)
The Cropwatcher Magazine (Ed. Paul Fuller) – Various 1990-1994
1991-Scientific Evidence for the crop circle phenomenon – Montague Keen (Centre for Crop Circle Studies 1991)
Journal of Meterology (Ed. Dr.G.T.Meaden) Various 1988-1994 (Artetech Publishing/TORRO)
The Circles Effect and its Mysteries – Dr.G.T.Meaden(Artetech Publishing/TORRO 1989)
Circles from the Sky– Dr. G.T.Meaden (Artetech Publishing/TORRO 1990)
The Goddess of the Stones – Dr. G.T.Meaden (Souvenir Press 1991)
Cropcircle Apocalypse – John Macnish (Circlevision 1993)
*The Demonic Connection – Toyne Newton and Charles Walker (*Badgers Books 1987)
The Crop Circle Enigma (Ed. Ralph Noyes)-(Gateway Books 1990)
Crop Circles-A mystery solved? Jenny Randles and Paul Fuller (Robert Hale 1990)
Controversy of the Circles- Jenny Randles and Paul Fuller (BUFORA 1989)
The Beckhampton Group Newsletter (Ed. Alan Rayner and later Robert Irving) -Various 1990-1993
Round in Circles –Jim Schnabel (Hamish Hamilton 1993)
MUFON UFO Journal (Ed. Dennis Stacey)November 1995- Article re-Swangate by Jim Schnabel
Truthseekers Magazine 1995 'Interview with the Spiderman' – Matthew Williams (interviewing Robert Irving)
Others equally as informative were: Flying Saucer Review; Link-Up;The PROBE report*; Exploring the Supernatural*; The Unexplained*; Viewpoint Aquarius*. Of which those marked * are out of print and no longer available
I've left anyone out-my apologies. Let me know and I'll put it right in future issues of the book.
COMING SOON! Cereal Killers Book Two-*Into the Labyrinth* 1991-1993